1

Computers seem to be commanding more and more of our time and attention. Undoubtedly you've heard of them, you may have even used one, but do you really know why they are so important or how they actually work?

This book aims to make the basic technology and functions of computers understandable. While computers and technology will continue to develop, this book covers the basics that underlie present technology and forms a foundation for understanding emerging technologies and advances as they happen.

We do not cover every computer topic—to do that would require shelves filled with books. This book tries to cover the important concepts that are fundamental to a vivid understanding of computers. We have divided this book into four chapters that separate the information into four areas: **Uses**, **Components**, **Technology**, and **Evaluation** of computers. Each of these first three sections is divided into chapters that discuss the **Processing,** the **Storage,** the **Communication** of information, and the **Interface** (or interaction) of data and information on these levels.

While this book is arranged in these four chapters, it is not necessary to read from front to back. It is just as sensible to start at some point that intrigues you, at any place in the book, and jump around from topic to topic as it is to start at page four. We've provided **jump words** with directions that can take you to other places in the book where that topic, or a related one, is discussed.

Because the world of computers is so big, and one book cannot possibly cover all information, we've provided an annotated **Bibliography ▶130** that you can use to find books that allow you to explore more deeply a topic that interests you. We have tried to explain terms whenever we use them and keep the computer jargon down to a minimum, but to compensate for the technical nature of this topic we have included an extensive **Glossary ▶134** in the back integrated with the **Index ▶134**. Lastly, this entire book, including the illustrations and photos, was produced with a computer. Computers were used to write, edit, illustrate, and design this book. We have outlined this process for you in the **Colophon ▶142**.

modems ▶73

This is an example of a "jump" word. The marker is referring to page 73.

To find information on a specific topic, turn to the Glossary/Index on page 134.

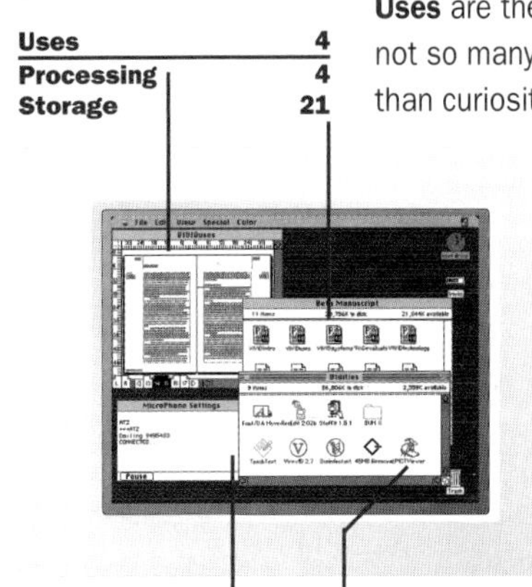

Uses is a good place to start for a novice.

Uses *(how people use computers)*

Uses are the reasons we have, build and buy computers. If there were not so many wonderful, significant uses, computers would be no more than curiosities and toys, and certainly not a part of so many people's lives. What computers can do (or help you do) defines how powerful they really can be. Most people don't go a day without using a computer (just picking up a phone and dialing a number engages a sophisticated computer system, as does making a plane reservation or bank transaction).

In **Processing ▶4**, we discuss the ways that computers can be used to manipulate information, whether you are writing, creating, designing, exploring or cataloging numbers, words, pictures, sounds, or music. In **Storage ▶21** you will learn about the ways of storing and retrieving information that make Databases and Hypermedia so interesting. **Communications ▶27** covers how computers interact with other computers and with groups of people to make work more effective. Topics such as electronic mail and groupware are discussed here. Although everything in this book has a relation to how people use computers, in **Interface ▶31** we cover the issues that face us now that a whole culture has developed around these machines. Issues such as Security, Computer Viruses, Privacy and Access are becoming of greater concern as we are provided with more and more powerful computers.

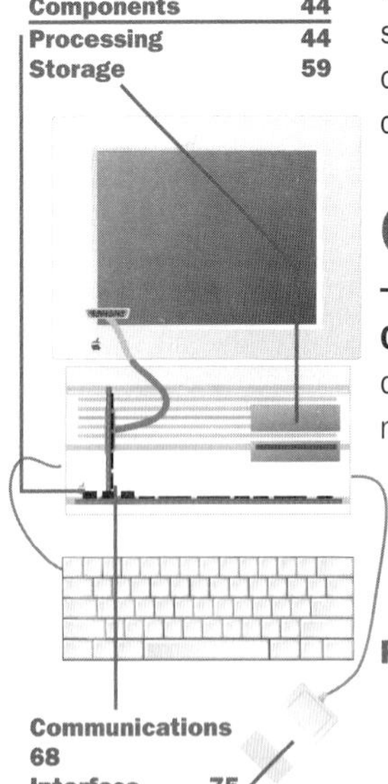

Components *(the parts of a computer)*

Components are the things that you can see and touch: the screens, discs, and computers themselves. These complex, sophisticated machines make possible the technologies discussed in the first section. It is how these technologies work together that make computer systems so powerful and fascinating. Operating systems, computer languages and other tools that allow computers to manipulate large quantities of complex information are explained in **Processing ▶44**, while the construction and workings of storage devices such as floppy disks, hard drives and CD-ROMs are covered in **Storage** ▶59. In **Communications** ▶68, networks, modems and other means of telecommunications are explained, and in **Interface** ▶75, user interfaces, and peripherals such as mice, scanners, keyboards, monitors and graphics pads are discussed.

Technology *(how computers work)*

Think of **Technology** as the basic advancements that allow computers to work. It is the applied research and science that are fundamental to all computing machines and electronic devices (including televisions, stereos, and automobiles). From the simple, but profound, **binary system** that organizes data, to the more complex assemblies of microchips, integrated circuits, and transistors, technology embodies the things you cannot see—what is inside the computer's housing, and what exists in the smallest scales of known science. The basics of circuits and "chips" are explored in **Processing** ▶90, how these devices store data is covered in **Storage** ▶104, and how they move data around with electronic technology is explained in **Communications** ▶108. The technology behind the ways computers receive and display information such as CRT (cathode ray tubes) screens and flat screen displays are discussed in **Interface** ▶113.

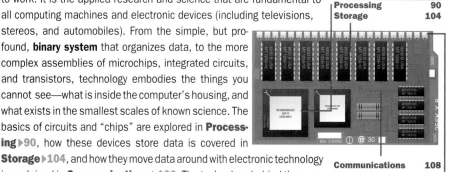

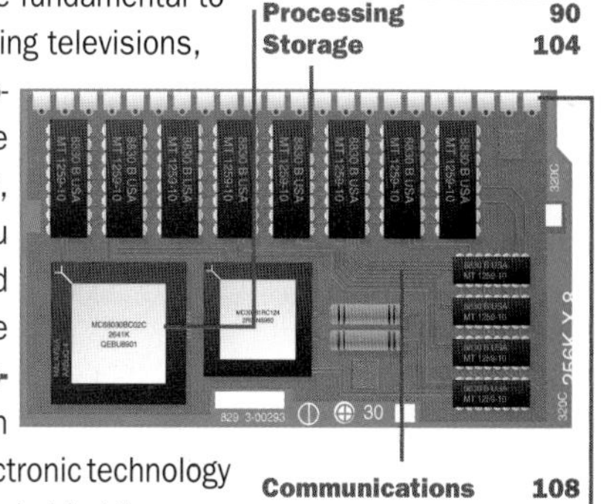

Evaluation *(how to buy a computer)*

The fourth chapter, **Evaluation** ▶116, provides some information to help you buy a computer, software, or related components, as well as information about upgrading a present system to a more powerful one. There are many different systems and software to choose from and it can be confusing and intimidating when trying to sort them all out. We have included some advice to help you evaluate your needs, find the information that goes into an informed decision, and develop an understanding on which to base that decision. Whether buying software or hardware, the key is to settle not for answers that just give you information, but for answers that help you understand what you are buying.

Uses | Processing

For most people, computers are only as interesting as they are useful. The vast majority of those who work with computers are users, not programmers or technicians.

App is an abbreviation of Application. When people refer to a computer "program", they usually mean "application".

To understand computers, you must understand that the computer is just a tool. The human race is and has always been a race of tool builders. The computer is just one of our grandest tools yet.

The range of uses for computers is ever–widening. First used as simple calculators for military and scientific applications, computers are now used to do things those early users could not have dreamed of: publishing, designing, creating music, films and art, controlling factories and robots and educating children. Because the range of computer uses is so wide, we've broken it into a few categories: Word Processing, Optical Character Recognition (OCR), Desktop Publishing (including Graphics, Art and Image Editing), Fonts, Entertainment, Music, Video and Animation, Accounting and Spreadsheets, Integrated Packages, Education, Utilities, CAD/CAM, Scientific Applications and Industrial Applications. **Storage** ▶21 and **Communications** ▶27 uses will be covered in the next two sections.

An **application** is a software product developed for a specific purpose (such as graphic design or financial modeling). It is roughly equivalent to the word **program** ▶57. The term *application* is used instead of the term *software* because software refers to any instructions or data in a computer (such as a file or the **operating system** ▶44–45). An application is specifically used to create files and work within them. Usually, it is a set of capabilities, commands and tools that create an environment for certain types of work on the computer.

Typically, applications are released in **versions**. As new capabilities are added, applications will have different version numbers in the application's name, such as *PageMaker® 3.0 or 4.0*. Minor upgrades (those that fix problems or incompatibilities or increase minor capabilities) usually add numbers after the decimal point, such as *PageMaker® 3.02* or *System 6.0.7*. The first number denotes the major version and the others denote minor upgrades. Higher numbers indicate more sophisticated versions.

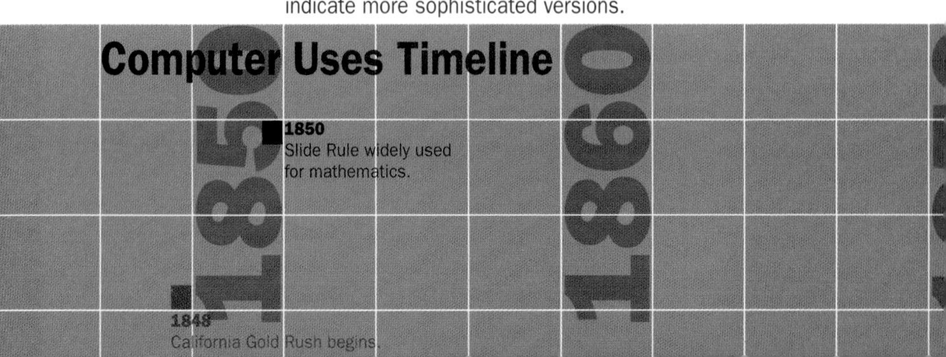

Computer Uses Timeline
1850
1860
1850
Slide Rule widely used for mathematics.
1848
California Gold Rush begins.

All applications are specific to the computer **platforms** (computer families) for which they were designed. Because platforms, system software, operating systems and interfaces are different, the same application cannot be run on any other platform. Many software publishers, however, release versions of their applications for different platforms, such as DOS, UNIX, Macintosh, OS/2, etc.... Usually, the features of the applications and the environment in which the user works with them are similar—even on different platforms. Often, files from an application on one computer can be transferred to and used by a different computer running a similar version of the same application. This allows a greater level of flexibility and effectiveness between workers using different computers.

Even when an application does not exist in a version on a different platform, information can often be transferred by saving the data in a **file format** ▸22 common to applications on both platforms. The formats can be industry standard formats such as **EPS** or **TIFF** ▸23 or application–specific formats such as Lotus 1–2–3 or Excel.

There is no end to the capabilities different applications and other software can have. We have tried to explain the most common and most important ones but this list is by no means complete. In time, whole new categories of software emerge; and as software, hardware and users evolve, capabilities change and expand.

Be cautious of 1.0 versions of applications. Many new applications (though not all) have not been completely perfected and may contain annoying ***bugs****. Also, beware* ***alpha*** *or* ***beta*** *software. This software has not been finished or tested and is meant for use only by developers. It may cause damage to your system or loss of data.*

Word Processing

Writing letters, memos or reports are the ways most people use computers. They manipulate words and text on a screen—primarily to print at some later time and store for safe keeping. Computers alleviate much of the tedium associated with typing, writing, proofing, and manipulating words. Because computers can store and recall information so readily, documents need not be re–typed from scratch just to make corrections or changes. The real strength of word processing lies in this ability to store, retrieve and change information.

This is what a typical word processing document looks like on screen.

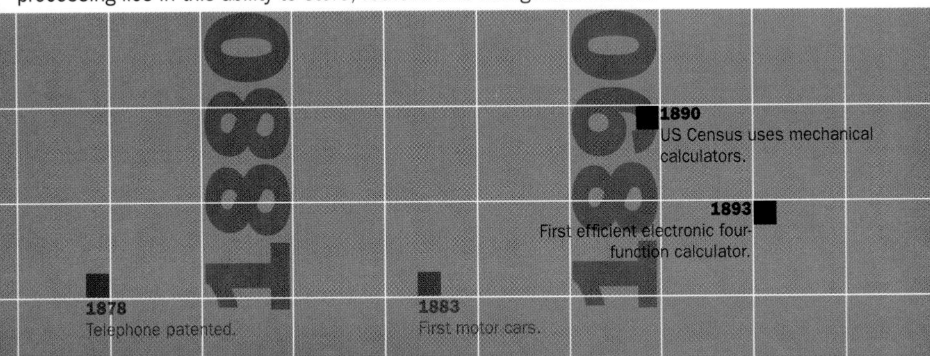

Word Processing

Great hardware and bad sof
terrible and disappointing
Likewise, powerful ^Rsoftw
^Bhardware^B will make you
the whole system out the w

^IMargin Note: To help eva

eat hardware and inadequate
erful **software** and bad **hardw**

To help evaluate your needs a

The top illustration is a non–WYSIWYG display while the bottom one is.

Many word processors now include capabilities to automatically create Tables of Contents and Indexes for long documents. Some even include tools that make cross–references and footnotes easier to create.

Typing is still necessary (at least, for now) to put the information into the computer initially, but once in, the need to re–type only applies to new information.

Word processing is more than just typing, however. Word processors have many features to manipulate text. Features such as *Search* and *Replace* allow users to find a particular phrase, word or character no matter where it is in a body of text. This becomes more useful as the amount of text grows. Computers can search much faster than humans can but they are not terribly smart about how they do it. Like most computer features, brute force is relied upon rather than intelligence. If a word processor is asked to find a specific word, it will find every occurrence of it without thought to context. Word processors do not replace a user's intelligence or judgment, but they do provide some fast and accurate assistance.

Word processors usually include different ways to view the text. Some include a view that displays the text with editor's marks that show hidden characters or commands (spaces, returns, paragraph endings, applied styles...). Many word processors include the ability to show exactly how the text will appear on paper when printed. This is called **WYSIWYG** (What You See Is What You Get, pronounced "wizzy–wig"). WYSIWYG shows **bold**, *italic*, underline and other type style characteristics on the screen so that the user can clearly see what he or she is typing. Another feature of WYSIWYG is the correct display of different **typefaces** ▸12 and format characteristics (margins, indents, super– and sub–scripted characters, etc...). This allows the user to plan the document more accurately and reduces the frustration of printing something that doesn't look right. These features are necessary if a user has any intentions of **desktop publishing** ▸10.

Many word processors now have so many features that they approach the capabilities of **layout applications** ▸10 for desktop publishing. They can import graphics, format multiple columns of text, run text around graphics, etc.... This can make a word processor useful or burdensome, depending on how well these features have

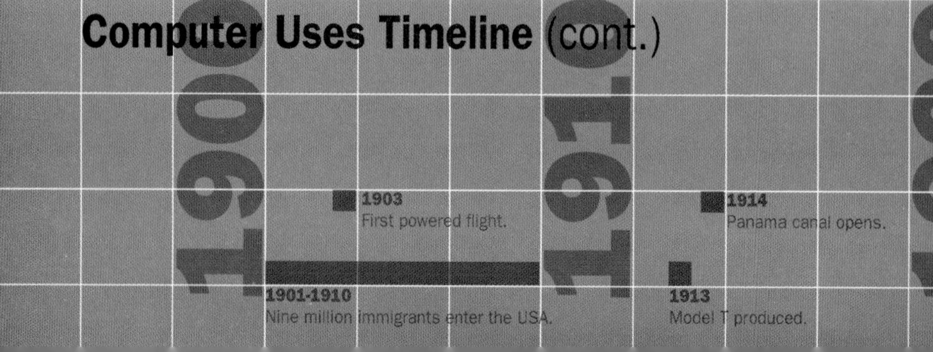
Computer Uses Timeline (cont.)
1900
1910
1903
First powered flight.
1914
Panama canal opens.
1901-1910
Nine million immigrants enter the USA.
1913
Model T produced.

been designed into the application. Many times, users do not need or want these features and they only get in the way. Other times, users may need to use them but cannot understand how to use or find them. Sometimes they are hidden under layers of other commands.

The major features that word processors offer are **spell checking**, **automatic hyphenation**, **mail merge** and, sometimes, **grammar checking**. **Spell checkers** can be used to compare words in the program's dictionary to those used in the user's document. The spell checker points out any words it cannot match, notifies the user, and allows him or her to make any changes—it sometimes even suggests possible correct spellings. However, this does not mean that all of the words in the document are spelled correctly. A word may be spelled correctly but still be wrong (*too* instead of *two*, for instance). This is a good first step at proofing a document because it can find many common errors, but users will still need to proof–read documents to ensure complete accuracy.

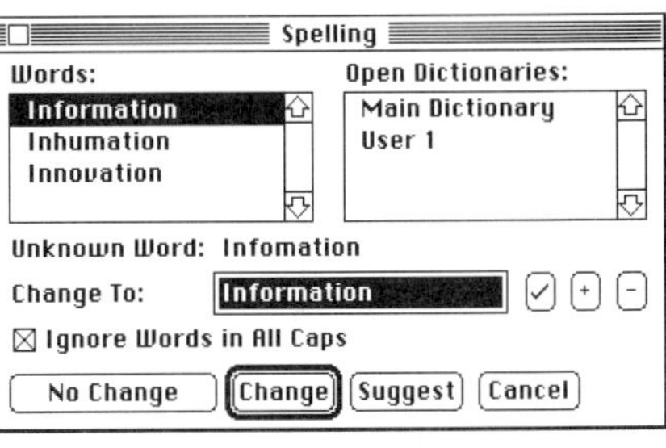

This is a typical spell checker window or dialog box.

Automatic hyphenation is the splitting of a word between two lines so that the text will fit better on the page. The word processor constantly monitors words typed and when it reaches the end of a line, if a word is too long to fit, it checks that word in a hyphenation dictionary. This dictionary contains a list of words with the preferred places to split it (usually in order of preference). If one of these cases fits part of the word at the end of the line, the word processor splits the word, adds a hyphen at the end, and places the rest on the next line. This happens extremely fast and gives text a more polished and professional look.

In the paragraph to the left, the word ***processor*** *is hyphenated .*

Outline processors are similar to word processors but they help users organize their thoughts. They allow users to expand and collapse hierarchies to reveal only the amount of work needed any time.

Many word processors now offer the ability to save styles of text. **Styles** (often called style sheets) combine multiple specifications for type such as: typeface, typestyle, size, hyphenation, color and other attributes. All of these attributes can then be applied at once to

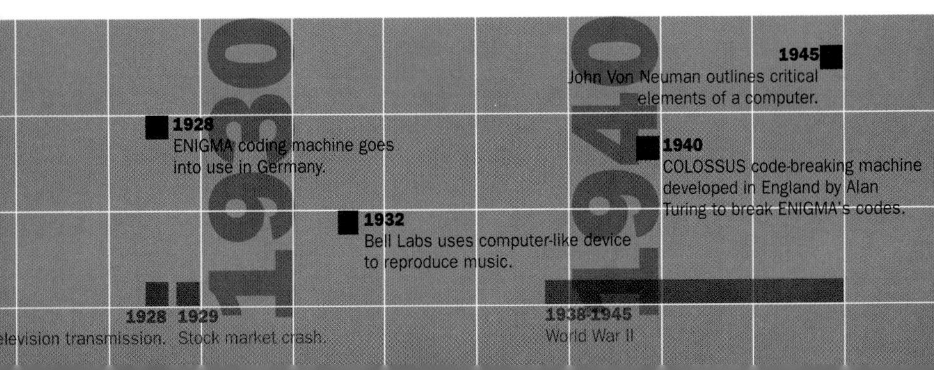

selected text by simply choosing the style. This saves the writer and designer time when formatting text.

Many word processors include an **on–line thesaurus** with which users can look–up different words to use in similar instances. Like a conventional thesaurus, this database of words contains definitions and suggestions of words with similar and opposite meanings. Some even include information about pronunciation and histories of evolving meaning.

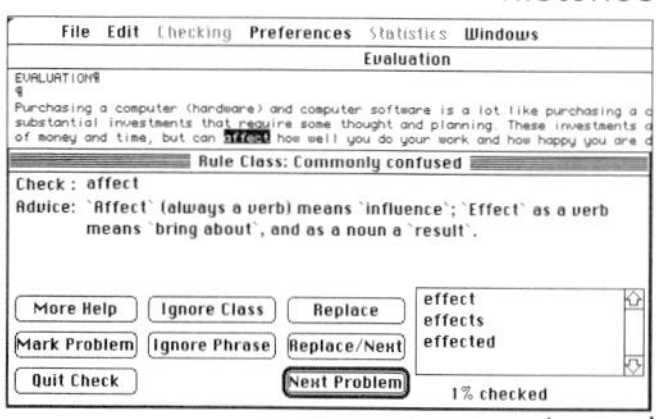

Grammar checkers are applications that attempt to check more than just spelling. They count words in sentences to flag possible run–on sentences. They look for words that show possible conflicts between verbs and subjects and they offer advice about corrections. Grammar checkers are a step beyond spell checkers, but they are still not a substitute for a human editor. Their power comes not from knowing every grammatical rule, but from questioning the writer about certain parts of a text. This gives the writer another chance to think about what he or she has written. This opportunity can be important because the computer provides an objective (and very naïve) viewpoint that can alert writers to problems that wouldn't be obvious to them otherwise.

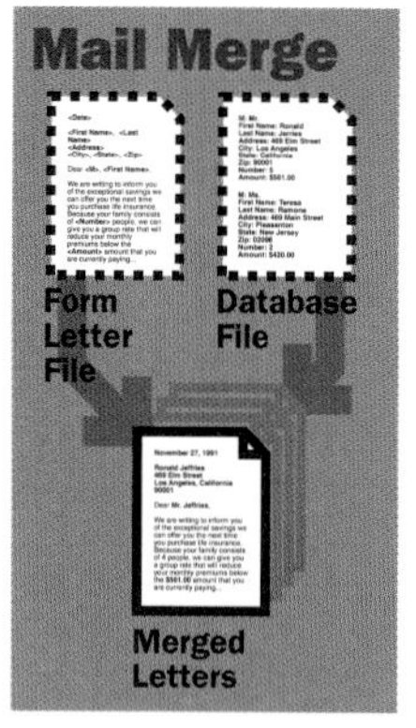

Mail Merge applications are largely responsible for the explosion of "personalized" junk mail. Form letters with designated spaces for names and addresses are stored as documents with links to lists of names and addresses of potential buyers or customers. By designating what information goes into which blank space, a computer can process a huge amount of correspondence substituting the "personal" information seamlessly into a form letter. The final document appears to be typed specifically to the person addressed. Although this has increased the amount of junk mail, mail merge is useful for large quantities of similar documents. It makes the processing and printing of these documents much more efficient for companies. Bills, notices, catalogs and account statements are all

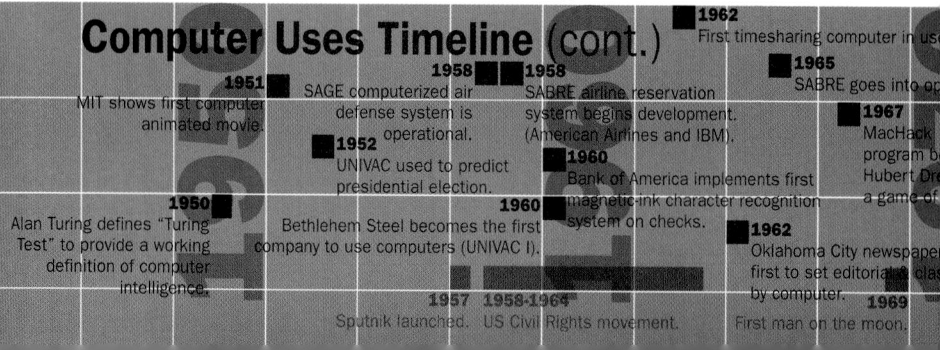

easier to control and produce with mail merge features, taking less time and money to do so.

Many word processors and **layout applications** ▶10 can even help generate tables of numbers or figures, sophisticated indexes and comprehensive tables of contents.

OCR

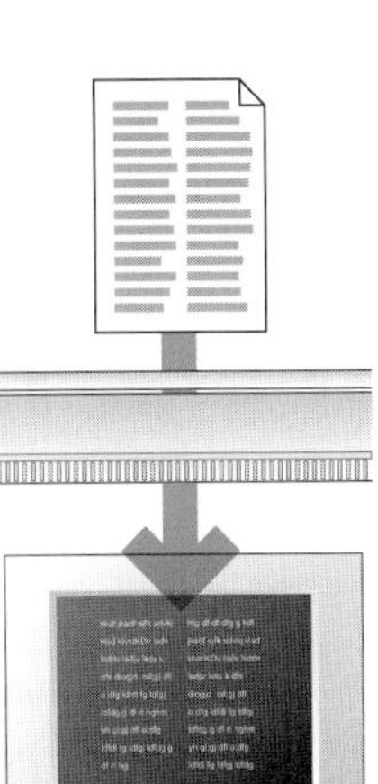

OCR translates written text into text that can be edited with a computer.

Optical Character Recognition (OCR) is a relatively new technology that allows computers to recognize text scanned into a system with a **scanner** ▶87–89 or digitizer. Scanned text is recognized by the computer as groups of dots rather than characters. A computer cannot normally understand the text and a user cannot manipulate it by typing. By scanning the text into a computer as a picture, OCR software can compare the groupings of dots, letter by letter, to stored pictures of letters or use rules to convert the scanned image into editable text. OCR applications are not yet 100% accurate. In fact, most cannot get more than 95% of the letters correct. However, they can be a real help in reading information from forms, manuscripts and other documents and converting them into data that can be stored in databases, edited as text or manipulated in many different ways.

Handwriting recognition is a technology just on the horizon. Like OCR, this feature can identify parts of scanned information (in this case, handwriting) and convert it into editable text. This is a fairly easy job for humans, but a daunting task for a computer. There are so many possible differences in every letter, from neat to sloppy, cursive to carefully printed, that developers are only now making headway in training computers to recognize them. Think about how hard it is to read the stereotypic doctor's prescription. Now you can begin to imagine what it is like for a computer to be able to read just evenly spaced and carefully drawn capitals.

While this technology is just now becoming available, its potential is great. Many people are fast with computer keyboards but

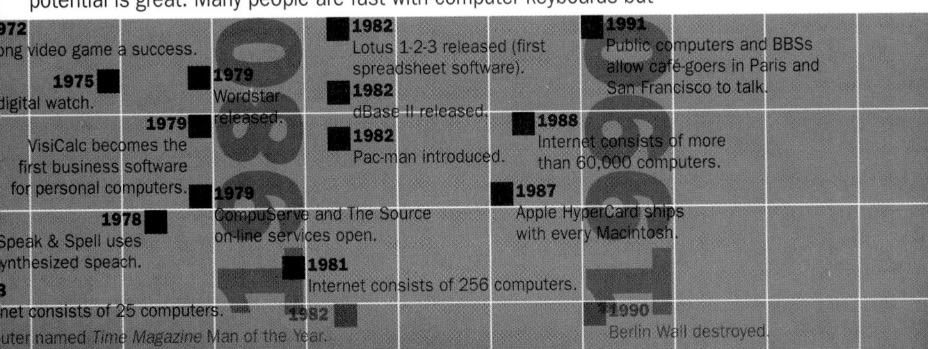
972
video game a success.
1975
digital watch.
1979
VisiCalc becomes the first business software for personal computers.
1978
Speak & Spell uses
ynthesized speach.
net consists of 25 computers.
uter named Time Magazine Man of the Year.
1979
Wordstar released.
1979
CompuServe and The Source on-line services open.
1981
Internet consists of 256 computers.
1982
1982
Lotus 1-2-3 released (first spreadsheet software).
1982
dBase II released.
1982
Pac-man introduced.
1988
Internet consists of more than 60,000 computers.
1987
Apple HyperCard ships with every Macintosh.
1991
Public computers and BBSs allow café-goers in Paris and San Francisco to talk.
1990
Berlin Wall destroyed.
1980
1990

don't find them natural nor easy to use. However, we are all familiar with writing. Potentially this could make computers more accessible to many people and make some forms of data entry easier.

Desktop Publishing

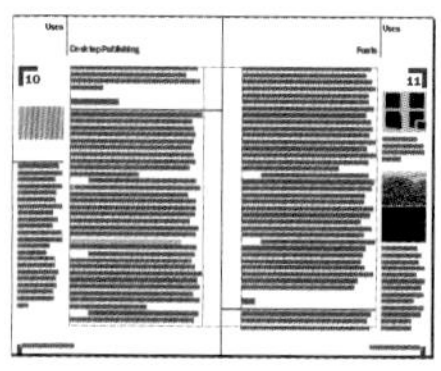

The only way to distinguish a good ***service bureau*** *from a bad one is by word of mouth. Talk to people in the industry about different service bureaus in your area. Ask service bureaus to show you examples of similar projects they have handled. Some service bureaus offer superb service and careful quality control. These are critical for quality publishing —especially for 4–color process work. If you are only printing laser copies, quality is not as crucial, but for sophisticated jobs look for a good service bureau well before you need it.*

Desktop Publishing refers to the use of personal computers to design, create, and publish books, newsletters, magazines and other printed pieces. Desktop Publishing is really a combination of a few different processes including **word processing** ▶5, graphic design, information design, output and pre–press technologies, and sometimes image manipulation. There are also many applications that support these processes, including font creation applications (that allow users to design and create their own typefaces, called **fonts** ▶11–12) and type manipulation applications (that allow users to modify text in visually creative ways).

Desktop publishing centers around a layout application. A **layout application** ▶143 is used to import text from word processing applications, graphics from paint and drawing applications, and images from scanning or image manipulation applications, combine and arrange them all on a page. They typically can bring in or import many different types of files. It is this ability to manipulate so many different items and control how they are used that makes layout software so popular and useful. This software is usually the last stop before a document is printed. Once composed and designed, these files can be printed onto film by high–quality devices, called **imagesetters** ▶86, 121, 144, and printed on a traditional printing press.

Because imagesetters are expensive and temperamental professional devices, most people cannot afford to buy their own. There are, however, companies called **Service Bureaus** ▶120 that specialize in printing other people's files on imagesetters just like copy stores make copiers available to others. Service Bureaus can offer a variety of equipment and services. Some offer imageset output, **laser printer** ▶85, 121–122 output, **color laser printer** output and even slide or **film recorder** ▶12 output. In addition, some have scanning and color **scanning equipment** ▶87–89.

Drawing applications differ from paint applications in the way they understand graphic objects. **Paint applications** see everything on screen as a collection of tiny dots or **pixels** ▶80, 114–115. They only

record the data necessary to reproduce each pixel accurately. Paint software understands the image to be one unified scene (not a collection of smaller images). **Drawing applications** on the other hand, understand the image part by part. Each object is drawn as a separate piece that can be manipulated without changing the other parts of the image. Objects are typically lines, circles, letters, images, and graphics. For example, the drawing application understands a rectangle as an object of four points connected by four lines. A paint application can only see that some pixels are dark and others are not and cannot manipulate the square as an object (only pixel by pixel). Because the drawing application understands the square as an object, the user can change it by selecting the points and moving them or deleting them. The original square can quickly become a triangle, circle or random and complex shape. The paint rectangle can be changed only by adding or deleting pixels or groups of pixels.

*The squares on the left repesent **draw** objects and those on the right represent **paint** ones.*

Image Manipulation ▸142 applications are sophisticated programs that act similarly to paint applications. They are used mostly to manipulate scanned photographs in complex ways. Images can be color–corrected for printing, combined with other images, subtlety changed to accent different parts or radically changed with visual effects. Blurry photos can be sharpened (to some extent), harsh ones can be subdued, and plain ones changed into exciting ones. As with most software, the imagination and training of the user is most important. The computer cannot make decisions about how appropriate a certain effect is or when an image is truly color–corrected.

Increasingly, photographs traditionally retouched by hand are retouched with computers because of the abilities to save work in stages and perform so many effects so quickly. The drawback to retouching photographs digitally is that it is very data–intensive, meaning it requires much processor attention, storage space and **RAM** (Random Access Memory) ▸44, 47, 104–108. As computers get faster and more powerful, this work becomes less tedious but currently it is still expensive and time–consuming to do well.

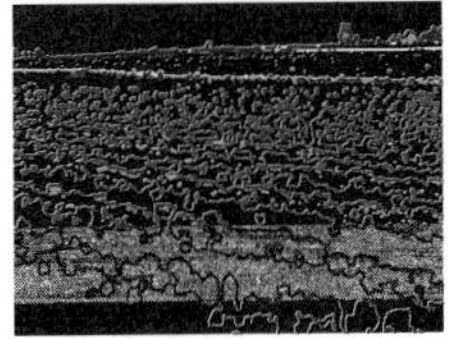

Many ethical questions have arisen about the use of image manipulation. One case involved National Geographic magazine's moving two pyramids closer together to fit them on the cover. Another involved TV GUIDE's using a photo compiled with the face and head of one celebrity and the body of another (without noting it).

Fonts

Fonts are a necessary part of desktop publishing and an increasingly popular aspect of computing in general. Fonts refer to the size and style of a **typeface** ▸12 (style of alphabet). Thousands of typefaces

Fonts

Every font (typeface) has its own distinctive characteristics.

exist in printed pieces, some simple, some elaborative and decorative, and hundreds are now available for use on computers. Some of the characteristics that define type include: **size**, **style** (**Bold**, *Italic*, Underline, etc...), **alignment** (flush left, right, center or both sides), and **typeface**. Layout and drawing applications, and some word processing and paint applications, can manipulate these characteristics and more. This control gives the designer many options in creating successful, quality published pieces. **Typography** (the design and manipulation of type and text) is far too complex to explain here. Refer to the **Bibliography** ▶130 for other graphic design and typography books for more in–depth information on fonts and type.

Computers control fonts in two ways: as bit–maps (the **display** or **screen font**) or in outline form (the **outline** or **printer font**). The computer may give different instructions to the printer to print the type and the monitor to display it. This often makes fonts a point of conflict in computers. Because the ability to use fonts is a recent capability for computers, the way applications deal with them is somewhat inconsistent. There are a few different font formats that describe these characteristics differently and some formats may conflict with others in certain computers or with certain applications.

Besides a few compatibility problems, however, typographic control has, in the last five years, reached the quality level of traditional (non–computer) methods. This is due to the development of **Page Description Languages** ▶85 (computer languages that describe how to print text and objects to different devices), faster and more powerful processors and toolkits built into the operating system that make these capabilities automatically available to applications.

Some Page Description languages (like PostScript™) are **device independent**. This means that they can speak to different output devices (printers, **film recorders** ▶89, imagesetters) and adjust the quality of the final output to the highest capabilities of the output device. **Resolution** ▶80, 84 is the measure of quality for output. This is a measure of how fine detail can be reproduced. Higher resolution means finer detail and smoother lines and type.

The typeface, type size, spacing and other type characteristics make a big difference in the message being communicated.

Entertainment

In the computer world, *entertainment* used to mean Computer **Games**. But now, with developments in video and sound technologies, it is coming to be more than just a toy. Computer controlled musical instruments and music software are revolutionizing how music is created and played. Advances in sophisticated animation technology are bringing capabilities to personal computers once held only by large, expensive equipment.

A new term, **Multimedia** ▸17, 23, 64, is the latest buzz–word for software and computer presentations that integrate voice, sound, music, video, text, images, animation and any other media in any combination. Although there is still much hype surrounding multimedia, the technologies that make it up are eventually going to change how people communicate information. Already another new term, **"info–tainment,"** has been coined to describe information that is more than just clear and understandable, but exciting too.

There are now applications available that help users create everything from simple slide shows to complex, sophisticated presentations. Because of the complexities of mixing sound, animation, video and graphics together, these applications can be a little daunting at first to learn. These applications offer great capabilities but just as in desktop publishing, there is no replacement for clear organization and planning. Beautiful colors and special effects can be seductive in the same way that the multitude of fonts can be, but if there is no substance or content to what you are trying to produce, all you can expect is glitzy garbage.

Some systems are geared more to playing mass–market presentations made by others, while other systems lean toward giving users as many capabilities to produce their own presentations. These tools include ways to input sound and images and integrate them easily and seamlessly.

The lines drawn between **presentation applications** (used for organizing and creating slide show–like presentations) and **animation** and **multimedia applications** (including tools for creating animation and integrating sound and video) are fairly fuzzy. This is still a new area of software and a great deal of evolution is still happening. The latest additions to the capabilities of these applications are **interactive tools** ▸15, 18.

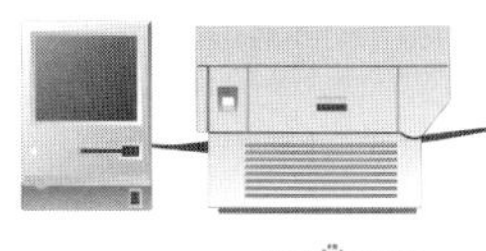

The boom in Desktop Publishing didn't get started until four products became available at the same time. The Apple Macintosh computer had been on the market for two years, but until Adobe Systems, Inc. released its PostScript™ page description language and Apple used it in its first laser printer, high–quality type and graphics were not available with a personal computer. Aldus Corp. completed the equation with a page layout application called PageMaker® that made these capabilities easy to use. The rest was, and will be, history.

Corporate Sales 1991

Computers and Music

Interactive tools allow users to control aspects or outcomes during the presentation. *Interactive* is an ill–defined word, but it generally refers to a user's control of aspects of a presentation. For example, a typical presentation might allow users to control which portions they see and how fast they move through it. It might even respond differently to one user's questions and answers depending on their experience or interests.

Computers and Music

At the heart of **Computer Music** is a code called **MIDI** (Musical Instrument Digital Interface). This code is a way of describing musical information universally so that both computers and musical instruments can understand the same instructions. Because MIDI is a universal standard, almost any kind of instrument (with a MIDI interface) can be used to create and play the instructions. A MIDI keyboard (electronic piano), for instance, can create MIDI code that describes the musical characteristics of what notes are played and how they are played. This code can be sent to another MIDI instrument, such as a MIDI trumpet, and played because both instruments speak the same language—MIDI. There are many different MIDI compatible instruments that can be used to create music, including MIDI string, wind and percussion instruments, and MIDI voice input devices (a sort of MIDI kazoo). This allows musicians to create music with whichever instruments they are most comfortable.

Connecting a computer to special MIDI instruments allows musicians to compose, mix and edit music electronically.

Once created, a computer can manipulate the MIDI code (with the correct software) into sophisticated, inspiring compositions. MIDI is a **16–channel, multi–timbral** code. This means that it can describe and communicate up to 16 different sequences of code simultaneously and play all concurrently. MIDI is **digital** ▶95 and **binary** ▶90, 95 (described with 1s and 0s), which is why a computer can manipulate it so well. This continuous stream of digital instructions is fast enough for instruments to reproduce sounds accurately in real–time. **Real–time** ▶29 means that the computer can process data fast enough so that the user perceives no time delay between giving instructions and seeing their result. Actions, in this case music, are produced while the user is creating them. This allows a musician to alter the instructions immediately and interact with the composition as it is playing.

Interaction ▸14, 18 is important here. The musician is not just playing previously recorded music, but creating it and changing it simultaneously—as with traditional instruments. The musician and instruments are responding to each other. MIDI adds the flexibility of controlling many instruments at once and manipulating them in ways traditional instruments can't be.

MIDI makes all of this possible by including timing data that helps the instruments synchronize correctly, as well as data about how each instrument acts. MIDI (like most computer codes and languages) is also very compact. A piece of music stored as MIDI instructions would take about 200 times less space in a computer as the same piece stored as high–fidelity, digitally recorded sound.

Most recording studios now have personal computers in them to control MIDI devices before, during and after recording and mixing. MIDI describes musical characteristics and doesn't sound "electronic" unless the musician specifically intends it to. Therefore, much current music that sounds traditionally played could very well be played on MIDI instruments and may have originated or been manipulated by a computer.

Video and Animation

Besides controlling music, computers have recently gained the abilities to control video and animation. **Video** refers to manipulating and showing moving images recorded with a video camera or captured from a television or video tape recorder. **Animation** refers to moving images on the screen that were gathered and combined from many sources.

Until recently, because television formats are different from computer image formats, personal computers could not manipulate images from these sources. Computers construct a picture in one of two ways; vector or raster. **Vector** ▸113–114 technology displays each of an object's components line by line, one at a time. The order in which objects are drawn may have nothing to do with their location on the screen. **Raster** ▸113–114 technology draws each row of the screen one at a time until the full screen is drawn (or redrawn). Neither the shape of the objects nor their location determine the order of drawing since the computer always starts at the top of the screen and draws across in rows until it reaches the bottom (and completes the image). In both cases, all the information about an image's appearance (shape, color, location) is stored digitally and translated into coordinates to be drawn on the screen.

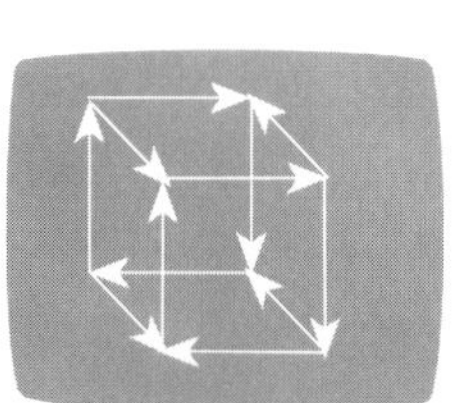

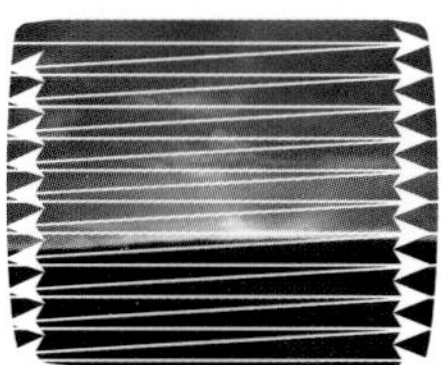

The top screen illustrates a cube drawn with vector technology while the bottom screen illustrates how raster technology displays images.

Video and Animation

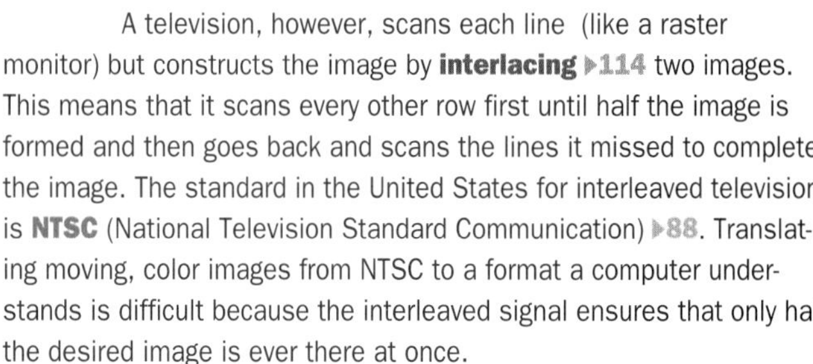

A television, however, scans each line (like a raster monitor) but constructs the image by **interlacing** ▸114 two images. This means that it scans every other row first until half the image is formed and then goes back and scans the lines it missed to complete the image. The standard in the United States for interleaved television is **NTSC** (National Television Standard Communication) ▸88. Translating moving, color images from NTSC to a format a computer understands is difficult because the interleaved signal ensures that only half the desired image is ever there at once.

In this example, two images (a sunrise and a field of tulips) are interlaced.

Despite the problems of translating so much information between different formats quickly, more and more computers are used for **video editing**. Computers have been used to produce professional quality editing for over eight years, but only recently has this technology become available on smaller, more affordable computers like personal computers.

Animation involves the movements of objects and pictures. Computer animation can take a few forms. At its most basic, it is the flashing of pictures in rapid succession that are slightly different to each other. Viewed as one continuous stream, these pictures depict motion in the same way that movie film or a flip–book does. This method offers little control and takes up a great amount of space. A more sophisticated approach is to describe the parts of the picture or scene as separate objects. By moving the objects across the screen and controlling how they interact with each other, animation can be achieved with much less memory or processing time needed.

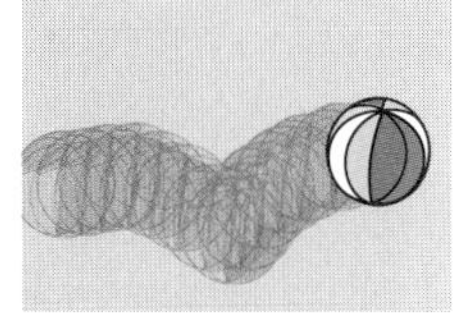

Animation applications are now available for personal computers. This software often allows sound to be edited into the animation as well, giving the final piece a complete and finished appearance.

Accounting and Spreadsheets

Because computers are great number calculators, they are ideal for applications that manage figures. **Spreadsheets** are flexible collections of boxes (called **cells**) that are containers for letters or numbers. These numbers can represent anything the user needs and can be part of complex equations. The cells are typically arranged two–dimensionally with rows and columns.

Spreadsheets are flexible because they allow most any data to be put into the cells (numbers, words, letters, equations, etc...). Equations can link numbers in different cells for automatic calculations. All of the data in a spreadsheet can be organized, managed and updated easily. Spreadsheets are also able to export data to other applications such as a **database** ▸21–22, 48 for further manipulation or a **page-layout application** ▸10, 48, 143 for inclusion in a publication.

Personal Workspace 91

	A	B	C	D	E	F	G
1							
2		1991					
3		January	February	March	April	May	June
4	Mon. Expense						
5	Car	$280	$280	$280	$280	$280	$280
6	Rent	$450	$450	$450	$450	$450	$450
7	Water	$30	$30	$30	$30	$30	$30
8	Cell. Phone	$337	$242	$75	$75	$75	$75
9	Phone						
10	Food	$200	$200	$200	$200	$200	$200
11	Bike	$250					
12	AT&T Carph	$8					
13	Business In	$112					
14	AMX-gold						
15	AMX-plt	$1,496	$500				
16	Doctor Bills	$133	$50	$50	$50	$50	$50
17	VISA-gold	$500	$500	$500	$500	$500	$500
18	VIVID						
19							
20							
21	Month Total	$2,451	$2,253	$1,585	$1,585	$1,585	$1,585
22							
23							

Accounting applications may use several different means to manage personal or corporate accounting data. Some mimic traditional accounting by arranging data in two–dimensional **ledger** sheets, very similar to spreadsheets. Others organize data into screens that are only possible on a computer. Most accounting applications include facilities for accounts payable, accounts receivable and check tracking. Some sophisticated applications also prepare tax returns, reports, profit and loss statements, controlling payroll or inventory, and fulfill many specific business needs. Some offer **statistical analysis** and **simulations** that allow users to predict the effects of certain actions. These applications provide easy access to related data combined with the ability to look at it in different ways and under different conditions.

Integrated Packages

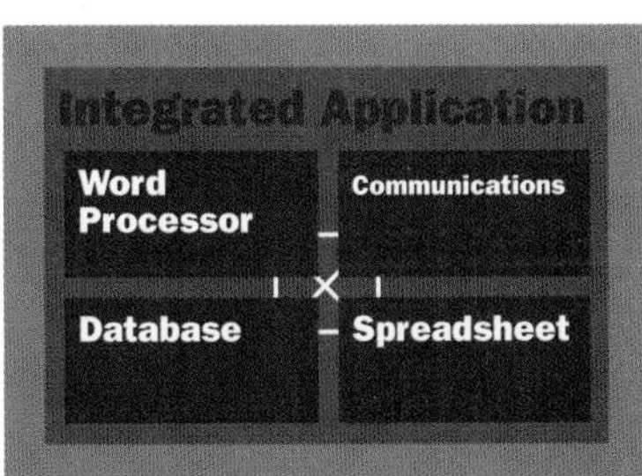

Some applications, called **integrated packages** or **integrated software**, offer several different functions that operate together. Usually, these include a **word processor** ▸5–9, **database**, **spreadsheet** and **communications** ▸27 capabilities. In effect, integrated packages are like having a few applications in one. These capabilities are linked so that they function together. This might allow a user to share information between a database and spreadsheet, for example. This limited form of **inter–process communication** ▸48 can provide greater productivity.

Education

There are many applications geared toward education and personal advancement. New terms, such as "**info–tainment** ▸13" and "**edu–tainment"** attest to a new view of education. This view is based on the realization that people cannot learn if they are not interested. By combining **multimedia** ▸13, 23, 64 with **interactive** ▸14–15

controls, it is possible to put people in better control of their educations. This does not mean that educational software lacks content. In fact, it is more effective to use animation, color and sound to teach some things that would make less sense merely as text.

Another aspect of better education is **interactivity**. This means that users and computers can respond to each other. Interactive software is often controlled by the user and can allow users to tailor it to their specific needs. Users can then learn at their own pace, as well as selectively cover only the information they need.

Applications already exist that teach typing, mathematics, science and medicine, and a variety of other topics. There are applications that help users enhance their brainstorming, thinking and creative abilities, and work through personal problems. There is no limit to what can be taught using computer tools if it is done with the understanding that computers can enhance learning but cannot make up for lack of organization or content.

Utilities

A hard disc crash may be caused by a number of things, including: water damage, smoke and dust particles or software and hardware malfunctions.

***Fragmentation** occurs over time as files are written and deleted again and again to a hard disc. Because of space limitations on the disc, many files get split into pieces and spread around the disc. You aren't aware of this but the computer is and knows where to find all of the pieces. **Defragmenting** the hard disc takes all of the pieces and writes them into one.*

Computers are intricate machines and require some special tools to keep them working efficiently. There are a variety of utilities available that help users stay organized and take advantage of a computer's full capabilities.

Back–up utilities help users speed the process of copying and cataloging the content of their **hard discs** ▶61–63 to **diskettes** ▶59–60 for safe keeping. Backing–up is important and should be done periodically to insure the safety of your information. While a hard disc rarely **crashes** ▶62 (seriously malfunctions), it is still a possibility. Ensure that you do not lose important information by backing–up at least once a week. Unfortunately, backing–up is all too often recognized as important only after it is too late.

If you lose data through a hard disc crash, a diskette gone bad or accidentally deleting the wrong file, a **repair utility** can often help. These utilities find lost or erased data—even on damaged discs and diskettes. When a file is deleted, the data is not usually erased. The system only marks the space on the disc as empty so that new data can be written over it. If the attempt is made directly after the accident occurs these utilities can often retrieve all or most of the lost data.

Other utilities can help **defragment** your hard disc, analyze and change the workings of your **system software** ▶44–45 and transfer files between different **file formats** ▶22–23. **Macro utilities** allow users to translate complex sequences of tasks into easy–to–invoke processes. Usually, combinations of keystrokes and commands can be condensed into one **key combination** or **function key** ▶79. This is especially useful for tedious and repetitive operations.

CAD/CAM

Computer–Aided Design (CAD) is a fast–growing category of computer applications. CAD software allows designers and engineers to plan, design and realize technical products such as microchips, integrated circuits, automobiles, houses, buildings and even molecules. CAD applications have **two–dimensional** (2D) or **three dimensional** (3D) capabilities, depending on the focus of the application. Software to design chips requires primarily 2D capabilities while designing buildings and cars requires mostly 3D capabilities.

Generally, 3D design is displayed with either wire–frame or with solid–modeling techniques. **Wire–frame** drawings are those that appear as lines that represent the edges of the object. **Solid modeling** is the rendering of the object's surfaces. There are many sophisticated methods that can be used to render 3D objects. Color, texture, lighting, viewing angle and opacity are some controls that these CAD applications offer to make the objects displayed look as "real" as possible. Solid modeling requires many more calculations and much more computational power than wire–frame drawings. Designers and engineers usually work in wire–frame and periodically produce solid model images to check their progress.

Associated with CAD, **Computer–Aided Manufacturing** (CAM) allows products designed with CAD systems to be fabricated under computer control. Automated manufacturing robots can control the production of a part with instructions from the CAM software.

Related to CAD and CAM (sometimes called CAD/CAM or CADAM) are **Computer–Aided Testing** (CAT) and **Computer–Aided Engineering** (CAE). This software simulates and tests a design using mathematical models before physical parts are ever built. This can save a lot of money and time eliminating errors earlier in the design process.

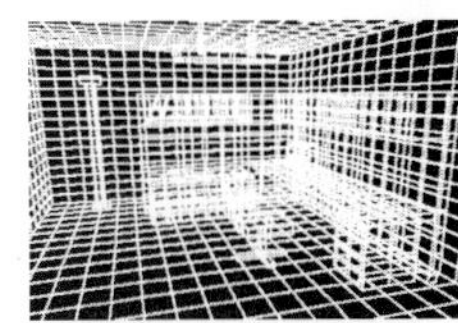

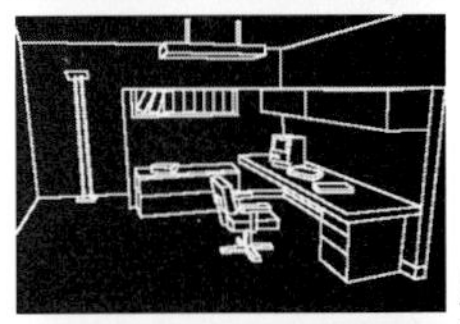

*The examples above show the different ways an object can be displayed in a CAD application. The top is a **wire–frame** model that only shows the object outlines. Under that is a **hidden–line** view that removes unnecessary lines for a clearer view. The other two show the same objects with **solid modeling** and **shading** and **shadows** rendered. Adding **reflection** and **texture mapping** would make the scene even more realistic.*

Scientific and Industrial Applications

More and more scientific and industrial applications are written to run on powerful **UNIX** ▶50 *workstations.*

Note: The more unique the task, the more custom programming necessary.

Scientific Applications

Most scientific research and development requires expensive, custom–created applications and software tools. Because most research is specialized, researchers frequently develop their own tools. Usually, these applications cannot be used by others doing different research. Basic applications that can be used as building blocks can sometimes be purchased, but more specific capabilities are usually self–built.

Almost all aspects of research and development use computers. Models for weather prediction, high–energy physics, simulating experimental mathematics and medical applications all use high–speed supercomputers to a large extent. Computers have aided in the development of everything from better skyscrapers to microscopic neurosurgery.

Industrial Applications

Computers are used to control manufacturing machinery, robots, assembly lines, inventory, phone switching networks, etc.... Like scientific applications, **industrial applications** are usually custom–built or proprietary. Because the nature of the work is so specific to each circumstance, it is unlikely that the same applications can be used in different environments or for different uses.

One of a computer's greatest assets is its ability to store large amounts of data in such a small space. Typically, a single high–density (HD) diskette can store 1400 pages of text. Images and sound take much more space, but data compression ▶23, 28 techniques use mathematical equations to squeeze digitally stored pictures and sound into smaller files.

Databases

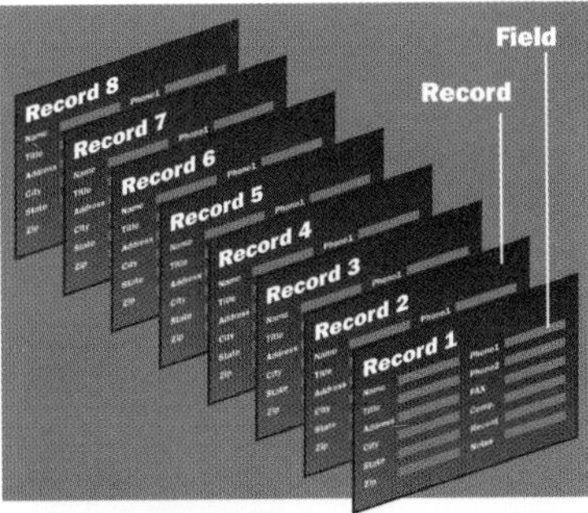

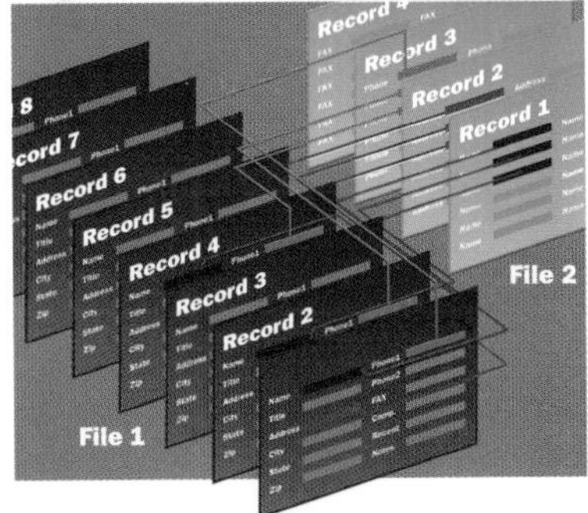

*The top illustration is an example of a card or record from a **flat file** database. The illustration at bottom is from a **relational** database and shows links between different fields in different records.*

A **database** is a computer file (or set of files) that contains varied data in a pre–described form. Each piece of data is held in a **field** labeled to describe the type of data it is. A set of fields is grouped to form a **card**, **form** or **record** that holds data that pertains to a particular subject.

Basically, there are two different types of databases; flat file and relational. A **flat file** database stores information in fields grouped on a card or record. The database does not necessarily understand the data in each field but it knows the organization of the records (like a card file). The user can then flip through the records or reorganize them but cannot manipulate the fields themselves (besides retyping the data or deleting it in each individual field). A **relational database**, however, is able to build links between all the components (including the fields and the data inside them) and can allow the user to manipulate and reorganize them in much more sophisticated ways. These links allow users to pull specific data from different fields easily and reorganize them into a new form. This extra power comes at a cost, however. Relational databases are usually more complex and harder to learn, but their abilities to transform data make them powerful and astounding.

A flat file is fine for a limited set of data like an address list that gets used in only one way. However, as the data gets more complex and cumbersome, a relational database can offer more flexibility and less repetition.

Database applications ▶17 allow users to configure databases in a way that makes sense to the user and makes the data manageable and understandable. Because the database application

understands the structure of the data, information can be reached quickly and efficiently in many different ways. Databases allow the user to search rapidly for specific data or reconfigure it into new organizations. It is crucial to keep the data up-to-date for it to be valid. Just because it is well organized, doesn't ensure its validity or importance.

File Formats

One important aspect of data storage is the form in which it is stored. This is analogous to energy storage. The form in which either is stored affects the ways in which it can be used. If energy is stored as electricity, many products and appliances can use it for power, but a gas stove or the majority of automobiles cannot. Choosing one form of storage may limit your options of use.

Fortunately, with computerized data, it is much easier to translate data into different forms. Many applications can "read" (open and use) and "write" (save and store) different file formats. This can allow you to translate data into different forms where it can be used by different applications for different purposes. As with applications, there are a few categories of different data storage types. There are many formats available for different types of data on a particular **platform** (family), but few formats are commonly used across computer platforms (by different computer families).

Text (words, numbers and punctuation) is one of the most common forms in which to store data because so much of a computer's use involves manipulating text. Most computers can write and read **ASCII** or **TEXT** files which are basic characters with a few special characters to mark tabs and returns. Some applications now understand **RTF** (Rich Text Format) which includes more sophisticated formatting instructions (such as font, style, size, indents...) to retain the structure of the document between different applications.

New formats for representing page–layout files are emerging. One proposed format called **SERIF** (Standard Entity Rendering Interchange Format) stores graphics, images, text, text styles and formatting, within frames in the file to be read by any **page–layout application** ▸10, 48, 143 that supports the format.

Graphics are still so new to computers that few standards exist that are common to different computers. **PostScript**™ ▸35 is quickly becoming a standard for most computers used for **desktop**

are mixes in different amount
of colors. In nature, a great a
possible, but a monitor is onl
about half of them. Still fewer
displayable) are able to be pri
process inks.

Video **acceleration cards** spe
process by placing lots of extr
high-powered processor on a
allows the card to process the
quickly (especially for drawing
like **video processing**, compu

ASCII (TEXT) example

(***Cyan, Magenta, Yellow,*** *and* ***Black***)
amounts to create a wide range of co
assortment of colors are possible, bu
displaying about half of them. Still fe
displayable) are able to be printed wi

Video **acceleration cards** s
drawing-to-screen process by
VRAM and a high-powered pro
video card. This allows the ca
drawing routines very quickly
drawing-intensive applications

RTF example

(***Cyan, Magenta, Yellow,*** *and* ***Black***)
amounts to create a wide range of co
assortment of colors are possible, bu
displaying about half of them. Still fe
displayable) are able to be printed wi

Video **acceleration cards** s
drawing-to-screen proce
special video card. This
drawing-intensive appli
processing (pre-press publish
separate and optional, it mus

SERIF example

File Formats

publishing ▶10. This format stores the instructions to recreate a graphic in the PostScript™ language. Each device that supports PostScript™ is able to interpret how that graphic or page should be displayed or printed. A variation of this is **EPS** (Encapsulated PostScript™) which packages the file in a form that can be imported into a different file. Sometimes, a low–resolution picture of the graphic is added so that it can be displayed on screens that do not understand PostScript™ directly. This allows the user to see and move the graphic on screen, but usually not to change it.

Images, such as photographs or scans, are commonly stored as **TIFF** (Tagged Image File Format) files. This format allows black and white, **grayscale** ▶80–82, and color images to be stored for use by most applications. Images take up more memory space compared to text. Full color (**24–bit**) images can be anywhere from 1 to 100 megabytes each, depending on the size and the **resolution** ▶80–82. Grayscale images are substantially smaller than color images and black and white images are smaller still but both are still massive in comparison to text. This is why **compression** ▶28 algorithms are so important. Any opportunity to encode these files into smaller space is welcome. It is possible to compress data for images and graphics up to 20 times without degrading the quality of the image. For high–end, professional publishing, many sophisticated systems store high–resolution color images in a **CT** (Continuous Tone) format. These files are even bigger than TIFF files because the higher resolution requires exponentially more data.

There are few standard formats for transferring database or spreadsheet data. Most applications can read a **tab–delimited** file in which all the data is in text form and each piece is separated by a tab space. If the user knows the form in which the data is arranged (either in cards, records, tables, etc...) the application can usually be shown how to reconstruct it, but any links or other features between the data will probably be lost.

There are, currently, no formats popular enough or complete enough to be called standards for **multimedia** ▶13 or **hypermedia** ▶24–26 data. Two proposed formats are **MIFF** (Multimedia Interchange File Format) which would store text, numbers, images, video, and sounds together in one file and **HIFF** (Hypermedia Interchange File Format) which would store multimedia objects with any embedded **links** ▶25. Unfortunately, neither has been standardized or widely used.

1–bit (Black and White) TIFF image (16Kbytes)

GrayscaleTIFF image (189Kbytes)

8–bit Color TIFF image (189Kbytes)

24–bit Color TIFF image (545Kbytes)

Database Publishing

Database Publishing

Database Publishing uses elements of the storage and manipulation abilities of a **database** ▶21–22, 48 and publishing capabilities of a **page–layout application** ▶10, 48, 143 to publish information–intensive products such as catalogs, price lists, and directories. The information from a database can be stored in a way that meets information management needs and formatted automatically to meet design and publishing needs. The automatic formatting is handled either by a special utility application or within the page layout application. This utility then composes the entire publication, pulling the information from the appropriate places in the database and arranging it correctly into pages. The information may include graphics and images, as well as numbers and text.

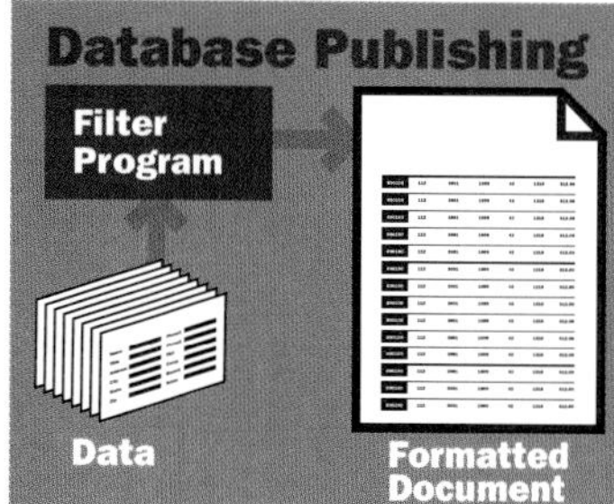

Usually, a set of instructions is written to arrange and format each piece of data correctly on the page to the design specifications. These instructions are either in the form that the utility application can understand and work with, or as a custom application written specifically for this purpose. With a specially developed database publishing utility, the information must be written into a special file by the database application in a format that the utility understands. This file will contain all the data separated by tabs or other special symbols. If a custom application is written, it may contain the necessary instructions to find the data in the database itself.

This works in much the same way as **mail merge** ▶8, but generates more complex **camera–ready** artwork that can go directly to a printer for large–scale printing and production. Because the computer does so much of the formatting and organization automatically, very large, information–intensive jobs can be handled more quickly and more effectively.

Ted Nelson coined the term ***hypertext*** *to mean electronic text that was flexibly structured and accessible in many ways. For over 20 years he has been developing hypermedia systems to allow people greater personal access to information. His latest,* ***Xanadu***™*, approaches key issues that most other systems ignore (copyrights, availability, franchising, control, royalties, etc...) Like many others, he was there long ago and waits (impatiently) for the rest of us to catch up.*

Hypertext and Hypermedia

For over twenty years the term Hypertext and the ideas that surround it have been in use, but only recently have they begun to be implemented. The term **Hypertext** ▶29–30, 78 refers to text on a computer that is not arranged linearly or sequentially. This means that users do

Hypertext and Hypermedia

not have to follow a predetermined path to use the information. Users can follow their interests by jumping from one topic to another at will.

The prerequisite needs for hypertext include links and vast amounts of information accessible from the computer. This information is not like a computerized *card catalog* in a library but more like a computerized library where the books and the information within them can be read on screen. **Links** are a connection between points in text (from one part in the text to another part). Users can jump from point to point with these links. Some links may connect to several points, giving the user a choice of jumps.

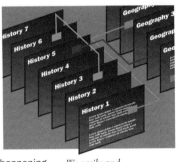

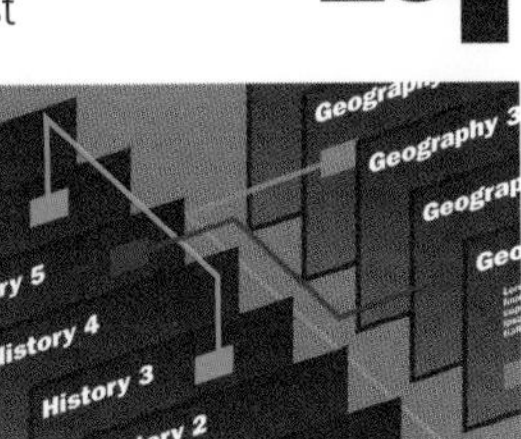

Adding pictures, graphics, animation and sound to a hyper–linked database creates something called **hypermedia**. Instead of only reading text, the user can hear and see things happening. Links may be from text to a photo, animation, sound or anything. This diversity provides a rich environment for learning and exploring.

We easily and naturally move from topic to topic in our conversations with others, but until recently this was not generally possible with computers. Hypermedia allows us to use this more natural thought process with computers.

Because users can change their search criteria at any time without being forced to complete a predetermined sequence or path, they can search information more quickly and more naturally. This is one of the wonderful aspects of hypermedia. Because the information, itself (and not just references to it) is **on–line** ▶29–30 (on the screen), the user can browse rapidly without having to search through books. This information can also be accessible to many people at once. Some systems may even allow users to write and **author** their own information (complete with links) and integrate it into the rest of the information available in the system.

There are many hypermedia products available already but most can only be used on separate **platforms** ▶22 (computer families). Some are merely hypertext, while others are full hypermedia systems. While some allow users to create their own presentations, others allow users only to read existing information. These separate applications are limited systems (so far), because they are not constantly linked to great databases of information. HyperCard® (from Apple Computer, Inc.) is the most successful of these products. It enjoys a wide base of published material in HyperCard form and is a good tool with which to access information on **CD–ROMs** ▶63–64 or in **databases** ▶21–22, 48 if that information is in a form HyperCard can read. There are not yet, however, any **on–line** databases that work with HyperCard.

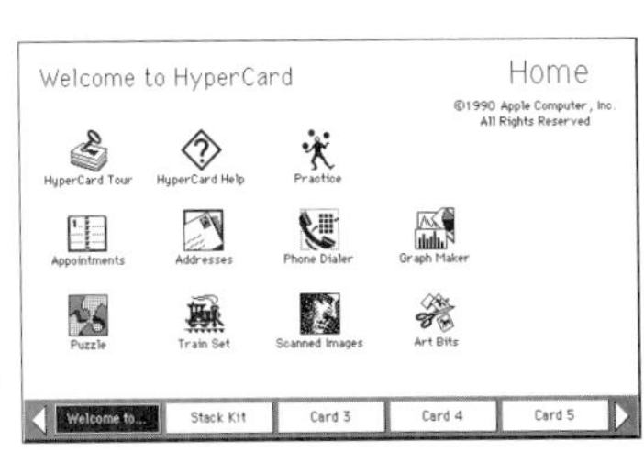

Screen shot from a HyperCard® ***stack***.

Hypertext and Hypermedia

A linked database like hypertext or hypermedia has its drawbacks too. The first is that there are none yet publicly available. They will eventually appear, but only after considerable development and support.

Another crucial aspect of a hypermedia system is **navigation**. With so much information available, it is easy for users to get lost or have trouble finding what they need. Great navigation tools and a clear interface are paramount to a successful hypermedia system. Also, there are other needs to be addressed to be successful, such as copyright protection, royalties, information integrity, and authoring abilities. The only system publicly announced that addresses most of these aspects is Ted Nelson's Xanadu® (now owned by Autodesk) and currently in development. It remains to be seen when hypermedia will be widely available.

*Vannevar Bush developed a concept of **multimedia** and **hypermedia** back in 1945 called the **memex**. This system proposed microfilm to accomplish many of the same things designers are trying to accomplish today with computers.*

Modems and Communications

Modems and networks are changing the ways users work with each other. One computer can empower one user and many computers can empower many users, but many computers communicating with each other empower all users to an even greater extent.

Cooperation is a fundamental necessity to achieving anything and computer communication tools offer increased cooperation between computer users. A new term, **groupware** ▸68–69, describes applications that allow many people to work together to achieve goals that are much more powerful and sophisticated than those they can achieve by themselves.

Modems and Communications Software

Users of **modems** ▸69, 73–74 need special **communications applications** to use with modems to connect their computers to other computers. These applications allow users to specify the phone number to dial and the transmission settings to match those of the computers they are dialing. **Baud rates** ▸69 (the speed at which the modem sends and receives data) can be set by the user. Some applications and modems may reset transmission characteristics themselves to the correct settings when connecting to other systems. This is sometimes called a "handshake".

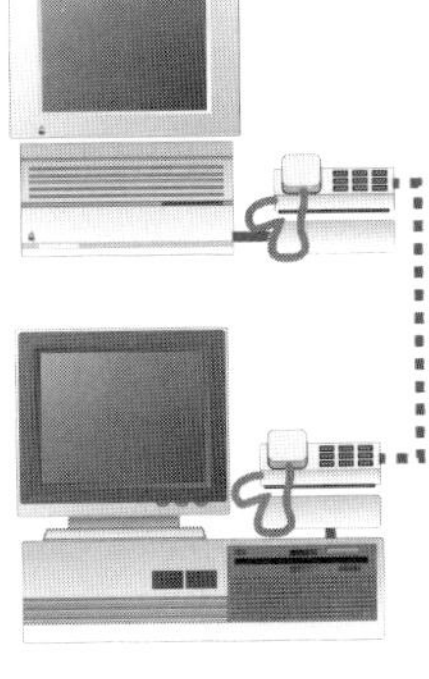

Although modems and communications applications have been around for a long time, they are not as easy to use as other applications or equipment and can be confusing to novices.

There are standard communication methods (called **protocols** ▸73) that are common to most computers and communications software. These protocols allow different kinds of computers to structure their information so that they may be mutually understood. A common protocol, is **VT100** which allows personal computers to emulate (appear and work as) a mainframe terminal. This text–based interface is common to mainframe computers shared by many terminals. Even if both connected computers aren't terminals, they can "speak" to each other by this (or any other common) protocol. This is called **terminal emulation** ▸69.

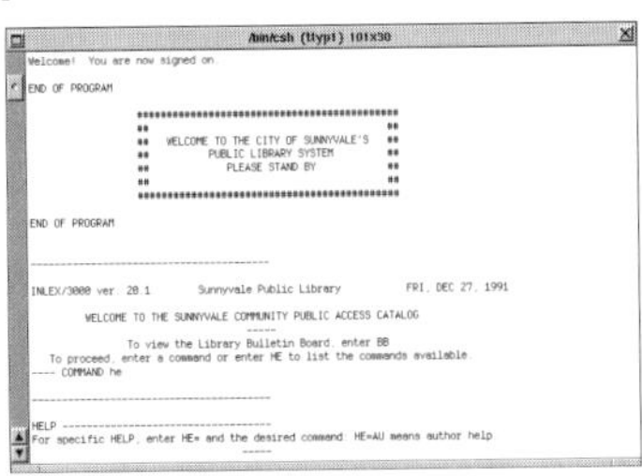

E–mail

Once connected, users can communicate by typing messages on the screen, send or receive files and access **networks** ▸70–73 and **servers** ▸71-72. Some communications applications are specifically used to access networks from remote or portable computers. This is especially useful for people traveling on business. They allow a user to dial in (usually requiring a password), access a company's computers, send and receive electronic mail, and even use the printers on the network. Generally users connected in this way work as though they were sitting at a computer in the office.

E–mail

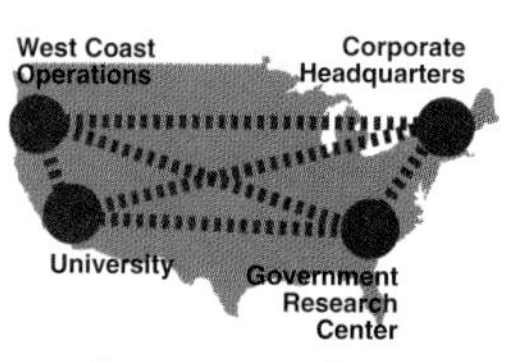

Wide–Area Networks (WANs) can substantially vary in size and geographic coverage.

One of the most basic communications applications is **electronic mail** (E–mail). These applications allow users to send messages to each other. Usually, the messages are short pieces of text, but some applications and systems support the ability to send documents or files within the message. A network of some kind is necessary for E–mail to function. Within a company, E–mail allows one person to send messages to another by specifying the **address** (the name or account number) of that person and then entering the message. Over a **wide–area network** (WAN) ▸73 the process is the same but the message may be sent across the street or across the country. E–mail messages may be stored in a host computer (such as a **server** ▸71–72), or in the computer of the user who receives the message.

Any **document transfer** (sending a document to another location) involves **downloading** the document to the network and having it routed to the correct address. This takes a little time. Large documents (especially those that include images or sounds) may require a lot of time to download, depending on the **transmission speed** of the network.

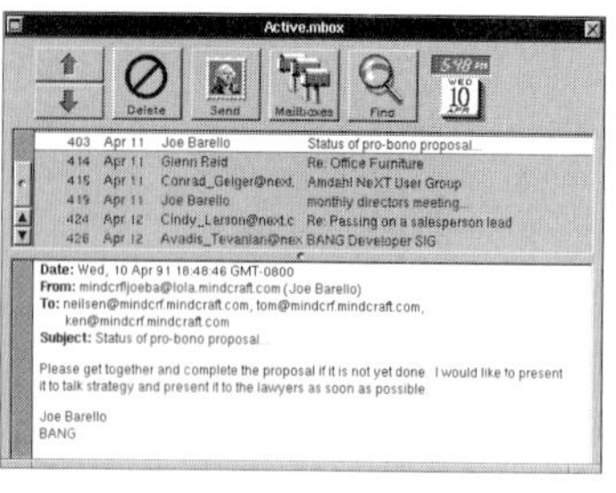

It is possible to transmit large files faster if they are first **compressed**. Image documents can be compressed to as little as a twentieth of their previous size and result in faster transmission times. Special **compression utilities** must be used to compress the file for transmission and **decompress** it once it has reached its destination.

Voice–mail is similar to E–mail except that it includes sending recorded sound in addition to text. Users can send verbal explanations of instructions. Voice–mail works very much like an answering machine except that the messages are stored on a hard disc or network. Others can leave verbal messages for you or you can leave spoken notes for someone else in case they aren't available then. Voice and E–mail can enhance productivity by allowing people to work and deliver messages even when they can't reach others involved.

Note: Voice–mail is most efficient for short messages and E–mail is best for long messages.

The ability to transfer written and spoken messages, files and data, can increase productivity among members of a team or workgroup. This is why **groupware** is referred to as **interpersonal computing**. Groupware allows users to share data and interact with each other simultaneously.

BITnet (a popular wide area network) stands for Because It's Time network, or sometimes, Because It's There network.

On–line Systems

On–line refers to applications used on a computer—especially by more than one person. An **on–line document** is one that exists on a computer. Many documents are only meant to be seen and used on the screen instead of on paper. A lot of documentation, especially technical notes, instruction manuals and directories are now being used on–line. This is a new and different environment for publishing materials. While the resolution of the screen is much lower than what is possible on paper, the costs and difficulty with duplicating the same information are also less. On–line documents may also include **multimedia** such as sounds, images and animation, and the cross–referencing and search capabilities of **hypertext**. These documents can, ultimately, be more flexible, valuable and easier to use than their paper counterparts and require less space to store. They are also much easier to revise and update.

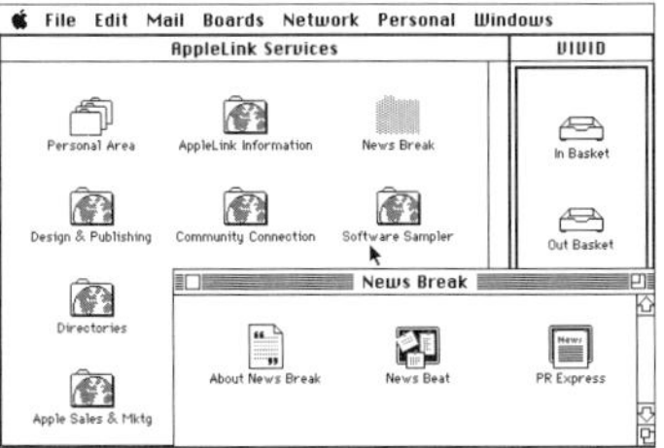

Many on–line systems offer immediate access to **databases** and vast stores of bibliographic and written information. Some dedicated systems offer continuous monitoring of the stock market in **real–time** (with little or no time lag). These give users immediate reports of the prices of stocks or other commodities.

BIX, CompuServe, The WELL, Prodigy, and America Online are all popular commercial BBSs.

Bulletin Board Services

While **Bulletin Board Services** (BBSs) are on–line systems, they are distinct because they are free–form discussions on remote, private computers. Other on–line systems tend to be more structured

Bulletin Board Services

information systems. Users access a BBS by dialing in over phone lines with a **modem** ▸73–74 and communications software. Once connected, users may have to answer initial questions to gain access or set–up an account for use. There are many bulletin board services that offer a variety of capabilities. Many offer on–line discussions (called **forums**) with other users on a variety of topics, including technical support and politics. Many offer social chatting with others currently logged–in on **talk–lines**. Some offer files, **freeware, shareware** ▸37–38 or other software for **downloading** to the user's computer. Some have on–line information such as weather, research materials, and news. Still others allow users to shop, purchase airline tickets and review stock market activities.

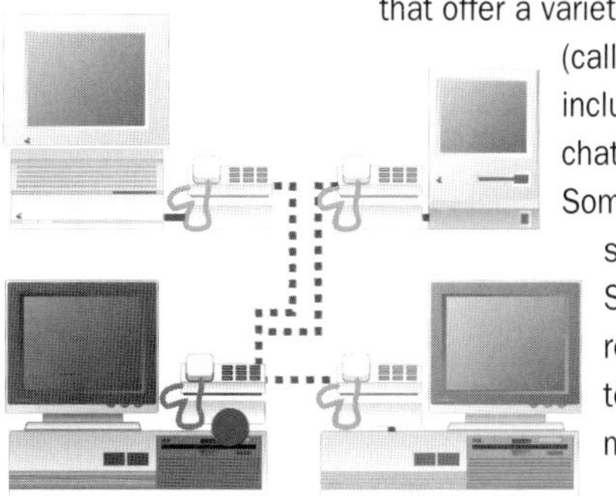

All BBSs consist of a computer connected to one or more telephone lines through modems. Most allow many people to use them simultaneously. All are managed by someone called a **sysop** (short for **sys**tems **op**erator) or moderator. A sysop is responsible for the organization and, sometimes, the content of the BBS. If users have problems, they can request help from the sysop by "paging" him or her (sending the sysop E-mail).

Computers, modems, BBSs and on–line systems allow more rapid and thorough communications. Paper documentation is diminishing as electronic communication increases. The advantages of electronic communication include lower production, storing and editing costs, as well as, faster transmission times and ease of updating. While the computer has actually created more paper use, the concept of even a partially paperless office seems distant. But, electronic communications, particularly E–mail, on–line systems and **hypermedia applications** ▸24–26, promise to make portions of this concept a reality.

Some BBSs are commercial and available for a monthly or yearly fee, while others are private and may be exclusive. Many private BBSs are free and offer all types of special interests. Whether the BBS is free or not, any long-distance charges incurred with the phone call will cost you additional money. You can find a list of BBSs in your area in a copy of Microtimes *or other local computer periodicals. Or, ask a computer dealer near you.*

Although computers can do many wonderful things, it is not likely that they will replace all human skills. Computers excel at searching, calculating and sorting massive amounts of data at high speed and almost tirelessly. They do not, however, have good recognition or judgment skills, nor do they deal well with novel situations.

There are those who claim that computers already possess the **intelligence** of insects and small creatures (no small feat when you consider that it took only 50 years of development for computers versus over 50 million years of evolution for nature). They can be extremely sensitive to certain stimuli and perform routine operations almost endlessly, but they are a long way from competing with humans in abilities like **judgment**, **creativity** and **intuition**.

Humans (and many animals) are tremendous **pattern** and **symbol recognizers.** Music, art, language, mathematics, and science all involve the manipulation of symbols and the recognition of patterns. When we are able to define symbols and describe patterns well, we are able to teach computers to do the same. This is why computers are so highly skilled at mathematic calculations. We have not been able to program computers to be intuitive or creative (in the sense we use for artists) because these are human skills that we do not yet understand well. There may come a time when computers are adept at "thinking" for us and are able to make sophisticated decisions by themselves, but that time is a long way off. For now, computers are allowing more humans to forget repetitive, menial tasks and concentrate on more creative ones that use the skills which we find unique and more interesting.

Humans are extremely flexible. We can adapt to new surroundings and situations quickly and fairly easily. Ask a typical computer what its favorite color is and it will not react at all. Type in the question and it will probably respond with a statement of error (if at all). If you were to design a program to accept the question and answer it, the answer would still be a product of what the programmer suggested and not a judgment. A computer cannot really offer an opinion (which can make it an objective assessor of data), and its programming reflects the programmer's own **biases**. This only underscores the point that what comes out of a computer is only as

In 1967, Mac Hack Four by Richard Greenblatt became the first computer software to receive honorary membership in the American Chess Foundation. This signaled one of the first situations in which computers challenged human problem-solving capabilities. Ever since, we have had to constantly redefine what it means to be human and exactly what constitutes a machine.

Artificial Intelligence

valid or accurate as what goes in (**garbage in, garbage out**). A computer cannot usually correct faulty or inaccurate data because it possesses few judgment skills. Also, just because information comes out of a computer does not mean that it is necessarily relevant or accurate.

Because researchers do not agree on a clear, complete understanding of what **intelligence** is, it is hard to decide how machines compare. Our definition has also changed over time as we learn more, define more and are challenged by the capabilities of computers. In fact, as computers acquire new capabilities, we typically adjust our definitions of intelligence so that these capabilities are no longer included. Human memory, for example, is no longer considered by many a component of intelligence, nor is simple symbol manipulation. The capabilities that make up intelligence, then, are always out of reach of machines because when machines acquire those capabilities, the capabilities are no longer included in the definition. This process is also applied to our **definition of life**. We continually evolve our definitions of ourselves as we develop more sophisticated machines.

Artificial Intelligence

The first reference to artificial intelligence occurred even before the first computer. In her paper outlining the workings of **Charles Babbage's** ▶93 "Analytical Engine", **Lady Ada Augusta Lovelace** presents and objects to the possibility that machines could ever possess intelligence because they have "no pretensions, whatever, to originate anything, only whatever we know how to order [them] to perform." **Alan Turing** ▶55, the grandfather of the computer, dubbed

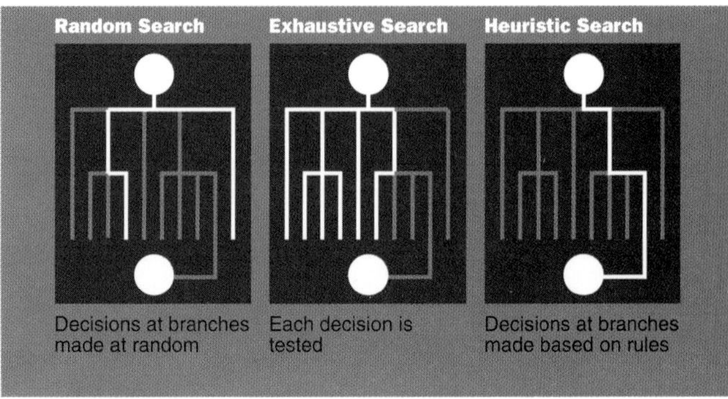
Random Search
Exhaustive Search
Heuristic Search
Decisions at branches made at random
Each decision is tested
Decisions at branches made based on rules

her reasoning "Lady Lovelace's Objection." This points out that computers, so far, possess no intent or self–motivation. These facts, however, speak more about consciousness than intelligence. Despite this, it is probably inaccurate to believe that computers will never possess any other aspects of intelligence.

The first artificial intelligence program was called The Logical Theorist.

Alan Turing developed what he called the **Turing Test**. This is a crude, working definition of machine intelligence. He theorized that if a human user was to interact with two computers (one real and one just a front for another person) and could not find any difference between the two, then the real computer possessed at least a measure of intelligence. Of course, this is an elusive target. The results depend directly on the abilities of the computer's software to deal with **context** and the interface between the user and computer.

Note that the abilities and perceptions of the tester also affect the results of a Turing Test.

Expert Systems

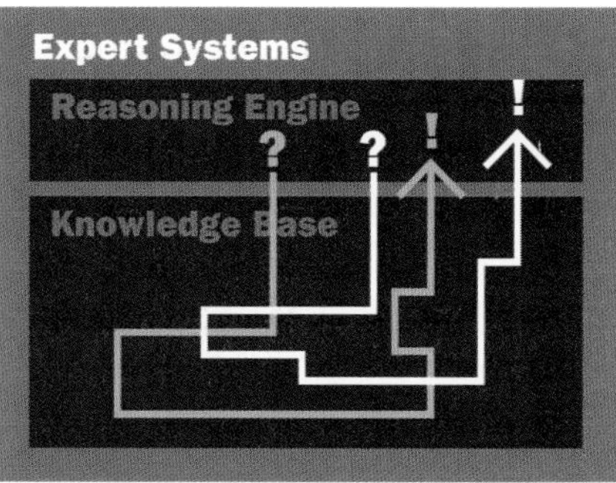

As described above, intelligence is a vague term with a constantly changing definition. There are, however, a few types of artificial intelligence (the building of computer software with human–like decision–making capabilities) that attempt to simulate some human decision–making processes. One is the study and development of expert systems. An **expert system** is a two–part application. The first part is a **knowledge base** that contains many instances of knowledge or facts. These have been carefully and methodically recorded from human experts or printed references and compiled into one file. The second part is a **reasoning engine**; a set of decision–making rules. When used properly, the reasoning engine consults the knowledge base for examples or facts that help it make decisions. These decisions are based on instructions provided to test for certain criteria and take different actions depending on the results. The rules are organized as **If/Then** statements about the answers.

Expert Systems have been used extensively for such things as diagnosing medical problems and automobile malfunctions as well as analyzing credit and geotechnical data.

For example, a medical diagnostic expert system might start by asking the patient, "Are you feeling all right?" The next instruction would instruct the computer to analyze the patient's answer and *if* the answer is "no", *then* proceed with the next question (possibly, "Where do you hurt?"). The expert system interacts with the user by asking questions and responding to the answers with other appropriate

questions until it has narrowed down the choices to one solution, piece of information, or advice.

An expert system is only as good as the programmer's instructions and information. A good expert system can quickly and accurately whittle down a specific type of problem to an appropriate solution, but it can easily be stumped if it receives answers it doesn't expect. Successful expert systems, properly used, have shown great value in diagnosing problems and advising solutions. They are often more thorough than humans typically are, but they have few resources with which to respond to novel situations. This makes them great aides but restricted ones.

Neural Networks

Another implementation of artificial intelligence is a neural network. **Neural networks** are an attempt to build pattern–recognition processes for computers to mimic the way humans recognize patterns. For example, we commonly recognize familiar people in a glance, but we are hard–pressed to describe how we do this in detail. These processes excel at dealing with novel situations and stimulation by breaking the input into parts and approaching the parts separately. A neural network builds an understanding from these separate parts much like humans do. Neural networks mimic the way humans see, hear and learn such things as language.

Humans are allowed to learn language gradually. We learn a little bit and get by without knowing every word or grammatical rule. We make many errors and learn to correct them with time. Eventually, as we learn more rules and expand our vocabularies, we make fewer mistakes. This is a natural process that allows us to function reasonably well while we are learning. If we were required to learn language as a computer must, we would have to learn almost every word and grammatical rule before we could speak our first sentence. This is because we currently require computers to be programmed with every rule and procedure in order to complete an operation.

A process of evolving understanding is new for machines. A neural network allows a computer to take in a great deal of stimulation it isn't necessarily programmed to deal with (such as "seeing" a picture it has never seen before or "hearing" a new type of sound.) Neural networks break data into discrete parts, make guesses at identifying the parts and build–up an understanding of the whole even though they may have never encountered data like it before.

Natural Language Processing

During a training process, guessed outcomes are compared with known answers. The computer then keeps the correct elements, disregards the incorrect ones and guesses again. After several tries, the neural network "learns" how to guess more accurately and with sufficient training, it can function quite well.

Already, neural networks have begun to simulate the pattern–recognition of human eyes and ears (although not nearly to the same degree of sensitivity). The rules that help them function are established through experience. In this sense, they are "learned" as opposed to given (as in the case of an expert system). There is great promise in neural networks to help computers begin to understand things we cannot explain well, but we are a long way from these developments. For now, neural networks have helped **OCR** ▶9 applications translate text accurately and industrial robots "see" parts on a production line.

Natural Language Processing

NLP (Natural Language Processing) is the capability of computers to respond to spoken or written instructions in "natural," human languages as if they understood these languages as well as the humans who use them. This is especially useful for automatic translation between different languages (such as French, Japanese, English, etc...) and requesting information from databases (called **queries**).

NLP involves decoding language into parts and determining the meaning of statements. This is extremely difficult to do because language can be abstract and contradictory. Although this poses a complex problem, the value of NLP is high because it allows users to use computers in ways similar to how they deal with other people. It means that less training will be required for people to use computers, making computers more accessible to more people, and thus, more powerful.

Copyrights

Most people think that when they purchase software to use (such as an **application** ▶4) they are buying that software outright. What they are really buying is not the software, but the right to use it.

Copyright laws have not kept pace with electronic media. The ease of duplicating software and the difficulty in creating and developing it are almost the opposite of print media. The copy machine

In 1969, Xerox Corp. hired Bob Taylor (the organizer of DARPA) to assemble some of the best and brightest people in the computer industry into a top–notch research organization. He staffed ***XeroxPARC*** *(Palo Alto Research Center)—the Camelot of computer research throughout the 1970's—which would found some of the most important developments in computers to date. Alan Kay developed his* ***Dynabook*** *concept there and developed the SmallTalk language with Adele Goldberg. Doug Engelbart made advances in his hypertext system and refined the* **mouse** ▶83–84*. Bill Atkinson developed a precursor to the* **Graphical-User Interface** ▶76 *and John Warnock developed the* **PostScript™** ▶22–23 *page description language there.*

Copyrights

has already made some copyright laws unenforceable and has hastened a new look at how they are written. Electronic media only exaggerates this problem.

SPA (the Software Publishers Association) researches and keeps figures on illegal software copying. They estimate that only half of the commercial software used with personal computers is used legally (is paid–for). SPA is very active in finding and prosecuting companies and individuals who use software illegally. (Telephone: 202 452 1600)

When you purchase software you are usually prohibited from making, selling or distributing any copies of it. Often, you are allowed to make one copy for use as a back–up or archive in case something happens to the original. Despite how easy it is to copy software, it is illegal and deprives software creators of compensation for the substantial time and money they invested into software development. Many people try to justify copying software with the argument that software is expensive. These same people, however, would never think of stealing the hardware necessary for computing (the CPU, keyboard, drives, monitor, etc...). Plain and simply, software would not be as expensive if everyone purchased copies legally.

Some software publishers use methods of **copy–protection** ▸126 to deter users from making and using unauthorized copies. Most common (and least annoying) is a dialog box that requires the user to type his or her name and registration number when it is used for the first time. Without the correct number, the software is unusable and once encoded, the software always bears that person's name, business name and registration number. This deters many unauthorized copies.

Copy–protection techniques attest to the conflict between trusting users not to illegally copy software and protecting the property rights of the publisher. If users did not make illegal copies there would be no need for copy–protection techniques.

Other methods of software copy–protection include: transmitting serial numbers across networks, requiring special diskettes or codes to be entered periodically and timed use. Transmitting serial numbers across a **network** ▸70–73 prevents two copies of the same application with the same serial number to operate on more than one machine in the network. This can be effective in multi–user, networked environments but not for single, **stand–alone** ▸70 workstations (unconnected to any other computer). Unfortunately, this often causes unnecessary traffic on networks and can slow network communication.

Other applications (especially **beta–test** ▸126 software) check the date from the computer's system and if it is past a set date, refuse to operate. This is known as a **time cut–out** and prevents use of out–of–date applications that may contain time–sensitive information or capabilities. Time cut–outs are a fairly common form of copy–protection on workstations but not on personal computers.

A sophisticated technique of copy–protection involving **host identification numbers** allows networks to keep track of what

Freeware and Shareware

computers are using what software and when. The identification numbers are encoded into the **EPROM** ▶106 (a special chip) on the computer's **motherboard** ▶108–109. Each computer has a unique number much like a serial number. The application software is encoded with the same number and will not run on any computer with a different number. A new copy of the application with a new identification number must be obtained from the software publisher for use on a new computer. This is a fairly unobtrusive and very secure copy–protection scheme and is used with relatively expensive and powerful applications.

Special software, running on a **server** ▶71–72 on a **network** ▶70–73 can respond to requests for applications from workstations or computers on the network. Known as **network checkout**, this licensing software counts the number of copies currently being used and compares that number to the amount licensed for use. If there are fewer copies in use than the maximum allowed, it will fulfill a request for another copy. If not, the request is denied. By periodically asking each computer what applications are running and what their identification numbers are it can keep track of how many applications are being used.

This sophisticated technique allows companies to operate more efficiently. Rather than buying a copy of an application for each computer, companies can effectively use fewer copies by distributing them over a network in this manner.

*Some software publishers offer programs called **floating licenses**, or **check-out licenses**, or **site licenses**. These programs allow companies to purchase many copies of the same software at a reduced price. Companies can use many applications, move them between different users and machines, while keeping fewer program disks and manuals around and still be legally licensed.*

Freeware and Shareware

Some software is published as **freeware** and users are encouraged to make and distribute as many copies as they like. These are usually public–domain **utilities** ▶18 (such as a **virus detector** ▶38–39) or a game of little market value. Many times, however, these are useful programs created by programmers who simply aren't interested in anything in return but the satisfaction of distribution. Be cautious with freeware that you know nothing about as it might be a **Trojan horse** or be contaminated with a **virus** ▶38–39.

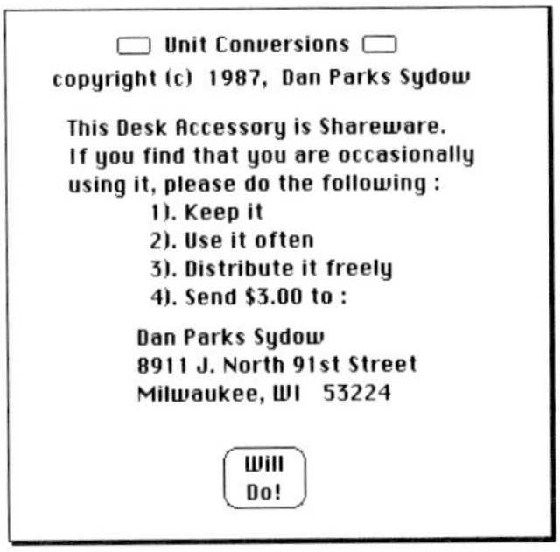

Unit Conversions
copyright (c) 1987, Dan Parks Sydow

This Desk Accessory is Shareware.
If you find that you are occasionally using it, please do the following :
1). Keep it
2). Use it often
3). Distribute it freely
4). Send $3.00 to :

Dan Parks Sydow
8911 J. North 91st Street
Milwaukee, WI 53224

Will Do!

Shareware is copyrighted software that is distributed on an honor system. Users are encouraged to copy and distribute shareware to others. Anyone who finds the software useful is encouraged or required to send in payment to the creator (the address is included in

the software). This is a good means of distribution because users can try the software before they purchase it. If it is not useful they can pass it on or discard it without any cost. Many great applications, utilities, games and other software are distributed as shareware. Most are small, very inexpensive—but sometimes invaluable—programs that provide a diverse range of capabilities that would not find publication or distribution in any other way.

One disadvantage of shareware or freeware is that there is little (if any) support. Both tend to be hard to find and learn about because these forms of software are inconsistently marketed (if at all).

Computer Viruses, Worms, and Trojan Horses

Lately, a type of computer software has been getting much attention in the media. **Computer viruses** are special software programs designed to replicate themselves and spread on a computer or network. Like biological viruses, replication is the major goal. Viruses actually attach themselves to applications and other software. This can permanently damage the software and be difficult to remove. While most are harmless, some are designed to cause problems in computers. Some search out specific files to destroy, some destroy indiscriminately and others cause problems inadvertently by inhibiting normal operations. Although these sound dangerous (and some are), most are rare and relatively harmless. Viruses are a nuisance more than anything else and should be a concern for users but not a worry.

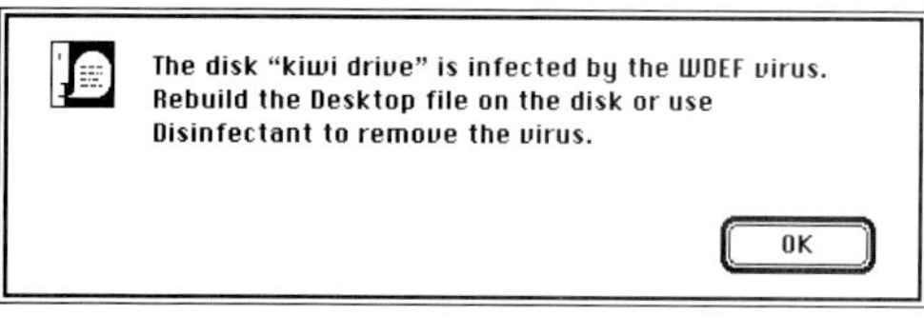

The disk "kiwi drive" is infected by the WDEF virus.
Rebuild the Desktop file on the disk or use
Disinfectant to remove the virus.
OK

Note: While viruses give computers a bad name and make users anxious, they are rare and mostly benign. For most users, viruses should be cause for caution but not alarm.

A **Trojan horse** is a related program but does not replicate itself. Its sole purpose is to destroy data or system resources. Usually, as the name implies, a Trojan horse is disguised as another application. Sometimes a Trojan horse may even be disguised as a **virus detector** or **destroyer**. Once running in your computer a Trojan horse goes to work destroying things, often without you knowing until it's much too late. Some wait for a specific period of time before they begin to operate and are known as **time bombs**.

A **worm** is a piece of software who's sole purpose is to replicate itself as often as possible. A worm is not immediately destructive like a virus or Trojan horse but they quickly fill extra space in memory and can quickly and easily render a system unusable. The

Internet worm did just this over the entire Internet government and university network. It brought the network to a halt but caused no destruction of files or data. Worms remain self–contained and do not usually attach themselves to applications or any other software.

The primary way to expose your computer to a virus, Trojan horse or worm is by sharing **applications** ▶4 with others or accessing an infected network. While infected networks are ***extremely*** rare, sharing applications is common. Viruses and worms usually don't infect data files.

There are many steps you can take to prevent infection and possible loss of important information. This includes not sharing applications with others, **backing–up** ▶18 your discs regularly, and not using unauthorized copies of software. If you exchange data with others, it is a good idea to get an **anti–virus utility** that checks for known viruses. These are inexpensive and updated often as new viruses are discovered. Some anti–virus utilities constantly monitor your computer for any suspicious activity that could be caused by a virus and notify you if any software is attempting to destroy data or alter resources without your knowledge. Anti–virals are especially useful, but not 100% effective.

Not all worms are intentionally written to cause damage. The Internet worm was written to "map" the Internet network (something that had never been done before). This would have calculated the size of the enormous network (something no one knows). Unfortunately, this remarkable idea never materialized because the program had a **bug** ▶**129** *in it (was written poorly) that caused it to copy itself incessantly. It quickly filled the available space on the network and brought it to a grinding halt.*

Ergonomics

Using a computer a great deal can affect more than just your workflow. It can profoundly affect your body. Like any activity, a lot of computing (especially without breaks) can lead to strain on many parts of your body. Research has only begun to explore what kinds of effects these are and to what extent they may be hazardous. Until the results are in, there are many things you can do to help prevent health problems.

Your **posture** is important. Your body will make you aware of the strain sitting at a computer can cause. Your lower back and shoulders will suffer the most. Taking the time to position your computer will help spare your spine undue stress. First, get a good chair; one that allows you to have both feet on the floor, adjusts to fit your lower back and allows you to move about and change positions easily. Position your keyboard at the same height as your elbows and the monitor just below your horizontal line of sight (you should look down slightly at it, not up). If you cannot adjust the desk surface to the correct height, adjust your chair to fit the desk's height and use a footrest to attain the proper dimensions.

Use these recommendations to fashion your main body position when computing. There are many possible positions and you should move around and shift positions often. Any position, no matter how "ideal," will get tiring. This is one area where being fidgety is all right.

Ergonomics

Take breaks frequently (at least 10 minutes every hour) and try to mix your computing time with other jobs so that you don't sit at a computer for long stretches. Learning and practicing a few good exercises can help greatly.

Computer Exercises
Heavy computer users may want to repeat these exercises every 15 minutes.
1. Start by sitting up straight and take a few deep breaths.
2. Bend over deeply to relieve your spine. Return to a straight position.
3. Roll your neck front and back and from side to side.
4. Clasp your hands behind your back and stretch your arms out behind you as high as you can.
5. Clasp your hands in front of you and stretch your arms above your head.
6. Bend over from side to side.

Your **eyes** are the next thing to tire quickly. Don't use a monitor that is fuzzy or distorts the image. If you cannot adjust the monitor's focus and need to, get a new monitor. Frequently change your concentration from the screen to objects of greater distance away. Look out the window, across the room or even up at the ceiling. Try not to stare at the screen for long periods of time. Use glasses if you have a prescription and get regular eye exams. Eating lots of carrots won't hurt either. **Eyestrain** not only causes tired eyes and worsened eyesight but can lead to headaches as well.

Give your eyes a chance to stretch every few minutes (no more than every 10 minutes) by looking out a window or across the room. Focus on objects far away once in a while.

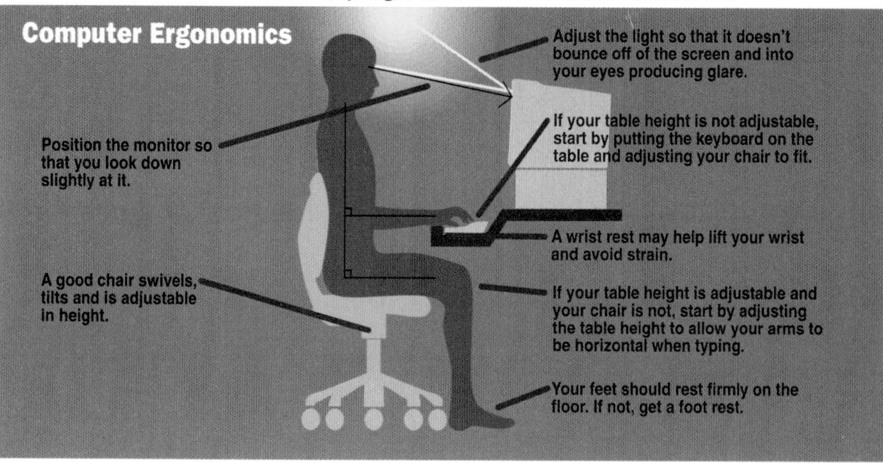

Computer Ergonomics
Adjust the light so that it doesn't bounce off of the screen and into your eyes producing glare.
Position the monitor so that you look down slightly at it.
If your table height is not adjustable, start by putting the keyboard on the table and adjusting your chair to fit.
A wrist rest may help lift your wrist and avoid strain.
A good chair swivels, tilts and is adjustable in height.
If your table height is adjustable and your chair is not, start by adjusting the table height to allow your arms to be horizontal when typing.
Your feet should rest firmly on the floor. If not, get a foot rest.

Keyboards may seem harmless but they are important contributors to strain. Heavy typing without breaks can lead to scores of **repetitive–strain disorders**. The most widely known of these is **carpal–tunnel syndrome.** This is a serious, destructive injury that

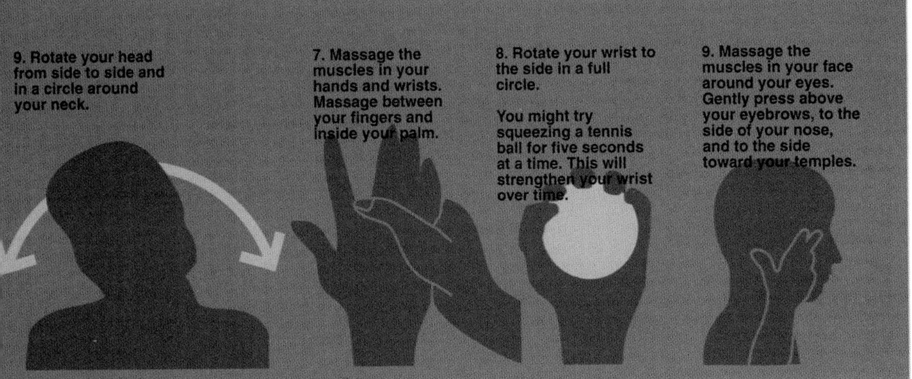

9. Rotate your head from side to side and in a circle around your neck.
7. Massage the muscles in your hands and wrists. Massage between your fingers and inside your palm.
8. Rotate your wrist to the side in a full circle.
You might try squeezing a tennis ball for five seconds at a time. This will strengthen your wrist over time.
9. Massage the muscles in your face around your eyes. Gently press above your eyebrows, to the side of your nose, and to the side toward your temples.

results in great pain and, possibly, permanent damage. It's hard to believe that typing could lead to such serious physical problems, but any action carried to excessive levels can be straining and dangerous. To avoid these kinds of injuries, keep your elbows and wrists supported and don't let them rest low on the edge of the desk. You might consider getting a special table at the proper height just for your keyboard and/or mouse if the one you are using isn't at the proper height.

Lately, researchers have begun to worry about the effects of the electromagnetic frequencies that radiate from **cathode–ray tubes** (CRTs) ▶113–114. These tubes are what generate the screen displays for video display terminals (monitors). All **monitors** ▶80–82, except flat–panel and **LCD displays** ▶114–115, emit **Extremely Low Frequency** (ELF) **radiation** ▶113. It is not clear how serious prolonged exposure to these frequencies of radiation can be (if at all) but recent results are not hopeful. To minimize your risk, stay an arm's length away from the front of the monitor when working. These radiation fields can be strong on the sides of the monitor. If you work in an office with many monitors, make sure that you sit no closer than 4' to any side of the monitor except the front. New monitors are being developed that cut down the ELF emissions but they are a little more expensive. **Radiation guards** are small screens that fit over the front of the monitor to block some emissions. While these guards can cut

Lighting, glare (especially from the screen) and noise will also play a big role in your working conditions. Get a good light (or a few of them) and place your screen so that you are not looking into glare from surrounding windows and lighting fixtures. You may need to use new sounds (such as soft music or an aquarium bubbling) to mask distracting sounds you cannot get rid of.

Beware of marketing schemes that try to convince you to buy a monitor with low ELF radiation. While there are many new products that actually work, many others are merely trying to capitalize on unknowing or confused buyers.

The most common form of illegal entry to a system is by using someone else's password. Never write a password down or give it to someone over the phone. Changing passwords frequently is also good protection. Structuring files so that only certain users can have access to sensitive information is also important. The greatest defense is to frequently monitor usage. Off-hour or multiple, unsuccessful attempts to enter a computer system may be signs of a possible intruder.

down some emissions substantially, they cannot eliminate all. **LCD** ▶118 and **LED** displays emit no VLF radiation. Incidentally, televisions have **cathode ray tubes** and emit as much VLF radiation, if not more, than computer monitors. Use these guides for televisions, as well.

These are important topics and should be explored in more depth by anyone using a computer. We've included a list of books and pamphlets on these subjects in our **Bibliography** ▶**130**.

Security

Computers are allowing us to change our culture so fast that we can hardly keep up with the advances. Copyright laws for published and printed information have been greatly affected by the use of copying machines. Pressure is being placed on lawmakers to rewrite these laws to reflect the capabilities of computers.

With so much information now being stored and processed on computers, it has also become important to make it appropriately secure. A knowledgeable programmer can gain access to credit histories, medical records—sometimes even military information—over phone lines with a modem, although this is not easy. Usually **passwords** are not enough to restrict people from unauthorized access to personal or "sensitive" information.

Organizations like the **Electronic Frontier Foundation** are already addressing how issues of access, privacy, security and civil rights are affected by our use of computers. Like any tool, computers are forcing us to reevaluate these and other issues. A new constitutional amendment has already been proposed that would protect electronic media and communications under the same constitutional rights that protect printed and broadcast communications.

Artificial Life

Some researchers are using computers to create software that controls electronic entities. These electronic entities have characteristics similar to biological organisms (such as ants) and play out scenarios in a hypothetical environment. These programs are capable of behavior that natural living organisms exhibit (characteristics such as replication, metamorphosis, consumption, adaptation to environment, movement and change), mimic biological processes and allow researchers to study evolution. The results are "growth" in the sense that the behavior evolves and is not decided at the beginning. These studies support theories that it is the pattern of behavior and not necessarily the behaviors themselves that characterize life.

Scientists look to artificial life research to help us understand what defines life and consciousness. This research may eventually provide us with more sophisticated computers—possibly "living" machines. But ultimately, it will have more important effects in helping us better understand ourselves and how we interact with others.

Access

Computers give many people access to a wide variety of information but access is sometimes an issue with computers. In the past, computers were very expensive and only used by technical experts and, thus, were easily controlled by a small group of people. Now, personal computers are empowering millions of individuals and bringing with them great changes. There are still those who wish to mystify computers and shroud them in a veil of complexity to keep them exclusive. While computers are complex and sophisticated tools, they are not mysterious or magical. If anyone tries to limit your access to information about them or your access to use them, they are doing you a great disservice and you should not stand for it.

There are plenty of sources of access to computers (schools, universities, libraries, community centers, copy stores, friends, etc...) and you should not feel that they are beyond your capabilities to use. Every day, computers are becoming easier to use (and thus more powerful). They are made especially for exploring and learning. Many people of all ages, abilities and interests are finding themselves learning things and doing things they never before imagined. This is why computers are powerful machines—not because of their processor speeds or memory capacities, but because they allow us to follow our interests and achieve our dreams.

Some people argue that we are rapidly losing some of our constitutional rights with regard to computers and electronic media. Rights of freedom, access, publishing, free speech, unreasonable search and seizure and due process have few precedents on-line and most law officials are inadequately educated and experienced with electronic media. ***Operation Sun Devil*** *(A Secret Service operation in the USA) at times typified this haste and ignorance with uninformed officers and attorneys. The results damaged legitimate companies and hurt innocent people. While the maintenance of copyright laws is important, so are the constitutional rights listed above. You should get involved and find out to what extent these rights affect you and have affected others. For more information, contact the Electronic Frontier Foundation* *(see page 133)*.

The Operating System is the software that controls the computer's hardware, manages the operation of programs, and coordinates the flow of data to and from disks and memory. Most of its actions are transparent to users; however, it also provides many commands and tools that you can use to control the operations of the computer.

RAM stands for Random Access Memory. A computer can access any part of this memory immediately. RAM is where the computer keeps data and instructions that it is currently working with.

The most basic parts of the operating system are stored in the system's permanent memory (**ROM** ▸105–106, disc, etc...) and loaded into the system's **RAM** (Random Access Memory) ▸104–105 when the computer is turned on. The ROM is a chip with the software permanently written into it. It cannot be changed nor is it lost when the power is turned off. The RAM is also a chip (or several chips) and is where the computer stores the software it is currently using. When the power is turned off, all the data in RAM is lost. There are few different types of RAM and ROM and these are covered in the **Technology chapter** ▸104.

The **operating system** ▸75, 118–119 (also called system

Operating System Capabilites

Start-Up Code These are the instructions that load when you turn the computer on and start the computer operating.	**Input/Output Functions** The operating system controls the flow of data in and out of the computer through ports for "reading," "writing" and "printing".
Memory Management These functions manage the movement of data within the processor and storage memories.	**Toolboxes (Graphics, Type, Comm., etc...)** Toolboxes make sophisticated functions available automatically to programmers.
File Management These capabilities allow users to organize files and applications to suit them and "keep track" of creation dates, versions, names and other attributes.	**Processes (IPC, Virtual Memory, etc...)** These are special functions that allow computers to do sophisticated and powerful manipulations of data.

Operating System capabilities.

software) defines what the computer is capable of processing—and how. It defines how files are organized, how memory is managed, how the **processor** ▸100–102 is used, how data is communicated between the

Computer Components Timeline

3AD
Abacus is invented in China.

1693
Leibnize develops the first mechanical calculator called the "stepped reckoner." It doesn't work but his concept of breaking down complex problems into simple pieces helps eliminate some of the tedium in mathematics.

1804
Jacquard develops an automated loom that uses punch cards.

1804-1808
Lewis & Clark expedition.

1800 1810

Operating Systems

distinct components within the machine, and how the **interface** ▶75 between the user and computer operates. The operating system functions as an intermediary by providing **system calls** for applications (like a word processing program). These system calls perform functions such as allocating memory space, opening, reading and saving files. **Applications** ▶4 are written for specific operating systems so that they can take advantage of these high–level functions built into the operating system.

Memory management is one of the most important functions of the operating system. The operating system is responsible for allocating (assigning) data to memory from the moment the computer is turned on. It loads the **system software** and other specified software into RAM at start–up. When the user opens (starts) an application, the operating system **allocates** memory space in RAM for that application's instructions and data. Likewise, when a file is opened, the data in it must be copied to RAM as well. When the user closes a file or application, the operating system **deallocates** that space in RAM, meaning it frees it for any new data that needs to be loaded into RAM.

The operating system also allows applications and system software to communicate in high–level commands (codes that are more complex than **binary** ▶90, 95 1s and 0s). Since all processes must be executed through the circuits of the chips and architecture, everything must be manipulated in binary. The operating system allows software programmers to use higher–level (and therefore, more understandable to human) commands and instructions and then translates them into binary in order to be usable by the electronics. Without this convention, software would be even more difficult and abstract to create than it is already. Some programmers still program in machine language for its efficiency, however.

The operating system is responsible for moving all data in and out of RAM. This includes looking up the appropriate **address** ▶104 for a specific piece of data needed. The **CPU** (processor) ▶100–102 will make requests to the operating system for data, and the operating system finds it in **storage memory** ▶106–107 and copies it into RAM. If there is no

The operating system forms a layer between the hardware and the software that runs on it. Some operating systems are very simple (like MS–DOS) and programmers must add many features themselves. Others (like UNIX) are robust with built–in functions (toolboxes) and allow many users to use one workstation at the same time.

0001	0000	Addresses
10001110	01110001	0000
10001000	00000001	0001
10111111	11100001	0010
10111010	00000011	0011
00010100	11111101	0100
[illegible]	01101110	0101
00000100	11001110	0110
10111001	11110101	0111

The data highlighted above resides in the address 00000101 (0000 x 0101)

1830

1840

[1]822
[C]harles Babbage begins to [b]uild the "Difference [E]ngine." This is a large and [i]ntricate mechanical machine [t]hat is able to keep track of [n]umbers with gears and cogs. [H]e receives some respect but [l]ittle support.

1834
Babbage abandons his Difference Engine, conceives and begins building his "Analytical Engine." This is much larger and more complex then the Difference Engine. It is able to perform many arithmetic functions instead of merely one. Lady Lovelace joins him and masterminds the programming of the machine.

1837
Electric telegraph invented.

Operating Systems

space left in RAM, the operating system will need to free room for the new data by copying some data to another form of storage (such as to disc). This is called **swapping** ▸48, 100.

In addition to swapping, the operating system keeps track of where all data is in RAM. Some operating systems can allow different applications and processes to share the same data so that less RAM needs to be used. All of this swapping takes time and the current operation remains unprocessed until the data is available. Having a lot of RAM available is an advantage. The more data that can be used without swapping, the more programs (applications) that can be loaded into RAM at one time and the more efficient the operations.

Swapping

Data in RAM

Data on Disc

Data is swapped in large chunks (roughly 512–1024 bytes) at a time.

Multi–tasking refers to the ability of the operating system to have more than one **application** ▸4 running in memory simultaneously. Because there is usually only one **processor** ▸100–102, the computer can never actually process more than one thing at a time (**Parallel Processing** ▸112 is an exception). However, some operating systems are extremely fast and organized about how they shuffle instructions in and out of the processor and allocate memory. Because of this efficient switching (also called **paged memory management**, because it moves blocks of data around in chunks called **pages**) and **protected memory** (specifying memory space for all data so that, in the shuffle, nothing important gets lost or overwritten), the computer can actually simulate two or more operations happening at once. This is called "true" multi–tasking because the user cannot perceive any loss of functioning on the part of the processes operating concurrently. This allows some computers to play

Computer Components Timeline (cont.)
1860
1870
1854
George Boole publishes The Laws of Thought, the basis of Boolean Algebra and logic.
1848
California Gold Rush begins.

music, print a document to a printer, perform complex calculations, and still be able to play an arcade game with the user—all at the same time.

Part of the key to multi–tasking is a special processor (or set of processors) called a **co–processor** ▸102–103 dedicated to moving data around in the computer between the keyboard, mouse, displays, memory, and chips. These **I/O Processors** ▸102 (for Input/Output) are separate and extremely fast chips that take the data-moving responsibilities from the main processor, thus freeing it to do the more complex data processing.

One type of multi–tasking is **time–sharing**, in which the processor works with many users, at separate terminals simultaneously. The processor spends a fixed amount of time with each user. It looks at what needs to be done for one user, performs a few operations, moves to the next, performs a few more operations and continues this process, cycling through all of the users very fast. Users do not notice any real slow–down in speed until there are many users on the system. Time–sharing is usually found on **mainframes** or **minicomputers** with many users who have the same priority of usage.

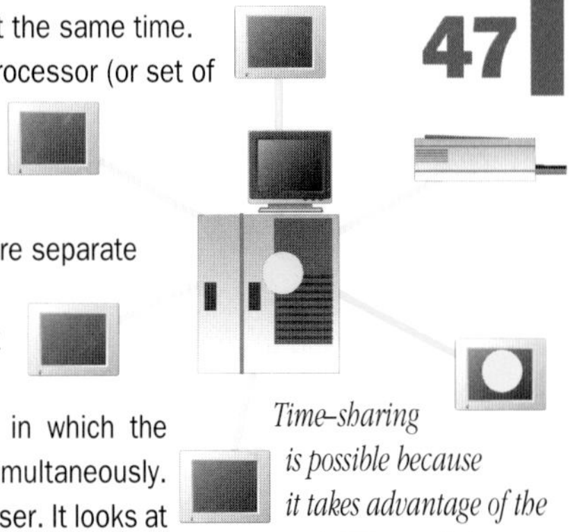

Time–sharing is possible because it takes advantage of the speed difference between users and processors. The CPU's clock speed is so fast that humans seem to move very slowly (to a computer). This allows the CPU to do other things while the user is typing information or manipulating data.

Virtual Memory ▸107 is a feature that allows the computer to simulate having more **RAM** (Random Access Memory) ▸104–105 than it actually does. RAM is necessary for the computer to operate on large problems or large amounts of data and to handle data that requires complex processing. If there is only a little RAM available, the processor must constantly swap blocks of data into and out of RAM from storage

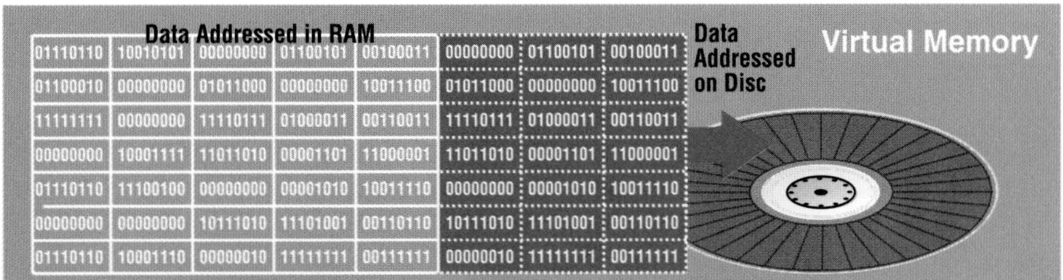

Virtual Memory

Data Addressed in RAM					Data Addressed on Disc		
01110110	10010101	00000000	01100101	00100011	00000000	01100101	00100011
01100010	00000000	01011000	00000000	10011100	01011000	00000000	10011100
11111111	00000000	11110111	01000011	00110011	11110111	01000011	00110011
00000000	10001111	11011010	00001101	11000001	11011010	00001101	11000001
01110110	11100100	00000000	00001010	10011110	00000000	00001010	10011110
00000000	00000000	10111010	11101001	00110110	10111010	11101001	00110110
01110110	10001110	00000010	11111111	00111111	00000010	11111111	00111111

1880

1878
Telephone patented.

1890

1883
First motor cars.

Operating Systems

With Inter–Process Communications built into the operating system, currently open files can access data in other files without having to open that file and start–up its application. It is even possible to have some of this communication occur automatically (such as updating prices in a catalog). IPC allows an application to control other applications and inform them of its status.

memory (on disc). This takes the processor away from its processing duties and slows everything down. Some very large applications or files may not even be able to be used if the available RAM is so small that the most basic data cannot be shuttled into RAM at one time.

To compensate, with virtual memory, the operating system can exclusively reserve memory space elsewhere (such as on a hard disc, or diskette) and use it as swap space. This can tend to slow things down a little, because reading and writing to a disc is slower than to RAM chips, but most of the time it is not noticeable. It is effective because it simulates RAM chips (which can be expensive) with less–expensive, more abundant, but slower, storage memory. With fast **I/O** (Input and Output) **devices** ▶102–103 and fast **bus speeds** ▶111–112 (the rate at which data can travel through the system), the swapping can be almost imperceptible.

Inter–Process Communications (IPC) (sometimes known as Inter–Application Communications) involves writing and using special message commands in the operating system that allow different processes and applications to communicate with each other. For example, if you are using a **page–layout application** ▶10–11 and you want to update a price that came from a **database** ▶21 file, the page–layout application might send a **system call** ▶45 to the operating system to ask

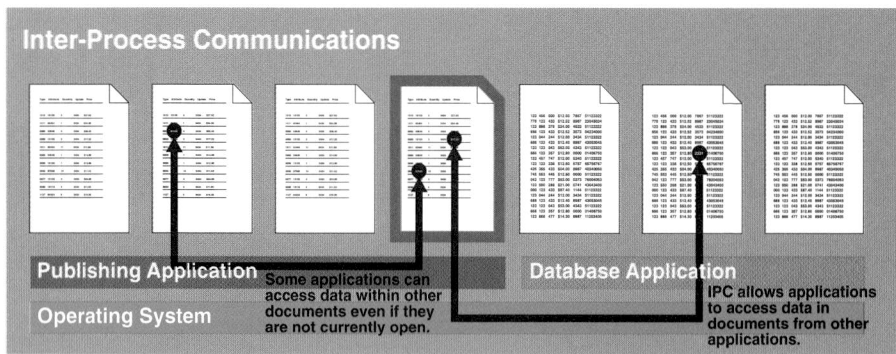
Inter-Process Communications
Publishing Application
Operating System
Some applications can access data within other documents even if they are not currently open.
Database Application
IPC allows applications to access data in documents from other applications.

Computer Components Timeline (cont.)
1900
1910
1903
First powered flight.
1914
Panama canal opens.
1901-1910
Nine million immigrants enter the USA.
1913
Model T produced.

the database application what the latest value for that number is. The database application would look up the value and pass the information back through the operating system, which would notify the page–layout application of the new price. The page–layout application would then replace the old value with the new one.

The user only had to invoke one command to initiate all of this communication between applications and the operating system. Without IPC, the user would have to stop using the page–layout application, launch (or start) the database application, find the value and write it down on a piece of paper, close (or stop) the database application, restart the page–layout application and type in the new value. IPC allows users to work more fluidly with their applications and make the computer do the odd jobs. This also allows the computer to reflect more how people think and work. People, by nature, perform many tasks at once while sharing information between those tasks (i.e., talking while cooking a meal).

The messages that go back and forth between applications must follow a standard and agreed–upon form and language.

The capabilities necessary for this type of communication are often written into the operating system. If they aren't, then the two applications will not be able to share information. Once there, they are ready to be used by any process at any time. The operating system doesn't know what information the message contains—only where the destination is and how big the message is. The application that receives it is ultimately responsible for knowing what to do with it.

Operating Systems:	UNIX	DOS 5	Win 3	Mac 7	OS/2 2.0	PenPoint
True Multitasking	●				●	●
Pseudo Multitasking			●	●		
Inter–Process Comm.	●		●	●	●	●
Virtual Memory	●		●	●	●	●
Graphics Toolbox	●		●	●	●	●
Comm. Toolbox	●		●	●	●	●
Memory Limitations	Few	Many	Med	Med	Few	Med

1930
Model 1, the first electromechanical computer is developed at Bell Labs.

1928
ENIGMA coding machine goes into use in Germany.

1940
COLOSSUS is used in England to decipher the German military's ENIGMA codes. COLOSSUS is a primitive computer developed by a team led by Alan Turing.

1941
Konrad Zuse independently develops two electromechanical calculators while in exile in Austria.

1943
Harvard Mark 1 (Bessie) is able to multiply two 32 digit numbers in 3 seconds. This $500,000 computer is 51 feet long and 8 feet high.

1928
television transmission.

1929
Stock market crash.

1938-1945
World War II

1930

1940

There are a few standard operating systems that different computers use, and some that are specific only to certain machines.

One of the most versatile and widespread operating systems is UNIX. Developed at AT&T Bell Labs by Ken Thompson and Dennis Ritchie, it has been distributed for a very low cost to universities, corporations and research centers, and is now a standard for these institutions. It is a complex system that usually runs on workstations powerful enough to take advantage of its sophisticated features. Some of UNIX's features include: ***multi–tasking****,* ***virtual memory*** *and* ***inter–process communication*** *(IPC).*

An application can, if properly programmed, bypass processes in the operating system and use its own processes. Some applications, for instance, have capabilities usually found in advanced operating systems (like virtual memory) even though the operating system does not. In this case, the capability is written into the application and evoked from it.

Operating systems often include utilities that make software writing more efficient. Some have sets of commands, called a **toolbox,** ready to evoke certain processes. An operating system may have a few, different toolboxes for specific functions: one for managing type (size, style, font...), one for managing communications, one for managing the display and what is drawn on it, one that manages the interface that the user sees, etc.... Applications use these built–in functions so that programmers are not required to recreate them on their own.

Firmware

If hardware is the actual, physical components of a computer (chips, boards, etc...) and software is the set of instructions (encoded into binary) that run through these components, then **firmware** is a type of software that is resident in specific hardware. Firmware manages the cooperation between the hardware and the software. All IPUs and **CPUs** ▸100–102 have their own, distinctive firmware that allows them to do their jobs. Firmware is a set of low–level commands that cannot be separated from the chips they run on.

Basically, a user will invoke a function in an application (like drawing a line) and the application will make a **system call** ▸45 to the operating system, which invokes instructions on the firmware, which tells the chip exactly how to process the instructions and data. The result is passed back up the chain of command, being interpreted at each level, until the user receives the result (the screen displaying the line drawn).

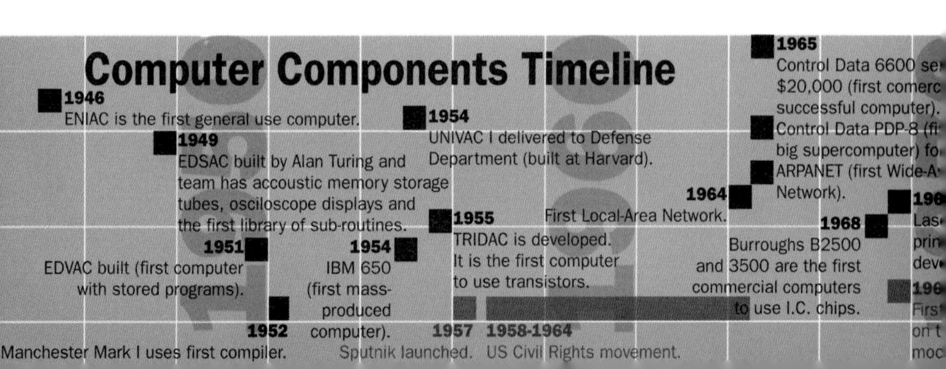

Computer Components Timeline
1946
ENIAC is the first general use computer.
1949
EDSAC built by Alan Turing and team has accoustic memory storage tubes, osciloscope displays and the first library of sub-routines.
1951
EDVAC built (first computer with stored programs).
1952
Manchester Mark I uses first compiler.
1954
IBM 650 (first mass-produced computer).
1954
UNIVAC I delivered to Defense Department (built at Harvard).
1955
TRIDAC is developed. It is the first computer to use transistors.
1957
Sputnik launched.
1958-1964
US Civil Rights movement.
1964
First Local-Area Network.
1965
Control Data 6600
$20,000 (first
successful computer).
Control Data PDP-8
big supercomputer)
ARPANET (first Wide-
Network).
1968
Burroughs B2500 and 3500 are the first commercial computers to use I.C. chips.

Computer Languages

Each level is a necessary step in the process. Sophisticated software would be nearly impossible to write without **high-level languages** ▸52, 55 and the system calls available in the operating system.

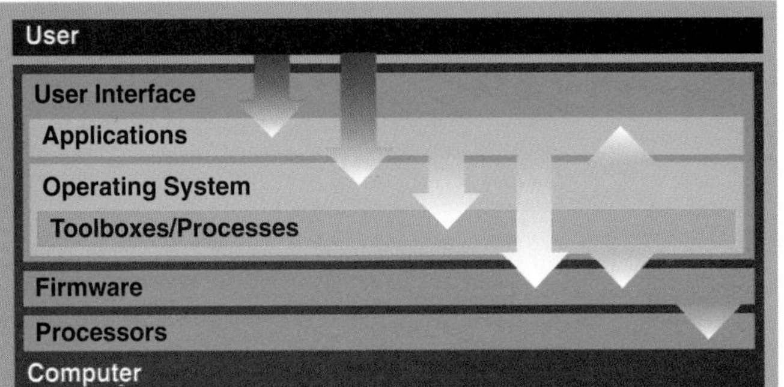

Without the operating system, each application would have to communicate directly with the firmware in the chips and thus be written differently for each type of computer. Also, applications could not share the processes available in the operating system and would have to be written with all of these processes included. Therefore, the applications would necessarily be much bigger, more cumbersome and repetitious because these processes would be duplicated in all applications (taking up even more space). If a CPU's design were changed, or a new CPU was to be developed, every application would have to be rewritten in order to run on it. The same is true for the operating system. Without firmware, each operating system would have to include all of the instructions necessary to communicate directly with each chip. Again, the result would be more space taken in memory to contain all of these instructions, duplication of instructions, and less compatibility with different computers.

The firmware forms a buffer between the operating system and the processor. This buffer allows both to change independently without those changes adversely affecting the other.

The user interacts with the computer through a series of processes that make computers easier to understand. The **User Interface** ▸75 *is what the user sees, hears and touches. Even when using an application, the user is often interacting with the interface. This is supported by various* **toolboxes** ▸50 *for special functions. The Operating System is what controls all of the various elements that the user sees, and it communicates directly with the computer.*

The firmware is the software written for a specific processor that allows the Operating System, Applications, and any other system processes to communicate with the processor, and thus, have data processed and instructions carried out.

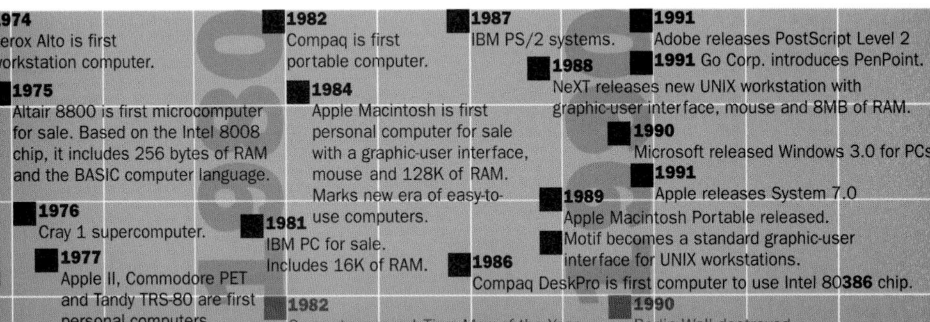

1974
Xerox Alto is first workstation computer.
1975
Altair 8800 is first microcomputer for sale. Based on the Intel 8008 chip, it includes 256 bytes of RAM and the BASIC computer language.
1976
Cray 1 supercomputer.
1977
Apple II, Commodore PET and Tandy TRS-80 are first personal computers.
1981
IBM PC for sale. Includes 16K of RAM.
1982
Compaq is first portable computer.
1982
Computer named Time Man of the Year.
1984
Apple Macintosh is first personal computer for sale with a graphic-user interface, mouse and 128K of RAM. Marks new era of easy-to-use computers.
1986
Compaq DeskPro is first computer to use Intel 80386 chip.
1987
IBM PS/2 systems.
1988
NeXT releases new UNIX workstation with graphic-user interface, mouse and 8MB of RAM.
1989
Apple Macintosh Portable released.
Motif becomes a standard graphic-user interface for UNIX workstations.
1990
Microsoft released Windows 3.0 for PCs.
1990
Berlin Wall destroyed.
1991
Adobe releases PostScript Level 2
1991 Go Corp. introduces PenPoint.
1991
Apple releases System 7.0

Computer Languages

When Grace Hopper (the mother of modern programming, designer of the first compiler and the creator of the COBOL language) was touring a computer center in Osaka, Japan, she was separated from the rest of her group. Knowing no Japanese and finding no one who spoke English she was finally able to communicate with the limited commands of COBOL, like MOVE and GOTO, because the programmers at the center used COBOL regularly.

Computer Languages

Almost all hardware in a computer processes data and instructions as collections of 1s and 0s. Through the years, programming has moved away from this machine–readable form of language to others which are more natural to interact with. Computer languages have become quite sophisticated and some are now approaching the structure of spoken languages (like English).

Computer languages allow programmers (and advanced users) to manipulate the capabilities of a computer in a more "natural" way. Eventually, all manipulation of computers comes down to moving 1s and 0s. This is a very tedious and abstract level of computing. Languages allow users to manipulate the 1s and 0s more understandably.

Spoken Languages (English, French, Japanese, etc...)
E.g.: Yo. What's up? Have you seen this report?

Very High–Level User Languages (HyperTalk, etc...)
E.g.: put name and the date into message box

High–Level User Languages (Pascal, BASIC, COBOL, etc...)
E.g.: if symbol=true then arc (12, 230, 50)

C, Ada, LISP...
E.g.: if (i++)else (g=1)

Forth, ALGOL, Assembly Languages
E.g.: mov r1,3b mov r2,fb jmp c5

Low–Level User Languages, *E.g.: 00100011 10111010*

There are quite a few languages used for programming computers. Some are called **low–level languages** because they manipulate the binary commands (1s and 0s) more directly. These tend to be harder to learn and use. They also tend to have smaller vocabularies (fewer commands are ready–made). **High–level languages** ▸55 have commands and vocabularies that are more like spoken languages. One instruction in a higher–level language corresponds to many instructions in lower–level languages.

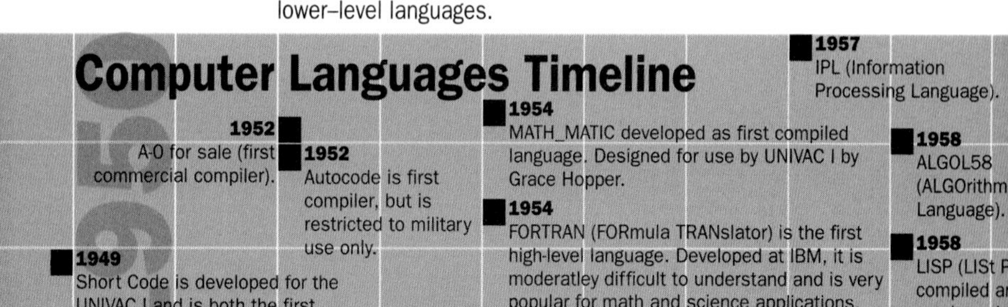

Computer Languages Timeline
1950
1949
Short Code is developed for the UNIVAC I and is both the first interpreted language and the first assembly language. It uses mnemonics and subroutines.
1952
A-0 for sale (first commercial compiler).
1952
Autocode is first compiler, but is restricted to military use only.
1954
MATH_MATIC developed as first compiled language. Designed for use by UNIVAC I by Grace Hopper.
1954
FORTRAN (FORmula TRANslator) is the first high-level language. Developed at IBM, it is moderatley difficult to understand and is very popular for math and science applications.
1955
FLOW_MATIC (first business language).
1957
IPL (Information Processing Language).
1957
1958
ALGOL58
Language).
1958
1958-1964

Some high–level languages (such as COBOL or HyperTalk) can almost be spoken and understood like human languages because the codes they use are so similar to words used in natural languages (i.e., *if answer is "yes" then put date into field CurrentDate*).

Computer languages have their own logic built into them—much the same as spoken languages. Each reflect their own implementations of **Boolean Logic** ▶93–94. Some languages emphasize certain aspects of programming and thus are better suited for programming certain types of applications. Some languages are designed around or are modifications of other languages and result in families of similar languages.

Because a computer only deals with electronic pulses in binary code, all languages must eventually be translated into binary commands. A computer's operating system will handle operations that it has been programmed to process. If an application can just translate its needs into **system calls** ▶45 the operating system can do the rest of the work. Otherwise, the application will be responsible for translating all of its commands down to the firmware itself.

Source Code
Compile
Object Code
Link
Machine Code

Original software is written in source code but needs to be in machine code to be used. A compiler will translate the software into object code and then machine code so that it can be ultimately used by the computer. An interpreter takes the source code and translates it into machine code while it is actually running.

PROGRAMMER
Instructions written in high-level computer language. (Source Code) This is what a programmer writes.
COMPILER
PROGRAM
Instructions compiled and packaged into a "program" for a specific computer platform. (Machine Code) This is the software you buy and use in your computer.
USER & COMPUTER
Computer "runs" the program (Instructions ready to run at any time).

There are two ways of translating languages: compiling and interpreting. **Compilers** ▶55, 57, 102 translate instructions (in the form of **source code**) written in a specific language so that it can be executed (or processed) by a specific processor. A compiler will actually rewrite the instructions into something called object code. **Object code** (sometimes

1960
ALGOL60 completed. Very popular in Europe but most of US is comitted to FORTRAN.

(Common Business Oriented ...ge) developed by US Defense Dept. ...sed in business because it is easy to ...d able to handle very large data files.

...e). Used largely for Artificial Intelligence. Both ...it is written as a series of intricate, nested lists of ...eat at manipulating symbols, but difficult to read.

1964
PL/1 and APL languages designed.

1965
BASIC (Beginner's All-Purpose Symbolic Instruction Code). Most well-known high-level language in the world. Both compiled and interpreted, it is easy to learn, but its lack of structure makes it inappropriate for large, complex programs. Developed at Dartmouth and based on FORTRAN.

1965
Simula language designed.

1969
FORTH language developed. It is powerful and flexible but difficult to read and learn. Compiled and interpreted, it is available now on almost any computer platform.

1969
First man on the moon.

1970

Computer Languages

called **target code**) is a low–level form of the instructions a specific processor can understand without further translating. The object code must contain all necessary instructions and be *linked* to all references at this point to be complete. Once compiled, the instructions cannot be changed. To make a change, one must go back to the **source program** (the original instructions), change the portion desired, and recompile the instructions into new object code. It is the source program that contains the logic computation designed to solve specific problems in a form that a compiler is designed to understand. It cannot contain any commands or instructions that the compiler has not been designed to recognize. Most applications are written in languages that are compiled.

An **interpreter** translates (or *interprets*) each command as it is

An interpreter processes everything at the time of execution. This means that it takes extra time to convert the instructions into machine code when running. However, since an interpreted language is constant from one application to another, it allows interpreters to run the same instructions for different **CPUs ▶100–102** *instead of requiring different instructions specifically for those different devices.*

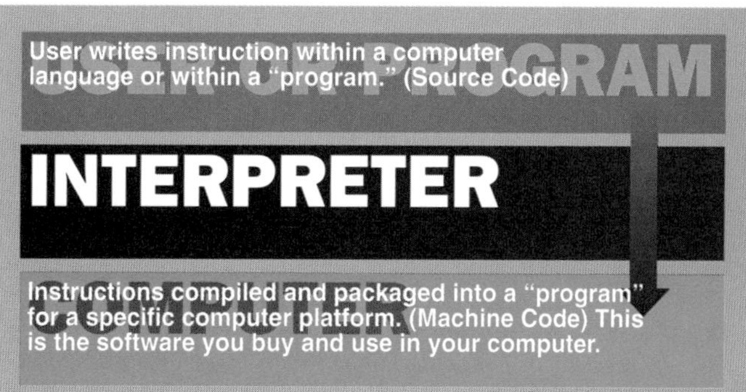
USER OR PROGRAM
User writes instruction within a computer language or within a "program." (Source Code)
INTERPRETER
COMPUTER
Instructions compiled and packaged into a "program" for a specific computer platform. (Machine Code) This is the software you buy and use in your computer.

encountered and sends it directly to the processor. This is ultimately a slower way to translate a high–level language than a compiler because the interpreter has to translate the instructions into machine–readable instructions each time it is executed (run). New commands, if properly stated, can be created and interpreted as they are encountered and sent to the processor to be executed just like previously defined commands. This flexibility is ideal for commands that are rarely used or could not have been expected at the time the language was written. One aspect of interpreted languages, however, is the ability to make changes directly in

Computer Languages Timeline (cont.)

1970

1970
Pascal (named after the famous mathematician). This block-structured language is easy to read and moderately easy to learn. It requires a fairly disciplined approach to programming.

1972
C developed at Bell Labs. This very portable language is small and very efficient. Popular for use in developing operating systems and commercial applications (especially for mini, micro and personal computers).

1973
Prolog language developed.

1975
BASIC becomes immensely popular with the emergence of personal computers.

1979
Ada language developed and named after Lady "Ada" LoveLace. Based on Pascal, this highly structured, modular language is fairly easy to learn and very readable but not efficient.

the source code without having to compile it. This also means that the changes do not have to be compiled into machine–readable form.

All languages have a **command set** that is a list of predefined commands that can be called upon and used. Common commands are already defined and ready to be used by programmers. More specific or sophisticated commands may not be defined in languages with small instruction sets and require combinations of instructions to accomplish the set task.

A **machine language** is a processor–specific, low–level computer language. It is very difficult for people to read, write and understand and works with only a specific **processor** ▶100–102. Programs written for one processor cannot be used by any other type of processor unless the two processors are **binary–compatible.** This means that the two processors process binary code in an identical manner. Machine language is similar to **object code**, except that it is typically written at this level and not just translated to this level by a **compiler**. Because machine code is so abstract, most programmers choose to program in higher–level languages. It is too difficult for people to keep track of the complex sequence of 1s and 0s.

An **assembly language** is a higher–level language than machine language and is processor–specific like machine languages. Assembly languages usually contain some words, letters or symbols that represent commands. These are easier to remember and read than sequences of binary code. Data and numbers may be represented in decimal numbers (0–9) or **hexadecimal** ▶90 numbers (0–9, A–F) instead of just binary (1 and 0). Because of these devices, an assembly language is more compact, easier to read, write and understand than source code, but far from the coherence of a spoken language. Each processor manufacturer typically provides its own **assemblers,** which translate assembly code into machine code.

High–Level Languages are the most popular tools used by software engineers to program computers. These languages (such as C, Fortran, COBOL, BASIC, Pascal, and many others) provide the software

Alan Turing ▶32–33 *was one of the biggest heroes in the development of computers. He was the brain behind the COLOSSUS project in Great Britain that broke the Germans'* ***Enigma*** *codes during World War II. He led numerous teams that developed early computer languages. Like Charles Babbage before him, he designed a device that would have won him the honor of designing the first true computer if he had the resources and support he needed to complete it. He developed theories of computation and symbol–processing systems, as well as artificial intelligence. His government abandoned him despite his contributions during World War II and in deep depression, he committed suicide at 42.*

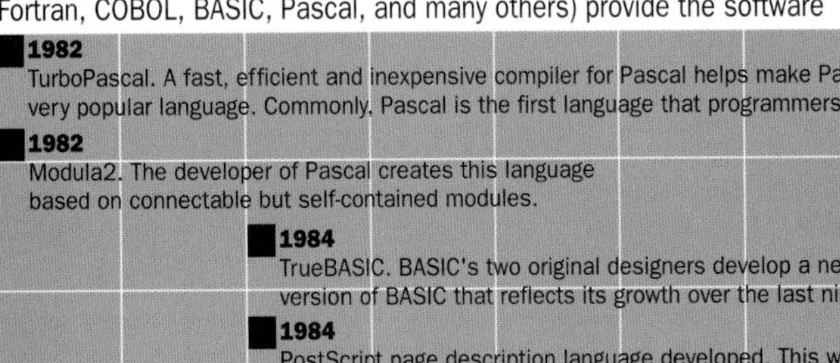

1982
TurboPascal. A fast, efficient and inexpensive compiler for Pascal helps make Pascal a very popular language. Commonly, Pascal is the first language that programmers learn.

1982
Modula2. The developer of Pascal creates this language based on connectable but self-contained modules.

1984
TrueBASIC. BASIC's two original designers develop a new, standardized version of BASIC that reflects its growth over the last nine years.

1984
PostScript page description language developed. This was one of the advances that made desktop publishing possible.

1982
Computer is named *Time Magazine* Man of the Year.

1986
C++ is an object-oriented version of C.

1990

1990
Berlin Wall destroyed.

*Programming **Objects** are like chess pieces. Each piece has data and instructions. A chess piece's data is its position and its instructions are how it can move. Changing the characteristics for one piece or adding a new piece with new instructions does not require changes in any other piece. Likewise, objects have their own instructions and changing how one object behaves does not necessarily create inconsistencies in other objects.*

*As with other professions, the title for those who develop software has changed over the years. While the term **Programmers** has been used for quite a while, the terms **Software Engineer** and **Software Developer** are the latest, politically correct titles.*

engineer with tools for performing specific functions without having to understand all the intricacies of the underlying hardware. This is very important because it separates the hardware designer from the software designers. A software designer can write an application to run on different types of computers as long as both computers support standard computer languages.

Object–Oriented Languages such as C++ and Objective C offer a new style of programming that will allow software engineers even more flexibility. Before object–oriented languages, software engineers were required to write complex and cumbersome programs. Small changes in the programming might have dramatic effects throughout the program. Instructions that referenced other instructions might not work under those changes. Object–oriented programming eases this problem by allowing programmers to organize applications as collections of **objects**, each with their own purpose. Objects are responsible for their own internal data but can share sets of data with other objects. Each object has specific functions which can be modified without changing the entire program. Object–oriented programs are more like a soccer team working together than a tennis player who is responsible for all aspects of the game. This tends to localize changes and problems. New functions and modifications to the program can be added easily because the obiects are independent of each other.

Logic

At the lowest level, all computer operations revolve around three elements: the logical expressions of **AND**, **OR**, and **NOT**. These are the basic components of logic and most other commands and processes are built as combinations of these. These simple logic statements correspond to logic circuits on an integrated circuit chip. The circuits are called **logic gates** ▶93–94, 97 because they regulate the flow of data through the circuits depending on what signals they receive. By doing this, they can simulate logical statements.

While all languages build on these logical statements, they are by no means identical. Each language approaches logic and programming in its own way and a programmer must accept that approach from the beginning. This is why so many different computer languages have been developed. One language may offer more convenience for a programmer or be better suited to a particular machine or problem to be solved.

Programming

Programming is essentially an attempt at creating a pattern of actions that can solve a particular problem. Most **programs** are combinations of **commands** ▶58 that instruct the computer what to do and **variables** that act as place–holders for data. The most basic commands have to do with inputting and outputting data and navigating around the instructions in a program. **Input** refers to the process of entering data into the computer and current program. **Output** refers to the program and computer returning or displaying data to the user or to some other place in the system. All programs have some way of inputting and outputting data in some form (numbers, words, binary code, etc...). Without this capability, a program would be extremely limited in what it could process.

Assigning **variables** is a way of symbolizing discrete inputs within the program (especially numbers). If a program computes a certain number (the date, for instance) that it will need later, it can be instructed to store it in a special container that will allow it to be retrieved and used later. This container is called a **variable** and it can be assigned almost any symbol or name to be referred by (such as the word DATE). The program can then forget all about it for the moment and look it up when it is needed. Being able to assign and reassign variables is extremely powerful to programs and programmers because it allows the programs to concentrate on the task at hand without having to keep track of lots of extra data that isn't immediately relevant.

To make different programs more efficient there are three basic types of variables: Character, Integer, and Floating–Point. Each variable is **declared** as one of these three types at the beginning of the program. This helps the **compiler** ▶55 compile the program more efficiently. **Character** variables store alphabetic characters such as words or names. **Integer**

Integer Operation:

561
+ 282
843

Floating–Point Operation:

561×10^{-5}
$+ e^{15}$
3.269×10^{6}

Lady Ada Augusta Lovelace ▶32 *was the first programmer. Daughter of Lord Byron, she excelled at mathematics at an early age. She was introduced to* **Charles Babbage** ▶32, 55, 93 *and his Difference Engine and immediately understood how the machine worked. She helped Babbage design the Analytical Engine and devised the basis of what would later be called programming. She also developed an early discussion of the possibility of Artificial Intelligence which Alan Turing named "Lady Lovelace's Objection."*

Programming used to be done with punch cards and was a very slow process. The sequence of cards was crucial. Consequently, dropping them on the floor was a disaster.

Programming

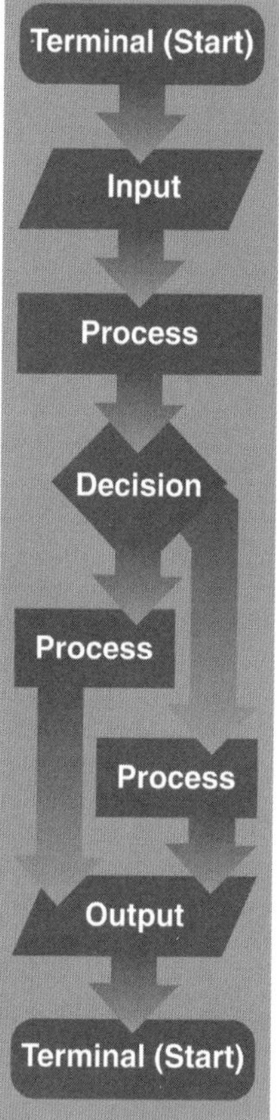

variables store integer numbers such as 1, 2, 6, 401, 1601, etc.... **Floating–Point** variables store numbers such as 4.333, 16^e and $4x10^{-5}$, etc.... This is the same as scientific notation. Each of these types of variables is treated differently by the computer to increase computer performance. Floating–Point numbers are the most complex and character data is the simplest. Some computers have special **processors** ▶102–103 just to calculate floating–point numbers because of their complexity. This is especially useful for graphics and scientific simulations.

After programs input data and assign variables, the next step is to perform some manipulation of the data. These manipulations are created as complex sequences of simple **logic** ▶93–94 functions. Within a program are **logic constructs** that allow extremely powerful manipulations of data to take place with very simple forms. The most basic is the **IF/THEN** statement. This works just like everyday conversations. For example, you might say to a friend "**IF** it's nice out tomorrow, **THEN** let's go to the beach." The structure of an IF/THEN statement in a computer program is the same. For example: **IF** Range_Window_One=True **THEN** Cursor=Box **ELSE** Cursor=Normal. The **ELSE** portion is an addition that adds more instructions in the case that the IF/THEN statement is not true. For example, you might say to your friend "**IF** it's nice out tomorrow, **THEN** let's go to the beach, or **ELSE** we could stay in and watch a movie." The IF/THEN/ELSE statement represents a way for the computer to make a decision. Other statements (or commands) allow the computer to **GOTO** or **JUMP** to another part of the program, **REPEAT** a section of instructions a number of times, or **OUTPUT** data in some form or another.

Complex programs that manipulate data in sophisticated ways all break down into fairly simple parts. These parts are statements that tell the computer what to do at any time. If a software engineer is using a certain group of statements or commands over and over, he or she can group these commands into a subroutine. A **subroutine** is a group of statements that is located within a program and performs a specific function (such as an alphabetical sort of data) and is called upon by the program when needed. The subroutine can be called upon by the computer at any time and as many times as necessary. Subroutines allow a software engineer to write more efficient, readable and modular programs.

Without the ability to store a computer's progress or a user's work, a computer would be fairly useless. A computer's ability to store data—in incredible amounts—is one of its greatest capabilities.

Diskettes

There are many different means to store data. The most common are hard discs and diskettes. **Diskettes ▸119** are portable disks used for storing small amounts of data in an easily transportable media. These are sometimes referred to as **floppy–disks** because the magnetic disk inside that holds the data is flexible. Floppy–disks used to be enclosed in flexible plastic sleeves. More recently, they are protected inside hard plastic cases like an audio cassette tape.

The disk that holds the encoded data is made of a flexible polyester plastic coated on one or both sides with a magnetic film. This film is where the data is encoded. **Single–sided** disks refer to disks that can only be used on one side and are abbreviated SS. **Double–sided** diskettes are abbreviated DS and can be used on both sides—doubling the capacity. A DS diskette can only be used by a diskette drive that is capable of reading both sides. There are a few notches in either the case (called a **jacket**) and/or the disk **hub** (the center). When inserted into the drive, a notch aligns the disk with the drive **head** (the part that "reads" and "writes" the data) and another is used to spin the disk. (Sometimes, these are the same notch.)

The coating on the surface of the disk is divided into concentric rings or **tracks ▸62**. Each track is less than $^1/_{100}$ inch wide. The head follows the tracks, much like on a phonograph and magnetizes the coating along each track to store data. The tracks are divided into **sectors** so that a drive can spin to the right sector, count in or out the correct number of tracks and find the spot that holds a particular piece of data very quickly. A record of where each piece of data is stored and how to find it is kept at the edge of the disk, called the **directory ▸62**.

At top is a $5^1/_4$" floppy disk used with IBM–compatible personal computers. To the left is a newer $3^1/_2$" diskette like those used with Macintosh computers, some IBM–compatibles and many UNIX workstations.

These disks are at half size.

Diskettes

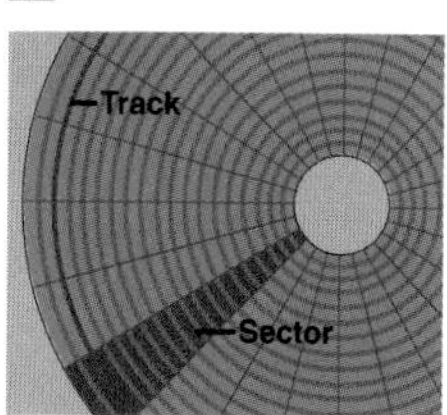

All disks must be ***initialized*** *when used for the first time. This sets up* **tracks** ▶59 *and* **sectors** ▶59 *in which to store data.*

Note: All disk illustrations are at half size.

The disk spins at approximately 300-360 revolutions per minute. At this speed, it is critical that nothing gets caught between the disk and the head. If something does, the disk may be scratched. As on a phonograph record, a scratch can cause a track or sector to be unusable. Cloth **liners** protect the disk from most particles and from the jackets. But, because the disks are flexible, the read/write head actually contacts the disk. This is why any particle (even dust or smoke) caught between the two can damage the disk. A scratch is called a **hard error** because it makes a physical scratch that is unrepairable. A **soft error** may arise if the coating has an impurity or is not properly formatted.

The disk must be formatted before use. **Formatting** (or **initializing**) is the process of writing the tracks and sectors into the blank disk so that it may be used by the drive for storing data. Most disk drives and system software can recognize bad sectors and block them from being used.

The capacities of disks are affected by how closely the tracks can be packed together. **High–Density** disks (HD) pack tracks twice as closely as standard diskettes. This means that the head in the disk drive is able to distinguish tracks half as wide. The coating for HD disks must be finer and more consistent to allow tracks this narrow. While double–sided diskettes can often be formatted for use as high–density diskettes because the coating is not as fine, they often make too many **soft errors** for reliable use. The notches in the corners of diskettes indicate whether the disk is write–protected. **Write–protecting** the disk prevents the drive from changing the data on it and, thus, accidentally deleting data. However, a write–protected disk can still be "read."

New, **Very High Density** Diskettes (VHD) are capable of storing from 2.88 MB to 21 MB per disk. However, the formats for these are still evolving and are not yet fixed as standards.

The notches in the edges of disks make sure the disk is inserted correctly and let the computer know what kind of disk it is and if it is locked.

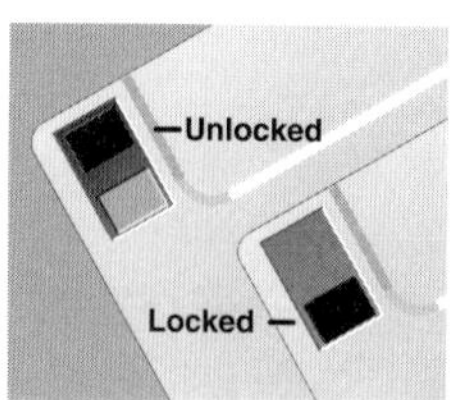

Hard Drives

Hard disc drives are large–capacity storage devices that can either be installed inside the computer or be enclosed in a separate box outside the computer and connected with a cable. Hard discs magnetically store and retrieve data in the same manner as **diskettes** ▶59–60 but, typically, at much faster speeds (commonly around 1 MegaByte per second). **Seek time** refers to the amount of time it takes the hard disc to find the right **sector** (place) where a given piece of data is stored. Seek times typically run around 30 milliseconds (3/1000 second).

Hard discs come in varying sizes and capacities. **Sizes** refer to the physical dimensions of the drive mechanism and **capacities** refer to the amount of data that can be stored in them. Drive dimensions (sizes) are measured by diameter and **height.** The diameters come in standard sizes (2.5", 3.5" and 5.25") and the heights are referred to in terms of a standard 3" high drive. **Half height** drives, then, are 1.5" high and **third height** drives are 1" high.

Hard drive capacities are measured in **megabytes** (MB) because of the great amounts of storage available. 20MB, 40MB, 80MB, 105MB, 200MB, 400MB, and 600MB are all common, although almost any size is possible. Currently, 40MB is a good amount of storage space for a regular user on most personal computers (but not a power–user). Users who store photos, sound and/or video clips fill space quickly and would need hard drives of much greater capacity.

The hard discs are made of iron and nickel cores with a thin, magnetic coating on both sides. This coating is similar to that on diskettes but finer and more consistent. This allows them to reliably **format** more tracks in less space. Because the discs are not flexible, the head cannot touch it or it will scratch the magnetic coating, causing a **hard error**. The distance the head flies above the disk's surface is, usually, around 2 microns (.000003148 inch) —so small that a particle of dust, hair or even smoke particles can wedge between the head and disc and scratch the disc.

From the outside, a hard disk looks like just another plastic box.

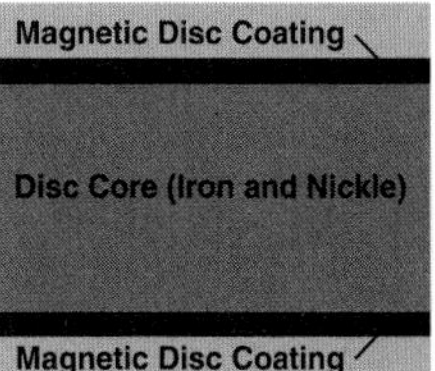

Discs are made of an iron and nickel core coated with a magnetic coating on both sides.

*A **megabyte** is 1,048,570* **bytes** ▶92.

*There is a great deal of confusion about the words **disc** and **disk**. **Disc** refers to a round platter used to store data as in a hard disc, video disc or CD-ROM disc. **Disk** is short for **diskette** and is used for floppy disks and diskettes. Both are fairly interchangeable in common usage.*

Hard Drives

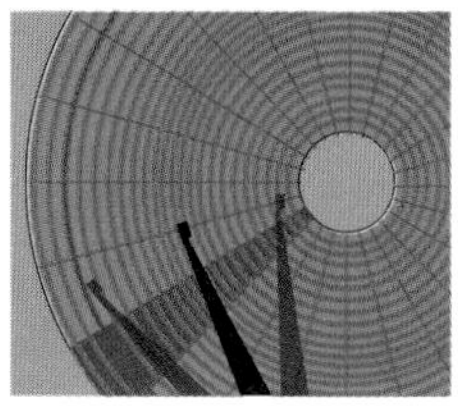

A typical disc spins at 3600 revolutions per minute. With a distance of only 2 micron between the head and disc, this is comparable to a jumbo jet flying at 150 miles per hour exactly 6 feet off the runway—continuously. Because of the possible catastrophe caused by dust or smoke particles, hard discs are sealed tightly to prevent exposure to anything that might get caught between the head and disc. **Tracks** ▶59 on a hard disc are, typically, 40 mills wide (4/1000 inch). This means that 250 tracks can be packed in one inch. With so many tracks packed this closely together, the head (which is mounted to a tracking **arm**) would need to turn slightly in order to align parallel with all tracks in all places on the disc. Because the head does not turn on the arm, the innermost and outermost tracks of the disc are spaced farther apart to prevent the head from "reading" a neighboring track by accident. The angle between the track and the head in these awkward areas of the disc is called **head skew**.

Hard discs pack a great deal of storage space in a small area because they use multiple discs (**platters**) stacked and spaced on top of each other. Multiple disc heads on arms (called **sliders**) reach between the platters to access both sides of each platter.

When a computer deletes data from a disk, it doesn't actually erase the data but notifies the **directory** ▶59 at the disk's edge that those sectors are available for new data. Because the data is not destroyed until new data is written over it, it is usually possible to **recover** it in the case of accidental deletion. Special **disk recovery utilities** ▶18 allow you to read the data in these sectors, even after you have told the computer to ignore it, as long as no new data has yet been written over it.

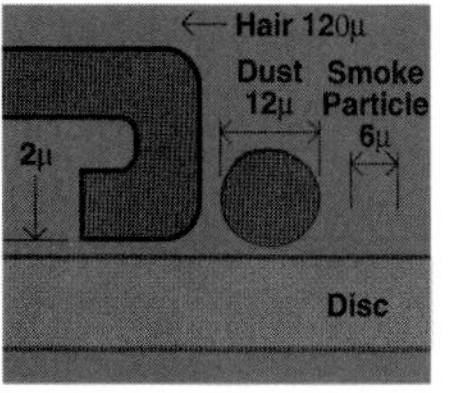

Note: The diameter of a typical hair is about 120 microns.

Sometimes, a hard disc is partitioned to create multiple **volumes** (areas of storage) on the same disc. **Partitions**, basically, are areas on a hard disc that are separated from each other and function as if they were separate hard discs. Usually, this is done in cases of a computer running more than one **operating system** ▶44–49 (such as UNIX and DOS or Macintosh). Because these operating systems are not necessarily compatible or interchangeable, each partition can run a different operating system without conflicts. In essence, the computer operates as if it had three different, incompatible storage areas, even though they are all part of the same disc. Another reason to partition a hard disc is to create an area in which to test **beta software** ▶36, 126. This software is usually unstable and unpredictable and can cause the computer to **crash** or lose data. To protect the computer and data in

---

Some new hard drives actually come on a board that fits into the computer like an accelerator board or **video card** ▶80.

storage, a special partition can be set up that keeps the beta software and its effects contained. Searching can also be faster on a partition because the space is smaller than the whole hard disc and this limits the amount of data that must be searched.

The opening in the front of a cartridge drive is all that distinguishes it from a hard drive.

Cartridge Drives

Some storage media combine the best attributes of diskettes and hard drives. **Cartridge drives** are high–capacity (approximately 45 or 88 megabytes) removable hard discs enclosed in a plastic cartridge. There is only one disc in each case but both sides are used. Cartridge drives are a little slower than hard drives but can offer more flexible storage options. Large capacities of data can be stored an a disc and ejected from the drive like a diskette. A fresh cartridge can then be inserted and used. This offers unlimited storage of data in 45MB or 88MB chunks. These cartridges are also handy for transporting large files (especially color images) to **service bureaus** ▸10, 123 where they are almost a standard medium of data storage.

The newest cartridge format offers as much as 88MB per cartridge. These drives are just now becoming widely used and available.

CD–ROM

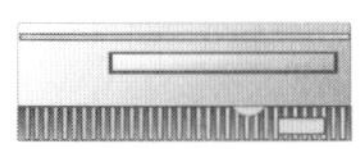

A **CD–ROM** (Compact Disc–Read Only Memory) disc is identical to a compact disc used for music. The data is stamped into a clear plastic disc in mass quantities, sprayed with aluminum to form an ultra-thin layer and encased in clear plastic. CD–ROMs are fairly inexpensive to produce and can carry incredible amounts of data. The typical 12cm wide CD–ROM disc can hold 550–660 MB of sounds, images, text, music, applications, or any combination of these data types.

Each Compact Disc can digitally store up to 74 minutes of stereo music.

CD–ROM

Actually, the data in a CD–ROM isn't exactly coded into 1s and 0s. Only the changes between 1 and 0 (and vise versa) are recorded. This means that if the current digits are 1s, when the laser encounters a pit, it marks each digit as a 0 until another pit is encountered.

Some CD–ROMs are only 3.5" wide and can store up to 128MB of data. The data on a CD–ROM cannot be changed or "written" to. It is only for "reading" data. It is a good vehicle for large amounts of published information that doesn't change often (if ever), such as encyclopedia, dictionaries, directories, and **multimedia** **▶13, 17** presentations. Some software publishers have started selling suites of **applications** **▶4** on a single CD–ROM, rather than on many diskettes. Other CD–ROMs contain whole libraries of fonts or artwork.

A CD–ROM has one track wrapped spirally from the inside to the outside of the disc. The track is a series of pits that protrude off the surface of the aluminum layer. These pits are "read" with a laser beam (a thin, concentrated beam of pure light). When the laser hits the smooth portions of the track it bounces back through the laser's lens. This **reflection** is read as a 1 in binary code. When the laser hits a pit, the light beam is scattered and does not reflect back into the lens. This is "read" as a 0. As the laser scans along the track, the reflections and pits create a stream of binary data (1s and 0s).

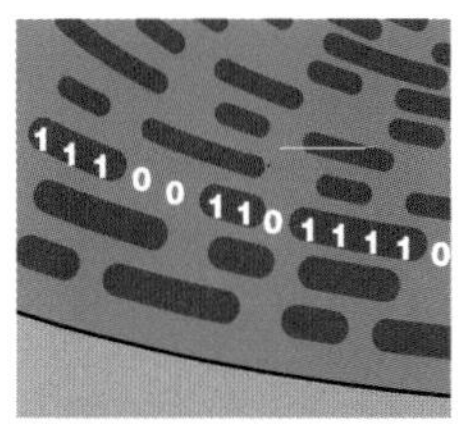

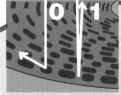

Video Discs

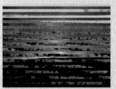

A **video disc** does not contain digitally recorded data. The sounds and images are stored in an **analog** fashion. When used in a video disc player for viewing on a television, the player reads the data and displays it on the screen in the same form as the signals the television normally receives for broadcast images (**interlaced** **▶16, 114**). Computer screens, however, use a different format to display images and the signals from a video disc must be translated into a digital form in order to be displayed on a computer. This takes time and a great deal of processing. Because of this, video discs are usually controlled by a computer but displayed on a television monitor instead of a computer screen. This allows the computer to tell the video disc which portions to display and when, without translating the data itself.

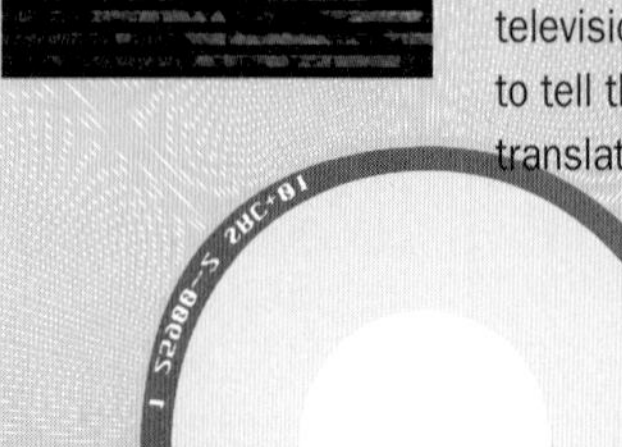

Note: All discs in this section appear at half size.

WORM Drives

WORM stands for **Write Once, Read Many**. It is an optical disc (similar to a CD–ROM) that can be "written" to once, but "read" many times. WORM discs are high–capacity (approximately 330MB–660MB) but slower than hard discs. They are used primarily for archiving data.

At the core of the disc is hard, clear plastic or glass. This is coated on both sides with metal and encased in glass or more clear plastic. A laser at high power can burn pits into the coating, but once cooled, the pits cannot be changed. This is why it is called "Write Once". The same laser, at low power, can then "read" the data (pits and smooth areas) much like a CD–ROM does (although the two formats are incompatible). The smooth areas reflect back into the laser lens (representing 1s) and the pits don't reflect back (representing 0s). The stream of reflections and dead spots are translated into 1s and 0s and represent a stream of data.

This technique allows users to store their own information onto an optical disc that cannot be altered (deleted, lost or changed) once it is written. When archived data becomes obsolete, those sections of the disc can be **marked off**. This means that the disc's **directory** is told to no longer access those portions.

Because of more complicated equipment, a WORM drive looks different than other types of drives.

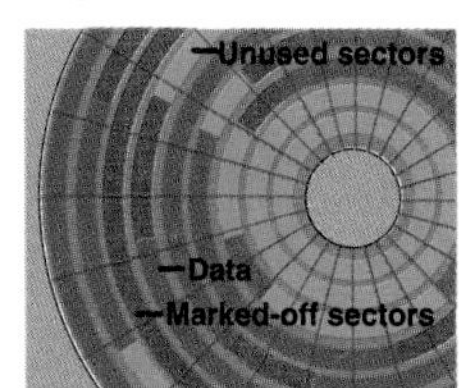

A WORM drive marks off old sectors on a WORM disk if the data is no longer valid.

RAM Discs

A **RAM disc** is not really a disc at all. It is a set of **RAM** ▸104–105 **chips** arranged on boards and encased in a box that either fits into the computer or connects to it with a cable from outside. The RAM chips operate exactly like the RAM on the computer's **motherboard** ▸108–109 (they are fast but they need constant refreshing and will erase if the power is turned off). A RAM disc is used when very large files need to be manipulated. Manipulating large color images or complex scientific equations are typical uses that may require a RAM disc. Otherwise, they are not too common. It is also wise to use an **uninterruptable power supply** with a RAM disc to protect the data in RAM if the power is suddenly cut off. RAM discs can come in any size, but they commonly start at about 80MB and go up from there.

A RAM disc is a plain and simple box and usually indistinguishable from a hard drive.

DAT Drives

Using DAT music tapes for storing data is not recommended. DAT drives turn the tape much faster and often go back and forth many times at high speeds. DAT music tape is not as strong as DAT data tape and may break or stretch.

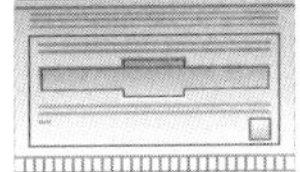

DAT Drives

DAT (Digital Audio Tape) cassettes can be used to store any digital data (whether it is a music album or a spreadsheet). DAT drives are now available to store computer data. These are usually used for **back–up** purposes and not for **real–time** use because they are too slow to effectively keep up with a computer's processor. They do, however, store a huge amount of data (approximately 2.3 gigabytes). This is equal to 2,300,000,000 bytes or about 1900 diskettes —all in a $^1/_2$ inch by 2 inch by 3 inch cassette!

Optical Discs

An **Optical Disc** is an erasable optical–magnetic disc. Although they are slower than **hard discs** ▶60–63, they have great capacities (approximately 600 MB) and they can be erased and written to like a diskette or hard disc. Also, optical discs are easily transported because they are enclosed in a case similar to a **cartridge**. A smaller (3.5") optical format is also used. This format has a storage capacity of 128MB and works the same way as the larger (5.25") format.

The coatings on either side of the disc's glass core are sensitive to both light and magnetic fields. A laser at high–power heats the coating so that a magnetic **head** can change the magnetic field along the disc's tracks and "write" data. Without the laser, the tracks are cool and can only be "read" from by the **laser**.

This is a fairly secure means of storing data that changes. Users who try to use them in place of hard discs are often disappointed at the slower operating speeds but these are getting faster as technology advances. These speeds are comparable to hard disc speeds of about five years ago.

Optical discs are promising because they cannot be altered in the presence of magnetic fields unless the laser is on to heat the coating. This means that discs can be transported through airport metal detectors without damaging the data on them. Hard discs and diskettes are all susceptible to strong magnetic fields and should be kept away from anything that might have magnetic fields strong enough to erase them.

Optical Discs combine the best features of all storage media except speed. They are erasable, transportable, secure, stable and have high–capacities. When the speeds are increased to hard disc levels of performance, they may become the preferred medium for data storage.

Storage Media Compared:

	Access Time	Data Transfer	Capacity (MegaBytes)	Size (inches)	Cost/MByte (dollars)	Rewritable?	Magnetically Vulnerable?	Stability (years)
Hard Drive	Very Fast	Med	20-500	var.	$3-$4	Yes	Yes	5
HD Disk	Slow	Slow	1.4	3.5"	$1	Yes	Yes	5
ED Disk	Slow	Slow	2.8-20	3.5"	$2.5	Yes	Yes	5
Cartridge	Slow	Slow	44-88	5.25"	$1.80	Yes	Yes	5
CD-ROM	Extrem. Slow	Very Slow	660-1024	5.25"	6¢	No	No	100
WORM	Slooow	Very Slow	200-1000	5.25"	23¢	Yes	Yes	100
Optical	Slooow	Very Slow	400-650	5.25"	28¢	Yes	No	10
3.5" Optical	Med	Slow	128	3.5"	77¢	Yes	No	10
DAT	Slowest	Extrem. Slow	750-1200	3"x2"	1¢	Yes	Yes	5
Flash Mem.	Instant-aneous	Faaast!	1-50	var.	$120	Yes	Yes	1

WORM Cards *are rectangular, credit card–sized pieces of optical material. Usually, the left–over pieces from the manufacturing of* **WORM** ▶65 *discs are cut into strips and arranged in rows on these cards. They are handy for recording information that can be easily transported. Some personal medical records are now stored on these cards so that physicians may have access to a person's entire medical history wherever they may be. Some corporations are also using the cards in place of money in company stores and cafeterias. Because the value on these cards cannot be added to (only subtracted from by* ***marking off****), they cannot be tampered with.*

Communications

Computers have long had the ability to share information. While this is nothing new, we are now seeing computer communication evolve to a much more sophisticated level.

When mainframes were the current technology, many users would use one computer simultaneously. This made it easy to share information because the information never had to transfer between computers—only between users. With personal computers, however, each user has his or her own computer and sharing information is a little more complex—especially if each user's computer is a different type.

Getting dissimilar computers to speak to each other can be a difficult task. First, the computers need some common physical form of connection (either a diskette format that each computer can recognize or a cable that plugs into each computer). Second, the computers must share a form of writing data that each computer understands. This is analogous to two people who speak different languages trying to communicate with each other. They need to reach some form of common ground in order to accomplish any exchange of information. Computer interactions are more limited since gestures, facial expressions and other means of information cannot be communicated.

Now that users are disconnected from each other by having separate personal computers, new software and hardware tools are reconnecting them. This enables better exchange of information, yet allows users to keep the autonomy they already have.

Both hardware and software components allow users to work alone and, when necessary, transfer information and work together. This is creating a new type of computer interaction dubbed **interpersonal computing.** Special software, called **groupware,** allows separate users to work together effectively whether they send mail, make comments, separately edit the same documents, or create documents, databases, and presentations simultaneously and interactively.

In any exchange, both the sender and receiver must come to some agreements about when data is to be transmitted, what data is to be shared, in what form it will be shared, who has access to it, and how to coordinate efforts. These issues of privacy, timing, organization, and format are at the core of all group activity—not just computerized group activity—although the technology adds another layer of complexity. Groupware allows groups of individuals to operate more effectively and, sometimes, achieve levels of interaction unattainable without computers. However, these groups are still vulnerable to the same basic human traits that make collaborative work a success or failure. Computers cannot make up for lack of organization or skills within the group.

The most basic form of computer connections are the cables and connectors that connect peripheral equipment (**peripherals** ▸71), such as printers, keyboards and monitors to the computer. Data sent through the cables is **quantized**. This means that it is cut up and sent in a series of short pieces called **packets** ▸73.

These packets travel at varying speeds depending on the type of cables and transmission. Speed is measured in bits per second or **baud**. The **baud rate** ▸27 is roughly equal to characters per second (1200 baud ≅ 120 characters per second). The common baud rates for **modem** ▸27 transmissions are 1200, 2400, 4800 and 9600 baud. Transmission speed is limited to the highest baud rate both connected devices have in common. For example, if one computer is capable of 2400 baud and another of only 1200 baud, they can only communicate between themselves at 1200 baud.

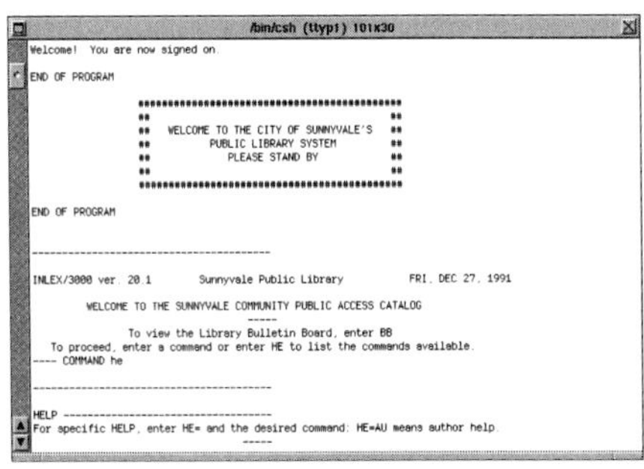

Communicating between two computers is a little more complex. Not only is the speed important, but the form of communication as well. If two computers are to communicate, they must have a common way of "speaking". Two computers from the same family have few problems because they share the same type of system software. But, two different computers (say, a Macintosh and a DOS–compatible) need some help.

Emulation is when a computer mimics the communication style of another. There are few emulation standards between computers. Some standards (such as VT100) emulate **terminals** connected to **mainframes**. This is common because so much data is stored on mainframes. Emulating one of these terminals allows a computer access to that information. If two computers can emulate the same format, they can communicate together.

Networks

Networks

Before networks and networking technology, users who needed to share data could only do so by copying it onto a diskette and handing it to another user. If a file needed to be sent across the room or across the street, the only alternative was to carry it on a diskette. This is jokingly referred to as **sneakernet**. Now, however, cables linking computers replace shoes and diskettes. These cables connect computers in groups called **networks** ▶37. Networked computers have many advantages over **stand-alone** ▶36 computers. These include **electronic mail** ▶28–29 (E-mail), sharing data and files, flexible and interactive work between users and faster communications.

Small networks are called **Local Area Networks** (LANs) because they are collections of a few computers connected within a small, physical area (i.e., a building or an office). A local area network can be as small as two computers or as many as a hundred or more. The more computers connected, however, the more traffic on the network. Computers send messages to each other over the network and many messages can slow down the performance in the same way that too many cars slow traffic on a freeway.

There are a few different ways a local area network can operate. One common scheme is called a token-ring. Computers and other equipment on a **token-ring** are hooked to each other one after another to form one continuous chain or ring. There is a piece of software called a **token** that gets passed between the devices. The token is no more than a pass that gives priority to the machine that possesses it at any time. The token is passed from machine to machine around the ring. A machine can only send a message or document on the network if it has the token. When it is finished, it passes the token to the next machine. The drawback of a token ring is that only one computer can use the network at a time. Every machine must wait until it is their turn. This can be a handicap with large networks of computers or if users pass big documents along the network.

In a token-ring, each computer or peripheral is attached in a chain.

Another network organization is called a bus. Basically, a **bus** consists of one cable that all computers and peripherals attach to at any place along it's length. The two ends of the cable do not need to be connected to form a ring. Most buses allow multiple computers to send messages at the same time.

The computers package the messages with codes that allow other devices to tell who the message is for. In this way, many messages may be sent along the bus at the same time. Each device (computer, printer, modem, etc...) is capable of determining which message is meant to be "read" by it. Too many messages can slow down the network speed, however. It is possible that messages will collide with each other and need to be sent again.

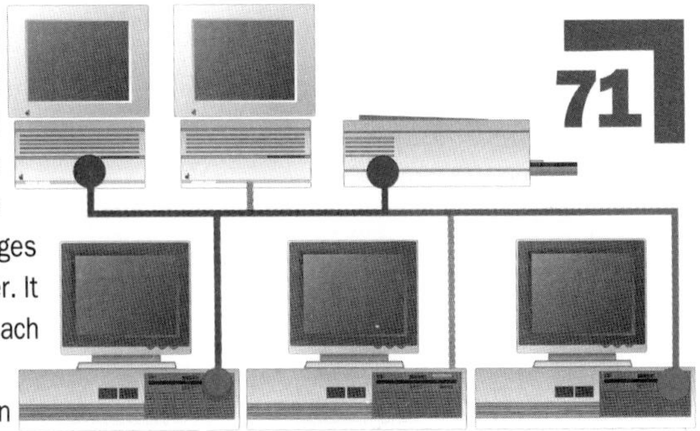

Star LANs are another common type of network. In this arrangement, each device is connected to one central device, called a **router** or **star controller**. The central device functions as a switching center since each machine cannot pass messages directly to another. This can be inefficient for many offices but it offers a great deal of control. Timing can be controlled easily to prevent any messages from colliding with another.

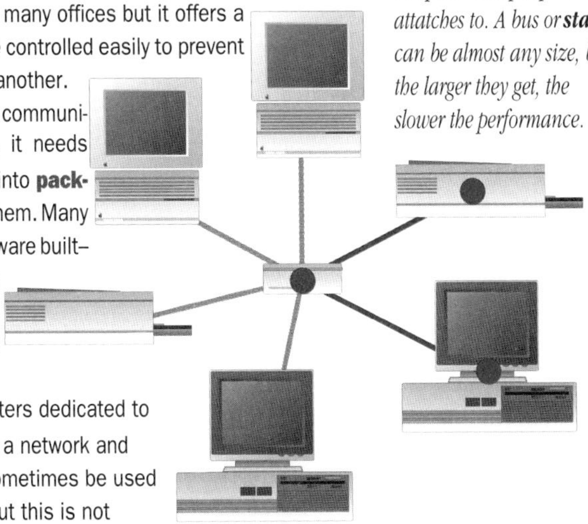

*A **bus** is basically a backbone that each computer and peripheral attatches to. A bus or **star** can be almost any size, but the larger they get, the slower the performance.*

In order for any device to communicate with another on a network, it needs special software to quantize data into **packets** ▶69, 73 and send and receive them. Many computers now come with this software built–in and all that is required are the cables to connect them. Others need extra software and special hardware to connect to others.

File Servers are computers dedicated to managing the communications on a network and storing common files. They can sometimes be used as a normal computer by a user but this is not recommended because it slows down the file server considerably. The server acts as a traffic controller and directs the flow of messages between computers and **peripherals**. Many times, the server will have a **hard disc** ▶60–63 or other storage device used to store common files and applications. This allows all users on the network to access these files. Users can also drop off files from their computers to the server where others can pick them up. Servers may also direct the flow of documents to printers, although this is less common. A server is a very effective way of enhancing users' capabilities.

Networks usually dedicate their fastest computers to be servers.

Servers come with special software that allows them to manage the flow of communications and the access each user has to

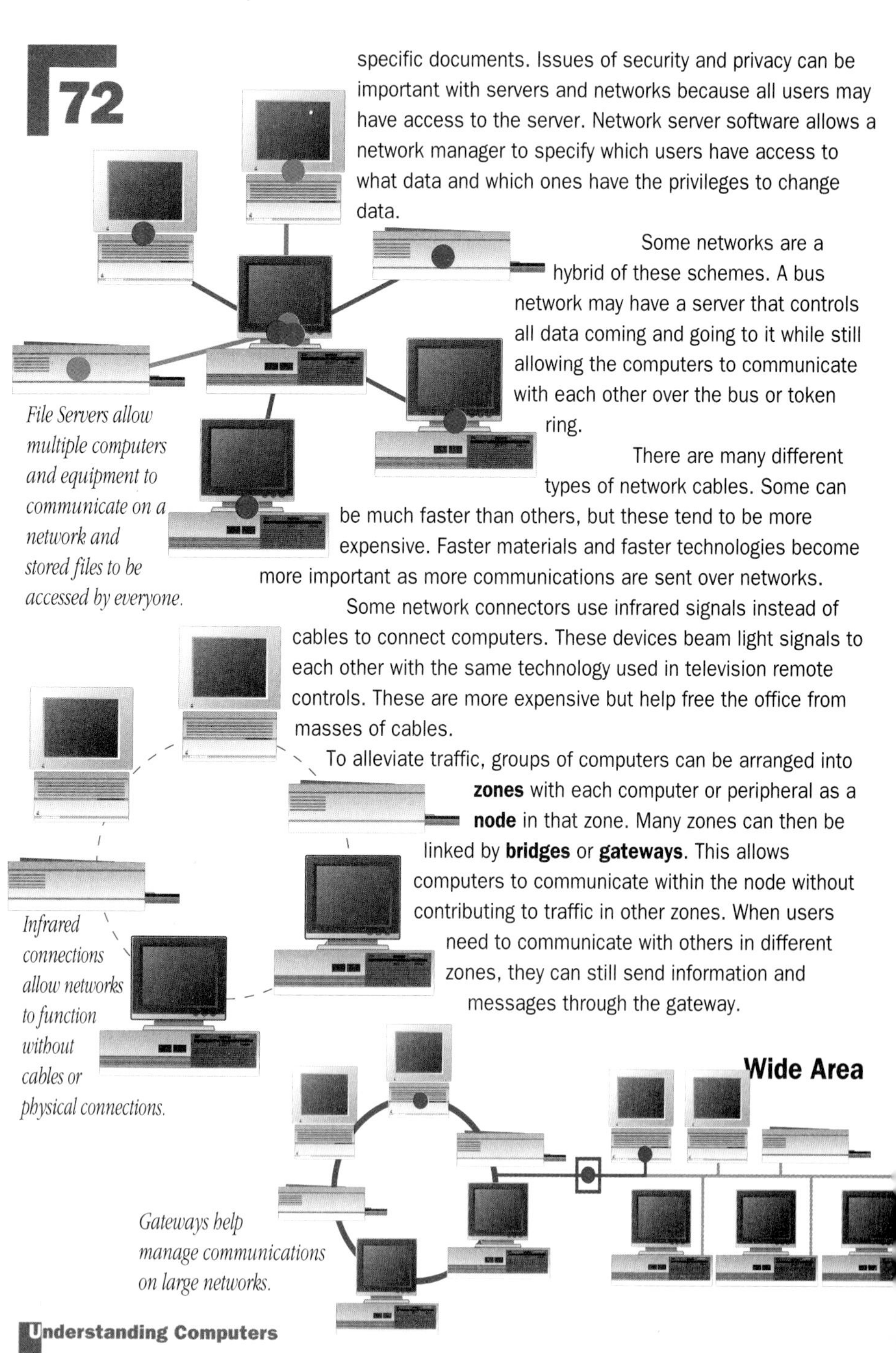

specific documents. Issues of security and privacy can be important with servers and networks because all users may have access to the server. Network server software allows a network manager to specify which users have access to what data and which ones have the privileges to change data.

Some networks are a hybrid of these schemes. A bus network may have a server that controls all data coming and going to it while still allowing the computers to communicate with each other over the bus or token ring.

There are many different types of network cables. Some can be much faster than others, but these tend to be more expensive. Faster materials and faster technologies become more important as more communications are sent over networks.

Some network connectors use infrared signals instead of cables to connect computers. These devices beam light signals to each other with the same technology used in television remote controls. These are more expensive but help free the office from masses of cables.

To alleviate traffic, groups of computers can be arranged into **zones** with each computer or peripheral as a **node** in that zone. Many zones can then be linked by **bridges** or **gateways**. This allows computers to communicate within the node without contributing to traffic in other zones. When users need to communicate with others in different zones, they can still send information and messages through the gateway.

File Servers allow multiple computers and equipment to communicate on a network and stored files to be accessed by everyone.

Infrared connections allow networks to function without cables or physical connections.

Gateways help manage communications on large networks.

Wide Area Networks

Networks

Wide Area Networks (WANs) are networks that cover a big area. Usually, they communicate over dedicated phone lines to link computers and local area networks. **Internet** ▸39 and **ARPAnet** are good examples of wide area networks. These are government–sponsored networks that link researchers, developers, military installations and contractors across the country.

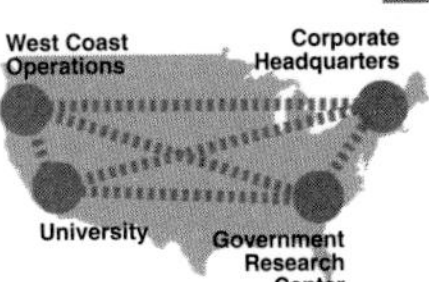

A wide–area network can connect geographically distant users as if they were "right next door."

Ethernet

Developed at Xerox PARC (where local area networks were pioneered), **Ethernet** uses a special **protocol** for sending data. Ethernet tends to be faster and more efficient than many other types of networks. It is capable of handling greater volumes of network traffic. Ethernet also allows all devices to send data virtually simultaneously. If collisions of data do occur, they are detected and retransmitted quickly.

The first computer to use ethernet was Xerox's Alto.

Modems

A **modem** ▸27, 69, 121 is a device that allows a computer to send and receive data over a phone line. This is critical when connecting with other computers, a **BBS** ▸29–30 (Bulletin Board System), or a remote network. A modem can be installed either on a board that fits into a computer or in a separate, external box. A modem connects to a phone line and to the computer. This allows the modem to transmit data signals over standard telephone lines. Once the modem calls and verifies the connection at the other end, it **quantizes** ▸69, 71 the data into packets and transmits it to the other computer.

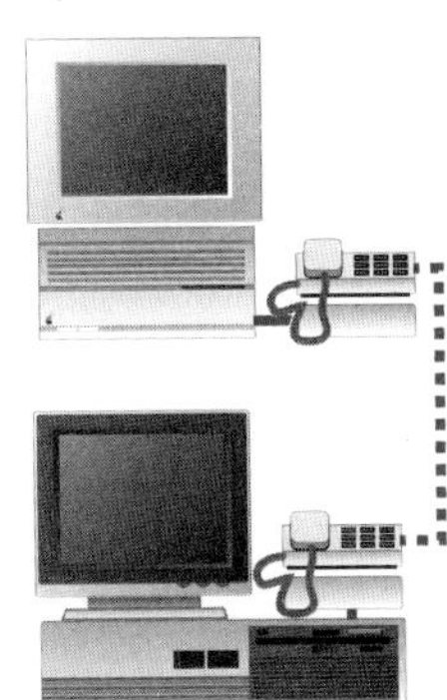

Modems can connect separate computers.

Most modems can only connect one computer to one phone line. However, new modems, called **net–modems**, connect to a network and allow many computers to share one modem and one phone line. These computers can only use the modem one at a time, though. Also, any computer connecting to a network with a net–modem can access **printers** ▸84–87 and **file servers** on the network.

A net–modem allows users on a network to share one modem.

Modems

A computer connecting to a network in this way has access to anything any computer on the network does, just as if it were in the same office.

Recently, with the advances in cellular communications technology, portable **cellular modems** have become available. These allow users to access networks and others wherever they may be. As long as cellular modem users are within range of a satellite or a local cell site, they need not be physically connected via a phone jack.

A **FAX–modem** is a modem with software and hardware that can emulate a FAX machine. This allows users to receive FAX transmissions directly into their computers. It also allows users to FAX documents from their computers. A fax–modem is not able to FAX a paper document or print one to paper like a traditional FAX machine. The document must already exist in the computer to be sent and can only be displayed on the screen when received. A **printer** connected to the computer, however, can be used to print a FAX when received and a **scanner** ▸87–88 can allow the user to put a paper document into the computer by taking a picture of it.

ISDN (Integrated Services Digital Network) *is a transmission scheme for digital text, sound, voice and video data over phone lines. The phone companies are looking at implementing this system in the 1990s to speed transmissions. This protocol supports sending diverse types of transmitted data in great quantities at great speed. In the future, these capabilities may be available in all homes and offices in many parts of the world. Already, two new standards are developing that support even greater speeds. One is SMDS (Switched Multimegabit Data Service) and the other is FDDI (Fiber Distributed Data Interface).*

Interface

A system interface refers to the part of the system the user actually uses: what he or she touches, sees and hears (so far, smell and taste have not been used in any commercial systems). This is the bridge that allows a computer, applications, information, system software, and users to interact or communicate. Each operating system ▶44–45 has an interface of some kind. Some interfaces can operate on different types of operating systems. A system interface usually refers to the interaction between the user and the system software or application.

Components / Interface

The interface between the user and the physical computer is just as important, however. This physical interface usually consists of a keyboard and display. In the past, punch cards and spools of magnetic tape were used. An interface may also include some type of screen pointing device such as a mouse, light pen, or joystick.

User Interfaces

Basically, there are two types of system software interfaces in use today, although we will briefly touch on two more that are emerging. The first type is called a **command–line interface**. It is a series of lines of alphanumeric text (and codes) that form the basis for **queries** (questions from either the user or computer), **comments** (answers) and **prompts** (statements). This is the oldest and most prevalent interface. Because the processor works on one instruction at a time and then moves on to the next, it makes sense to stack the queries, comments and prompts one after another on the screen. The computer types a statement or prompts the user for some input. The user then enters data or a new command. The stack of commands and comments scroll up (or down) and off the screen in order to make room for the next line. Unfortunately, commands in one operating system are rarely consistent with commands in other operating systems.

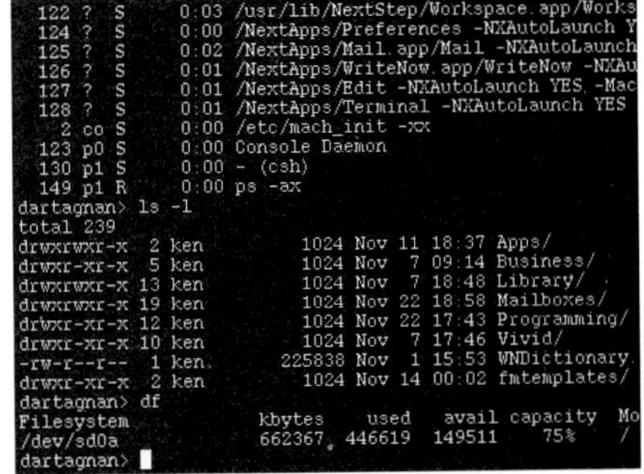
122 ? S 0:03 /usr/lib/NextStep/Workspace.app/Works
124 ? S 0:00 /NextApps/Preferences -NXAutoLaunch Y
125 ? S 0:02 /NextApps/Mail.app/Mail -NXAutoLaunch
126 ? S 0:01 /NextApps/WriteNow.app/WriteNow -NXAu
127 ? S 0:01 /NextApps/Edit -NXAutoLaunch YES, -Mac
128 ? S 0:01 /NextApps/Terminal -NXAutoLaunch YES
2 co S 0:00 /etc/mach_init -xx
123 p0 S 0:00 Console Daemon
130 p1 S 0:00 - (csh)
149 p1 R 0:00 ps -ax
dartagnan> ls -l
total 239
drwxrwxr-x 2 ken 1024 Nov 11 18:37 Apps/
drwxr-xr-x 5 ken 1024 Nov 7 09:14 Business/
drwxrwxr-x 13 ken 1024 Nov 7 18:48 Library/
drwxrwxr-x 19 ken 1024 Nov 22 18:58 Mailboxes/
drwxr-xr-x 12 ken 1024 Nov 22 17:43 Programming/
drwxr-xr-x 10 ken 1024 Nov 7 17:46 Vivid/
-rw-r--r-- 1 ken 225838 Nov 1 15:53 WNDictionary
drwxr-xr-x 2 ken 1024 Nov 14 00:02 fmtemplates/
dartagnan> df
Filesystem kbytes used avail capacity Mo
/dev/sd0a 662367 446619 149511 75% /
dartagnan>

User Interfaces

A **graphic-user interface** ▶35, 118 (GUI—pronounced "gooey") takes a different and more sophisticated approach to communicating with the user. A graphic interface replaces the

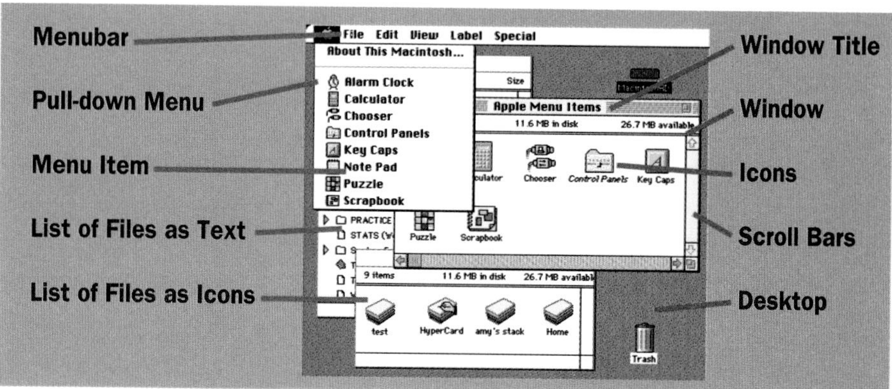

command–line interface with symbols that represent the most abstract functions in the computer. Typically, it will include a **menu** of commands and functions that may be used at any given time, **windows** that contain fields in which a user can type, draw, or store files, **buttons** that can be clicked (pushed) with a **mouse** ▶35, 83–84 or other pointing device to make selections, and **icons** which represent files, folders, discs, and software. Because file management is so abstract (all software, including applications, system software, utilities, and data files are written onto discs that the user never sees), icons are particularly powerful. **Icons** are graphic representations that distinguish different software. An application will have an icon that is different from any other and that may even represent what that application does (a page and pen for **word processing** ▶5–9, perhaps). Likewise, icons for files are usually related to the application that they were created in and will also represent what type of information is in that file.

Icons are a powerful interface element, not as pictures but as symbols. This is why they do not need to be exact, realistic illustrations to be effective. In fact, the less illustrative and the more symbolic they are, the better they tend to work.

A third type of interface is a variation of the GUI called a **pen-based interface**. These have just now become available. This type of interface uses a **stylus** ▶83 (pen) as an input device. Like a GUI, it allows users to enter information by choosing commands and pushing graphic buttons with the stylus, but it also allows them to write information with the stylus like a pen and paper. The system software automatically recognizes the written characters and translates them into editable type (see **character recognition** ▶9).

PenPoint™ screen shot courtesy of Go Corp.

People seem to be more comfortable with the interface they learn to use first and tend to dislike changing the way they work (whether it is a command–line interface or GUI).

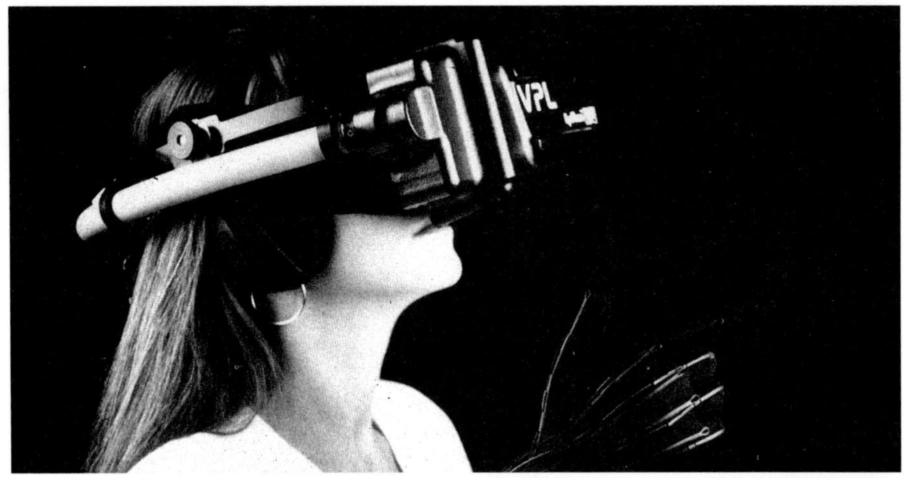

A fourth type of interface that is being developed is called a virtual interface. A **virtual interface** is one in which the user puts on a set of special goggles as a display, a controlling device (such as a glove) and a motion detector that allows a computer to sense when and how the user moves. What the user sees is a computer–generated world in which he or she can move. In addition, sound can be processed so that it appears to come from a specific place, moving with the user. This, plus more sophisticated controlling devices (such as suits that sense a user's body movements) provide the user with a remarkable computer–generated world. While these interfaces are still experimental and require extremely powerful computers, they offer great promise in being easy to learn and use, and will enable users to do things they could not do before. Actually, some of the experimental uses involve designing buildings or molecules around the user from the inside–out and representing abstract, non–physical elements such as vast data in a **database** ▸21–22.

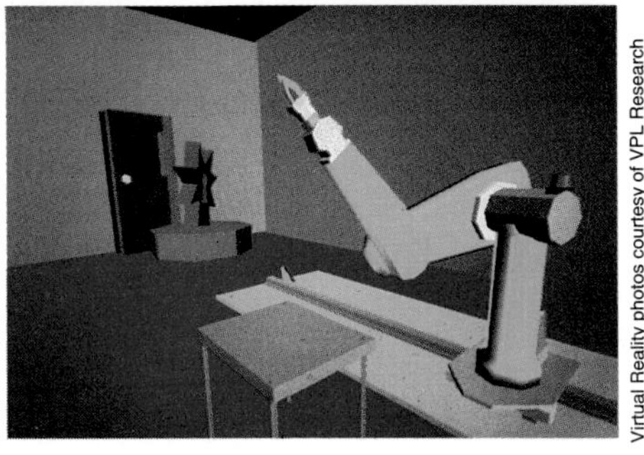

Virtual Reality photos courtesy of VPL Research

A virtual interface allows the user to participate in the interface to a greater extent.

These developments, however, are a few years away from being common—especially for personal computers.

Keyboards

Douglas Engelbart ▸35, 111 *can be credited with developing the* **mouse** ▸83–84 *(pointing device) and starting the field of human augmentation research (interface design) when no one else was interested in how humans and computers were to interact. He has championed* **hypertext** ▸24–26 *with a rich system called* ***Augment*** *which has yet to be taken seriously. This thinker has consistently been years ahead of his time and is usually and eventually proven correct.*

One of the most important aspects of the computer–human interface is the physical means we use to communicate with the computer and it uses to communicate with us. This includes the means to input data, receive acknowledgment of our actions, receive status reports about what the computer is doing and receive data from the computer in different forms.

The **keyboard** ▸41, 120–121, 128 is currently a standard item on almost all computers used to enter information and instructions. On many computers, it is the only way to communicate with the computer. The keyboard most commonly used is the **QWERTY keyboard**. It is called QWERTY because the first five letters at the top left of the keyboard are the letters Q, W, E, R, T and Y. It is only used because most typists have been trained on it. It was actually arranged, by its inventor Christopher Sholes, to be difficult to use. On 19th Century typewriters he found that the type bars would jam as people typed faster. To relieve the typewriter's inability to work fast, he jumbled the key arrangement so that the most commonly used keys (E, T, A, O, N and R) were harder to reach and, thus slowed down the typist.

Q W E R T Y

Many keyboard arrangements have been developed since, such as the Dvorak simplified keyboard by August Dvorak in 1932, and the Maltron keyboard by Lillian Maltron and Stephen Hobday in the 1960s. The former is arranged so that the most commonly used keys are under the strongest and quickest fingers. This can increase the typist's speed by as much as 50%. The Maltron is unusual because it is split into two groups of keys that allow the hands to be placed in a more comfortable position. Some keyboards even adjust the height and angle of the keys to maximize comfort and speed.

This is a standard QWERTY keyboard layout that comes with most computers. There are subtle differences between different keyboards.

Recently, some keyboards have been introduced that can be configured by rearranging parts and adding different keys. A numeric set of keys can be swapped for a track ball, function keys can be added, or keys can be switched from left to right. This allows a user to modify his or her keyboard to suit personal needs.

The computer keyboard has special keys that are not found on a typewriter. They may have words such as *control*, *option*, *escape*, or special symbols. Many times they are used to issue commands in **key combinations** ▶**19** (pressing two or more keys simultaneously to instruct the computer to carry out a specific function). This can be easier for some users (especially advanced users) than using a mouse or other pointing device to choose a command from a menu. **Modifier keys** are used in combination with other keys or a pointing device in order to change its actions. They may specify to the computer a special symbol (many foreign characters and symbols are specified this way) or may constrain the pointing device to a certain movement or function. Other keys include **function keys** that are separate keys with distinct actions attributed to them. These may include single commands (like launching an application or turning on and off the computer), or sequences of commands that perform many processes at once. Mostly, these keys can be programmed by the user with the aid of **macro utilities** ▶**19** to perform new and specific functions.

Not all computers use modifier keys or key combinations and few, if any, are consistent between computer platforms (computers made by different manufacturers). In the case of a graphic–user interface with a **pointing device** ▶**83–84** (such as a mouse), key combinations are not necessary to learn right away. A user shouldn't feel as though he or she must memorize them all. They can save time for actions that are done often, but users usually learn these as they need to and as they become more comfortable with the system and applications they use.

Macros *are sets of commonly performed steps that can be executed together with only a single keystroke.*

The unusual Maltron keyboard arranges keys so that the hands and wrists do not get as tired. Many typists are much more productive with arrangements like this.

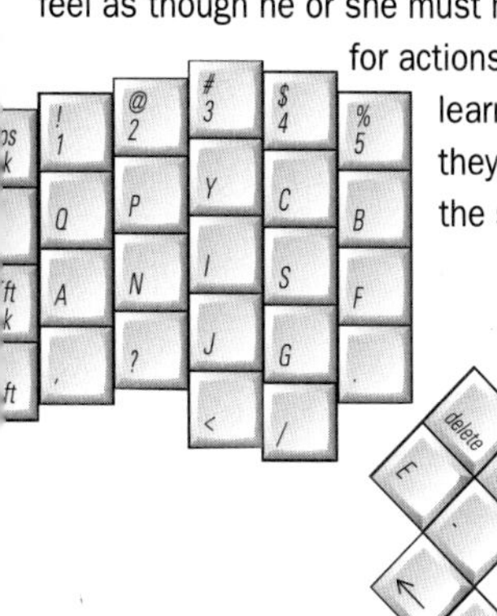

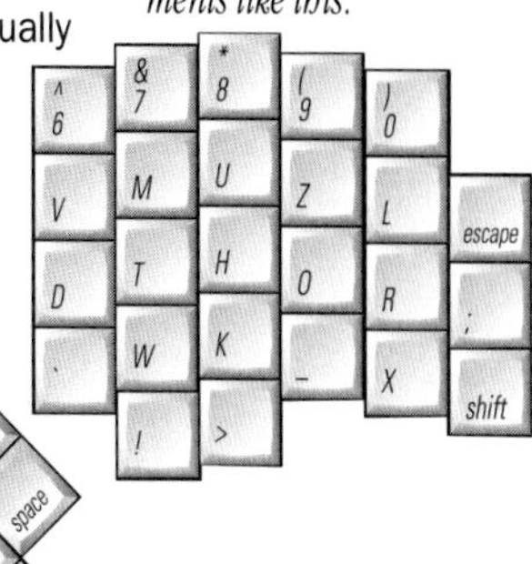

Monitors

Monitors

There are many terms for a computer's display screen: **monitor**, display, CRT (Cathode Ray Tube), etc... However, they perform the same function: they are presently the primary means for the computer to communicate with the user. Some are built-in to the computer and others are attached by a cable. Monitors can display one color (these are called **monochrome** ▸115-121), just gray tones (these are called **grayscale** ▸87-88, 121 monitors) or color. All monitors need special circuitry or a special circuit board called a video card between them

and the computer in order to be used. The **video card** ▸82, 88, 121 allows the monitor to decipher the instructions that the computer sends it in order to display what the computer intends. Although a monitor looks much like a television, it is usually capable of displaying images at higher resolution (finer quality and detail).

Resolution ▸12, 88, 113 refers to the size and quantity of the **pixels** ▸11, 114-115 (picture elements) on the screen. Each pixel is a square or rectangular dot that is capable of turning on or off, or displaying one color (in a color or grayscale monitor). It is the smallest unit of display. If there are more and smaller pixels, a monitor is said to have a higher resolution because resolution is measured by how many pixels fit into a square inch. Higher resolution monitors are capable of displaying finer, smoother images, graphics and text.

The size of a monitor's screen is measured in the same way televisions are (from top corner to opposite bottom corner).
*A **landscape** display is wider than it is tall. A **portrait** display is taller than it is wide. A **double-page** display is big enough to show two full 8.5" by 11" pages next to each other at actual size.*

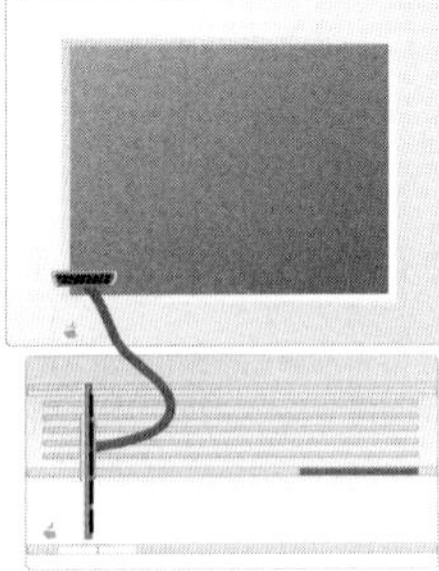

The video card is located inside the computer and connects to the monitor so that the computer can display images and text.

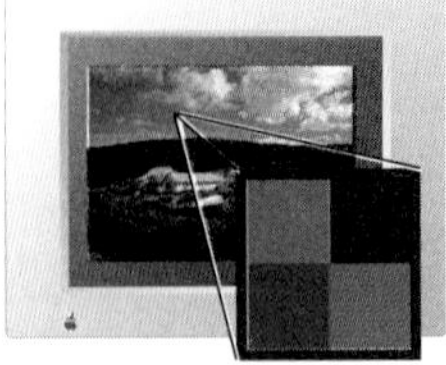

Images on screen are made from tiny pixels.

An 8-bit monitor is able to display 256 (2^8) different colors (represented by all of the colors on this page.)

A 4-bit monitor can display 16 (2^4) different colors (represented by the colors in the square to the left.

The two squares to the left represent the two colors a monochrome (1-bit) monitor can display (black and white), and the next biggest square represents the four colors a 2-bit monitor can represent.

A black and white monitor (or monochrome monitor) is called a 1-bit display (or 1-bit deep). This means that it only takes 1 bit of information to distinguish between the two possible states of the pixels (on or off, black or white). Monochrome monitors are usually faster than color monitors because the processor has less data to process. Actually, some monochrome monitors may not be white but green or amber. However, they are still capable of only one color and black–whatever that color may be. Monochrome monitors are much less expensive than grayscale or color monitors of the same size.

Some displays are 2 bits deep (taking 2 bits to distinguish a pixel's color) and can display black, white and two shades of gray (light and dark). These four combinations are all that are possible with 2 bits of information ($2^2=4$). A monitor can be built with almost any **bit depth** ▶88, but **8-bit** ▶120-121 and 24-bit are now becoming standards. A monitor that is 8 bits deep is capable of displaying 256 colors at once ($2^8=256$), which is an acceptable range of colors. In order to show images that are composed of more colors, a monitor can **dither** the image. This means that the computer reassigns patterns of colors within its limited color range to approximate the intended colors as closely as possible. This is similar to how pointillist painters (such as Seurat) painted.

Grayscale monitors are able to display a large range of grays. Usually, a grayscale monitor will be capable of displaying 256 different grays including black and white. This is enough to represent an image to the quality of a black and white photograph (although more grainy because of the resolution).

A **24-bit monitor** ▶23 is capable of displaying 16,777,216 different colors at the same time ($2^{24}=16,777,216$). It can do this by referring to colors with a code number 24-bits long. For example, the computer and monitor may understand a particular shade of red as 011010001001110110110010. 16 million colors is slightly more than humans can distinguish at once and this is why 24 bit color is often referred to as **true color.**

A **32-bit monitor** is actually 24 bit color plus 8 extra bits that can be used to perform special effects like transparency or masks (objects that temporarily cover portions of an image). This is especially useful for processing and displaying images for electronic photo retouching and video production.

A 24–bit monitor is able to display over 16 million (2^{24}) different colors at the same time. This would take almost 26,000 pages of colored squares like those on this page to represent them all.

The top image is shown in full color as it would be displayed on a 24–bit or "true color" monitor. A system with fewer capabilities needs to dither the image in order to display it with fewer colors. This second image is an 8–bit version of the same photo above.

There is really no difference between green, white or amber monochrome monitors. Research cannot confirm whether one color is easier to read than the others. The choice is based on personal preference.

Monitors

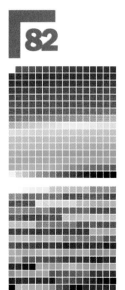

System CLUTs are used by the computer to keep track of colors. For a system that has only limited color display capabilities, CLUTs have to be switched in order to display enough colors to approximate an image.

In order to display or assign any color, the computer's operating system must be designed to reference colors with multiple–bit codes. Using a 32–bit monitor and video card on a computer with an operating system that only addresses 8 bits will not result in true (24 bit) color. The reverse is possible, however. A monochrome, grayscale or 8 bit monitor can usually be used on a computer with an operating system that addresses 8, 24, or 32 bits. Even though the monitor cannot display all of the information, it can display an approximation. For example, a computer designed to process 32–bits paired with an 8–bit monitor, can only display 256 colors at a time, even though it understands more than 16 million. The computer can pick and choose from those 16 million which colors to put in that list of 256 and refer to them with something called a **look–up table** or **color look–up table** (**CLUT**). These 256 colors are changeable based on what colors will most fit the display needs at a time, but the monitor can only display 256 at once.

Like all devices on a computer, the monitor must communicate with the processor and must be capable of interpreting the processor's instructions. This takes time and can cause a delay between what is happening in the processor and what is happening on the screen. To help speed these communications, some video boards have extra memory chips called **VRAM** (Video Random Access Memory) and their own processors (called **Video Processors** and **Graphics Accelerators**). These processors help the monitor process complex instructions (especially color) and help the monitor to keep up with the computer.

There are different languages that monitors use to draw things on the screen. Few are compatible across **platforms** ▸5 (manufacturers or model lines). These languages not only communicate how to display graphics and text, but the elements of the **operating system's** interface as well (especially graphic–user interfaces). Therefore, many combinations of monitors and video cards are not compatible with all computers.

Video **acceleration cards** speed the screen–drawing process by placing lots of extra VRAM and a high–powered processor on a special video card. This allows the card to process the drawing routines very quickly (especially for drawing–intensive applications like video processing, computer–aided design, pre–press publishing and photographic retouching). Because an accelerator card is separate and optional, it must also be made for a specific computer and monitor combination.

Pointing Devices

Pointing devices have become popular input devices for computers (in some cases, they have become necessary ones). A pointing device allows the user to specify an exact location on screen. This makes drawing, image processing and a **graphic user-interface** ▶76–77 possible. A pointing device can even help make database and word-processing applications more functional.

There are two basic types of pointing devices, styluses and variations on moving ball devices. A **stylus** is a pen-like instrument that is used to either point to a location on the screen or on a **tablet**. A stylus may or may not have a cord attached to it depending on the technology it uses to communicate with the computer. The user can move the stylus anywhere on the tablet (a flat, relatively thin surface that is sensitive to the stylus) and the computer will be able to track the movement, usually with a **cursor** on the screen. The cursor is merely a representation on the screen of where the computer understands the pointing device is. Some styluses and light pens have buttons located on their shaft or in the tip that can be used to signal a specific function from the computer.

Tablets (sometimes called **graphics pads**) use a lattice of wires buried inside them horizontally and vertically to sense the position of the stylus. The wires either sense a magnetic pulse from the stylus when its button is pushed or come into contact when the stylus is pushed into the tablet surface. A **light pen** is a stylus that uses light to indicate to the monitor the location of the pen on the screen. In effect, a light pen uses the screen (monitor) as a tablet.

Moving ball devices include the **mouse** ▶35, 121, **joystick**, and **track ball**. Each uses a moving ball in some way to track the movements of the device and communicate them to the computer. The cursor displays this movement on the screen. The **track ball** and **mouse** both have two wheels that touch the ball and measure the amount of travel the ball makes in each direction. The mouse and track ball work well because they measure two-dimensional movement and the screen is essentially a two dimensional surface. **Joysticks** may or may not actually use a ball, but both types track movement in two dimensions by the use of wheels of some kind. This is why they are included in this category.

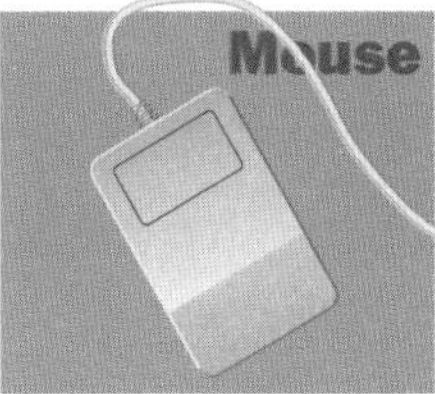

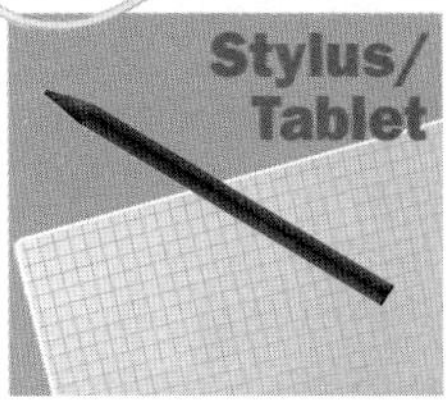

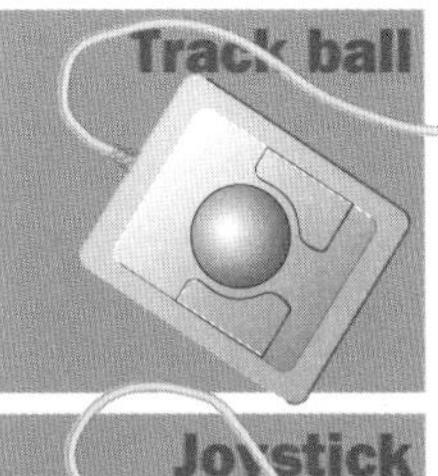

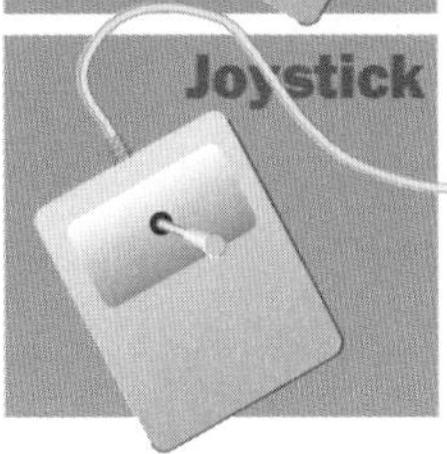

Pointing Devices

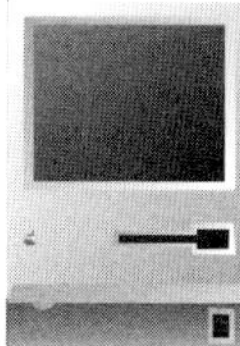

Steve Jobs is responsible for the development of the marvelous Macintosh computer. He led a small team of driven, talented and obsessed developers to create the best personal computer that could be built at the time. They incorporated scores of innovative, exciting ideas that resulted in a truly revolutionary computer. This was the first commercially successful computer to use icons, windows, a mouse and a Graphic–User Interface.

The benefits of pointing devices can be subjective. For graphic, artistic and visual applications, they are necessary, but for programming, text–based and data–based applications many people find them unnecessary. The mouse, and some track balls, allow the user to rest his or her wrist on the table surface and make fine movements with the hand. However, some users find them awkward or cumbersome (at least at first). Joysticks do not allow the user to rest the wrist and thus, are more tiring to use for extended periods of time. Light pens, particularly, are tiresome because they require the user to suspend his or her arm for long periods of time. However, the light pen allows the user to point directly to a location on the screen rather than a representation of it on a pad.

There are some special variations on the moving ball devices that allow the same functions in much less space. The **isopoint** is a combination of a sliding cylinder around a rotating cylinder that allows the user to control the cursor in the same two dimensions as a mouse or track ball. An isopoint, however, is less than one tenth the size of a mouse or track ball.

Another type of pointing system is called a **touch–screen display**. This is literally what it sounds like. The user is able to point to locations on the screen with his or her finger just like with a light pen and without any special equipment. The screen has a built–in lattice of very fine wires that are sensitive to the touch of a finger. This is especially useful for users that have never used any type of pointing device before. The drawback to touch–screens is that a finger is rather large compared to the pixels on the screen and is not appropriate for pointing to fine detail. Also, as with light pens, arms tire more quickly than with other pointing devices because they cannot rest on any surface.

Printers

There are many different types of printers offering a wide variety of output quality for many different applications. The quality of the printing is a result of the printer's **resolution** ▶12 (how small and how close together printed dots can be). **Dot–matrix** ▶122 printers print small squares on paper to form text, graphics, and images by pressing tiny pins against a ribbon. Dot–matrix printers tend to be noisy and low–quality. Even "letter quality" printers achieve no better than 72 dpi (dots per inch). This is, typically, legible for text, but poor for graphics

or images. Commonly, these printers require **continuous–feed** paper in rolls with holes down either side. This allows the tractor to pull the paper through the printer. Other printers are **friction–feed** and use rollers to pull the paper through, much like a conventional typewriter.

Color ribbons can be used on some of these printers, but the color quality is fairly poor and the range of colors is minimal.

An **ink–jet** printer uses a special printing head to shoot ink at the paper in controlled amounts. The ink is kept in reservoirs and fed to the printing head by tubes. This eliminates the need for a ribbon. Some ink–jet printers can print color because they have four reservoirs containing Black, Cyan, Magenta, and Yellow ink. These are the standard colors used in commercial printing that mix together to form many different colors. Cyan is a light–blue and Magenta is a bright red–pink. By mixing these four colors in varying amounts many colors can be achieved with fairly nice results. These, too, can be noisy (although not as much as dot–matrix printers) and may or may not require continuous–feed paper.

Laser printers ▶121–122, 143–144 have become very popular because of their high–resolution (up to 1200dpi). They are now almost standard for business communications and **graphics proofing** ▶142. Not only do they normally have a higher resolution than dot matrix or ink–jet printers, their quality is usually more consistent and fine. They are also faster and quieter. Laser printers use the same technology as laser copiers with the addition of a **graphics processor** that decodes the data sent from the computer and composes it into the desired text and images. This makes them acceptable for business uses such as correspondence, reports, newsletter, memos, and even resumés. They require little care and maintenance (the toner cartridge needs replacing periodically) and, generally, are trouble–free. They are, however, more expensive.

Some laser printers have paper holders for different sizes and types of paper, like a copy machine, but most have only one. Most can accept single pieces of paper **manually fed** into the printer, including envelopes.

Not all laser printers are alike. Depending on the **page description language** ▶12 they understand, printers may be able to print high resolution graphics and **fonts** ▶11–12, 143 or not. **PostScript**™ ▶22 has become one of the standard **file formats** ▶22, 23 for graphics and fonts. Just because a printer is capable of laser

There are many different models used to describe color on a screen

Red	50%
Green	29%
Blue	64%

RGB is the most common because it refers to the amount of light coming from a monitor's **red, green,** and **blue** light guns. Values for these colors increase as light gets brighter and closer to white.

Hue	191°
Lightness	55%
Saturation	12%

HSL refers to **hue**, **saturation**, and **lightness**. This color model is closer to those used in painting. Hue refers to the overall color (as in a simple color wheel). Saturation refers to how intense that color is (high values are bright, low values are grey). Lightness refers to how bright or dark these colors are.

Cyan	50%
Magenta	36%
Yellow	36%
Black	0%

CMYK is a color model used in traditional four–color process printing. These four pigments (**Cyan**, **Magenta**, **Yellow,** and **Black**) are mixed in different amounts to create a wide range of colors. In nature, a great assortment of colors are possible, but a monitor is only capable of displaying about half of them. Still fewer (about half of those displayable) are able to be printed with four color process inks.

This book is printed with CMYK (four–color process) inks.

Printers

72dpi

300dpi

1200dpi 2450dpi

Here are samples of the same type and images printed on four different kinds of printers. The first sample is from a 72dpi **dot-matrix** *printer. It is the most coarse and is not usually acceptable for business. The second is from a 300dpi laser printer. It is usually acceptable for business correspondance and proofing published pieces. The third sample is from a 1200dpi laser printer. It is possible to use this output for some publishing. The last sample is from a 2450dpi* **imagesetter ▸121, 144**. *This quality is mandatory for high–quality publishing and fine illustrations like those in this book.*

quality does not mean that it is capable of PostScript output. While many printers can **download** the font information required directly from the computer, most require special **font cartridges** installed in them in order to print special fonts. These printers are less flexible to work with and may be too time consuming and complicated for **desktop publishing ▸10** uses that require many different fonts to be used.

Thermal printers are high–resolution, color printers and use different technologies to achieve different effects. Some roll sheets of colored wax by the printing paper and melt the wax onto the paper wherever it is desired. The color is carried on four different sheets (Black, Cyan , Magenta and Yellow) and melted in tiny dots that overlap to form the illusion of many different colors.

Dye Sublimation printers use a technology that shoots a transparent dye into a special paper stock to create near–photographic color output. The dye exists as a solid. It is heated and changed directly into a gas that impregnates the paper next to it. How much dye is transferred depends on how much is heated. Because the amounts can be accurately controlled they do not need to be screened or **dithered ▸81** (like thermal printers). The dyes are transparent and can be laid on top of each other. These printers are still very expensive but offer great results.

Imagesetters ▸10, 121, 144 are used for the output of camera–ready artwork and negatives because of their extraordinarily high resolutions. Imagesetters use a **RIP** (Raster Image Processor) to image artwork and type at resolutions between 1200 and 2400 dpi. This level of quality is comparable to traditional typesetting and is necessary for high–quality publishing. Imagesetters can print to either photographic paper or clear **film**. The rolls of film or paper are covered with light–sensitive emulsions which are exposed to a laser. This laser draws the image or type onto the film or paper by burning off the emulsion. The film or paper is then processed much like photographic film.

Imagesetters are capable of processing images or type as either a positive image or **negative** image (where the white areas are imaged as black and visa versa). In addition, with **separating ▸144** applications, the artwork can be separated into the **four process colors** used in commercial printing automatically. This allows the designer to output directly to separated film negatives to be given to the commercial printer, saving time, materials and money.

Plotters come in all sizes and types. They are primarily used for construction plans, engineering drawings and other technical illustrations. They tend to be high quality for linework (like lines and curves) but not for filled areas or photographic images. This is because the ink is actually drawn onto the paper with fine pens held in a carriage.

Some plotters are upright and some are flat–bed. **Flat–bed** plotters are flat surfaces that a piece of paper is attached to. Pens move across the paper in both directions. The paper does not move during this drawing. Most flat–bed plotters are horizontal surfaces that sit on a table or desk, but some (especially big ones) are vertical and stand against walls.

Drum or **Upright** plotters stand vertically and have a drum that quickly turns the paper between rollers. Because the paper moves in one direction, the pens and carriage only need to move in the other direction, instead of two as in a flat–bed plotter. Between the movements in different directions of the pen carriage (or gantry) and the paper, the entire surface of the paper can be covered. Drum plotters also tend to be more compact, but make more noise due to the paper whooshing back and forth.

Scanners

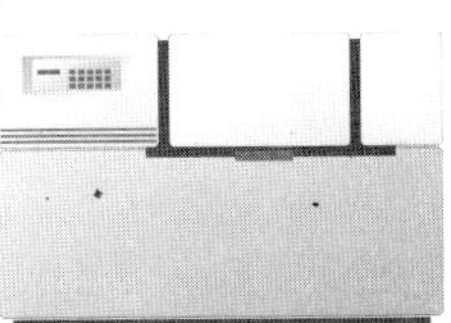

Scanners ▶10, 74, 142 are devices that "see" images and translate them into a form that can be displayed on the computer's monitor. The technology that allows a scanner to see an image is similar to that used in a copying machine. A laser scans the image in horizontal lines at set increments along the length of the image. When the laser beam hits white it reflects back to the lens and this registers to the scanner as a 1. When the laser beam hits black it scatters and does not reflect and this registers as a 0. In this way, the entire image can be translated into a matrix of 1s and 0s that describe the image.

Some scanners are able to "see" levels of gray as well as black and white. The **grayscale** ▶23, 80–82, 121 scanner not only registers whether the laser beam is reflected back to the lens, but also the amount of light that is reflected back. Lighter grays will reflect more light back than darker grays. By measuring the relative amounts of reflected light, the scanner can translate the image into values that represent the levels of gray at each point. The number of gray levels a

Scanners

scanner is able to read is identical to the **bit-depth ▶81** of monitors. For instance, a scanner than can "see" 16 levels of gray needs to be able to not only distinguish 16 different levels of reflected light intensities, but also describe those 16 distinct levels for the computer. This takes a **file format ▶22–23** capable of storing four binary digits for each point that makes–up the image. This is why grayscale and color scans take more room to store; they require much more binary code to describe.

A **color scanner** works the same as a grayscale scanner with the exception that it scans three times instead of one. Each scan past the image passes through either a red, green or blue filter. By combining the values for each of the three passes, the colors for every point of the image can be described. This takes a great deal of extra data, and thus, more storage space.

Some color scanners (like the Scitex) can scan with CYMK filters instead of RGB.

Resolution ▶12, is also a factor. Some scanners are capable of high–resolutions that result in fine and accurate detail. These tend to be more expensive. The higher the resolution, the smaller the units or points that can be scanned, and thus, the more of them that are scanned and stored. More resolution increases file sizes exponentially (as do more levels of grays or colors). A 24–bit color image is not 24 times larger than a 1–bit version of the same image, but 22 times larger. Also, a 300 dpi image is 17 times larger than the same scan at 72 dpi, not merely 4 times larger.

Video Capture

Another means of inputting information into a computer is to transfer it from video tape or broadcast television. This requires some sophisticated processing because computers and televisions understand images differently. Televisions in the USA understand **NTSC** code (National Television Standard Code) and in Europe, **PAL** and **SEACAM** (Phase Alternation by Line and Système Electronique pour Coleur avec Mémoroire). These are all **interlaced ▶16, 114** codes and are not compatible with the formats used to display images on computers. **Video Capture Boards** allow users to capture frames of broadcast television or from video tape, display them on a computer's monitor and save them in a form that the computer can understand. These boards fit into the computer like a **video card ▶80, 82, 120-121** or **accelerator board ▶62**. In fact, many combine the functions of all

three on one board or card. Some boards even offer **real–time** ▶14 **compression** ▶23 or decompression of video data so that continuous video can be displayed and stored (not merely single frames). This is much more intensive and sophisticated and these boards are correspondingly more expensive.

Film Recorders

Film Recorders are devices that output computer images to photographic film. This may include 35mm slides $2\frac{1}{4}$"x $2\frac{1}{4}$", 4"x 5" or 8"x 10" transparencies, or negative film. Most of these devices work by exposing the film to a small, high–resolution, grayscale display of the image. For color images, the film is exposed three times with red, green and blue filters so that the resulting image recorded to film is full color.

Other film recorders actually use a laser to expose the film (again, through filters if the image is to be in color). Because of the laser beam's accuracy and tiny size, the resulting images can be at higher–resolutions than with traditional film recorders. However, the movement of the laser beam requires many complex instructions and processing. Again, this results in more time and more sophisticated equipment.

Voice Recognition and Speech Synthesis

Recently, many advances in the technologies of **voice recognition** (having the computer listen to instructions in spoken language) and **speech synthesis** (having the computer respond with words and sentences) have made these abilities more feasible and affordable. There are, however, many problems to overcome before these will be available capabilities for personal computers. Advances in sound processing technologies (recording the speech and correctly identifying the distinct components) must be met with advances in **natural language processing** ▶35 (establishing rules to break down speech, analyze language and understand it) before this becomes a common way to interact with a computer. This will ultimately create computers that are vastly easier to use but require intense and sophisticated processing both in hardware and in software.

Processing

There are several counting methods used to make some levels of programming easier to read. ***Octal*** *(base 8) counts from 0–7 before it begins to stack numbers (10=8, 11=9, 12=10).* ***Hex*** *(base 16) counts 0–9 and adds six letters (A–F) before stacking. Hex (short for hexadecimal) combines both letters and numbers when counting (A=10, B=11,...F=15, 10=16). These methods arose from the need to efficiently address data with 8-bit and 16-bit processors. Different parts of the computer hardware and software use different counting systems.*

A computer can only count to two. At the heart of a computer's complexity lies a very simple process: when a computer works with large numbers, it translates them into groupings of the only two numbers it understands (1 and 0). This is called binary or base two mathematics.

Computers process data by converting it into electrical pulses. Each electrical pulse represents a small, important part of data that can be manipulated in vast quantities. A computer is a complex system of switches and electrical connections that can process these small pieces of data extremely fast. A typical personal computer can make between 2 and 25 million calculations in one second.

Binary Code

A computer must manipulate these two numbers (0 and 1) in order to form and process more complex numbers. The number **2**, for example, is represented as **10** because that is the next possible use of only these two symbols. **3**=**11**, **4**=**100**, etc.... In base ten (using the decimal system we are all taught in school), we count to 9 and then begin stacking digits next to each other (**1** and **0** become ten, etc...) In a **binary** ▶55 system (base two) one must start stacking these numbers much sooner (after the number 1).

The base two number system in not familiar to most people because we use a base ten number system every day. It is believed that people use the base ten number system because we developed methods of counting with our fingers.

The reason a computer manipulates numbers and data in base two is that it is easier to represent only two symbols in a machine compared to three or more. A **1** is represented by current flowing through a wire and a **0** by no current flowing through the wire. It is quite easy for a

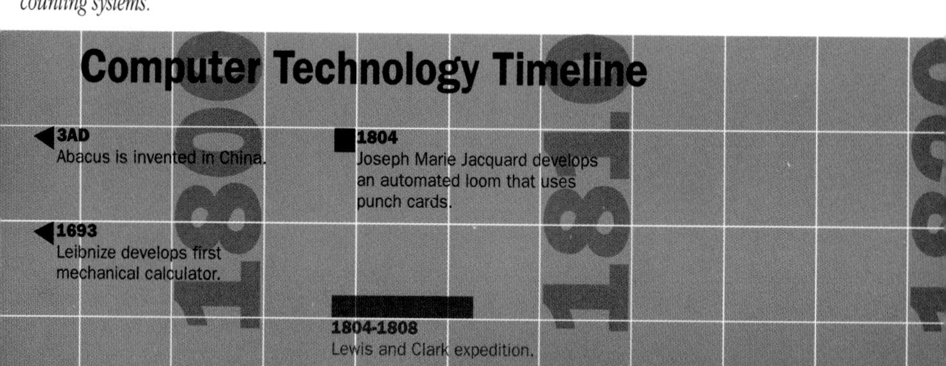

Computer Technology Timeline
1800
1810
3AD
Abacus is invented in China.
1693
Leibnize develops first mechanical calculator.
1804
Joseph Marie Jacquard develops an automated loom that uses punch cards.
1804-1808
Lewis and Clark expedition.

Binary Code

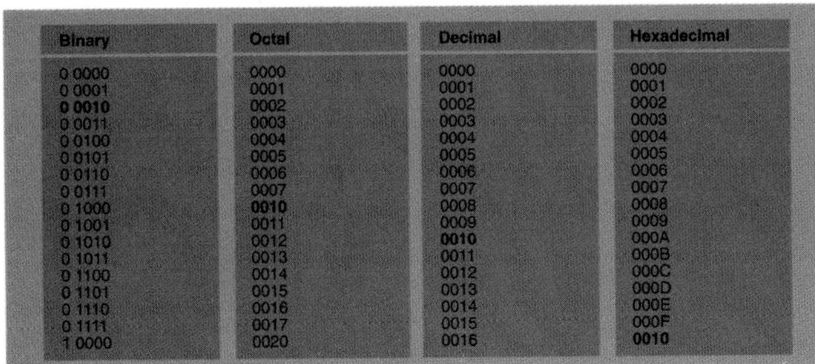

Binary	Octal	Decimal	Hexadecimal
0 0000	0000	0000	0000
0 0001	0001	0001	0001
0 0010	0002	0002	0002
0 0011	0003	0003	0003
0 0100	0004	0004	0004
0 0101	0005	0005	0005
0 0110	0006	0006	0006
0 0111	0007	0007	0007
0 1000	0010	0008	0008
0 1001	0011	0009	0009
0 1010	0012	0010	000A
0 1011	0013	0011	000B
0 1100	0014	0012	000C
0 1101	0015	0013	000D
0 1110	0016	0014	000E
0 1111	0017	0015	000F
1 0000	0020	0016	0010

machine to distinguish these two states. Building a machine that could distinguish varying levels of current would be much more difficult to do.

This physical model of electrical current (current=1, no current=0) is referred to as **on/off**. It is the most basic level of understanding how a computer works. It is the only way a computer can "understand" anything. Everything in this book, indeed everything about computers, is based upon this binary process.

While the simplicity of on/off allows the computer to process numbers and symbols, sophisticated systems must be designed for computers to manipulate more complex data.

Actually, there is no time that current stops running through a computer's circuits (unless it has been turned off), but it changes voltage level. The ***0*** *is represented by a very low voltage in relation to the* ***1****. Sometimes,* ***1*** *is referred to as a* ***high*** *voltage and* ***0*** *is referred to as a* ***low*** *voltage.*

ASCII Code

The next level of organization from binary is a system of grouping 1s and 0s into eight–digit codes that typically represent characters. These eight–digit groupings are made of 1s and 0s and are called **ASCII** (American Standard Code for Information Interchange) code. The term is pronounced **"ask–key"** and is a standard in all computers, although different computers have slightly modified versions.

Standard ASCII is only the lower 128 characters of the 8–bit counting system. The upper characters vary with different platforms. For example, European ASCII is slightly different.

Each digit (1 or 0) is called a **bit**. Keep in mind that it is actually a symbol that ultimately represents an electronic pulse going through a circuit in the computer. This is the smallest unit of data measurement for a computer (it does not mean anything to have half

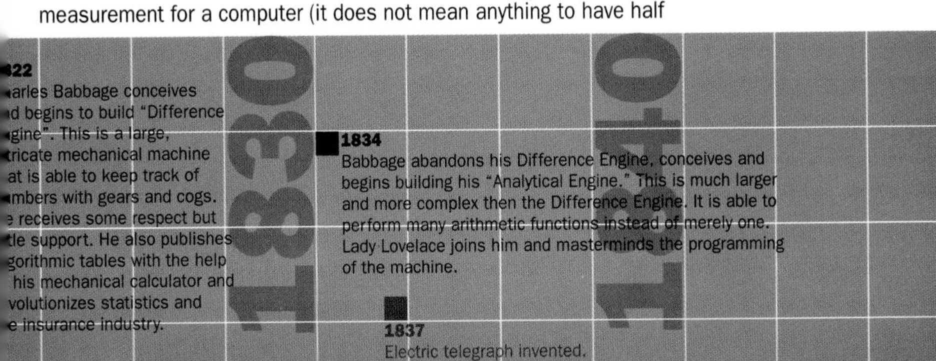

22
arles Babbage conceives
d begins to build "Difference
gine". This is a large,
tricate mechanical machine
at is able to keep track of
mbers with gears and cogs.
e receives some respect but
tle support. He also publishes
gorithmic tables with the help
his mechanical calculator and
volutionizes statistics and
e insurance industry.
1830
1834
Babbage abandons his Difference Engine, conceives and begins building his "Analytical Engine." This is much larger and more complex then the Difference Engine. It is able to perform many arithmetic functions instead of merely one. Lady Lovelace joins him and masterminds the programming of the machine.
1837
Electric telegraph invented.
1840

ASCII Code

A common use of the term ***byte*** *is in reference to a computer's physical RAM. "My computer has 8* ***Megabytes*** *of RAM." This means that their computer has Eight Million Bytes of RAM or 64 (8 x 8 = 64) Million* ***bits*** *of RAM space.*

This book contains roughly 1MB of information (not including the illustrations and photographs) and requires another 2–4 MB to read on screen or print.

0101 1011
nibble
byte

A ***nibble*** *equals 4 bits (although it is a rarely used term) and a* ***byte*** *equals 8 bits. Different combinations of bits and bytes can be used to represent a variety of different data (such as music, video, text, etc...).*

ASCII Equivalents

A	01000001	1	00110001	.	00101110
B	01000010	2	00110010	,	00101100
C	01000011	3	00110011	!	00100001
D	01000100	4	00110100	?	00111111
E	01000101	5	00110101	*	00101010
F	01000110	6	00110110	$	00100100
G	01000111	7	00110111	#	00100011

of a pulse). Eight bits together are called a **byte** ▸112. Humorously, four bits (half of a byte) is called a **nibble**, but this term is rarely used.

The best way to think of a single bit of data is to envision a light switch controlling a lamp. There are only two possible states or positions for the light switch to be in. These two states are simply, on or off. If the light switch is on, we could record a number 1. If the light switch is off, we could record a 0.

Therefore, a computer memory with 8 Megabytes of RAM is the equivalent of 64 million light switches. Try to imagine 64 million light switches. This gives you an idea of the scale and amount of data that a computer utilizes. The typical paperback novel represents about one million bits of information.

Only seven of the eight digits in ASCII are used for data. The first digit is used either for checking accuracy during transmission or is just ignored by the computer. With only 1s and 0s and seven places to arrange them, there are 128 possible code combinations that can be made. The first 32 codes are reserved for characters such as the space bar, return key, etc.... Each letter of our alphabet and many symbols (such as punctuation marks), as well as the ten numbers (0–9), have ASCII representations. What makes this system powerful is that these representations are standard from machine to machine. If they were not, it is unlikely that two machines could communicate data between themselves.

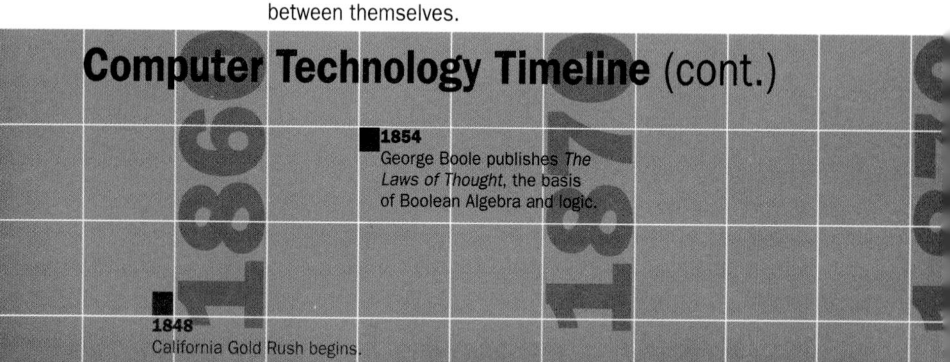

Computer Technology Timeline (cont.)
1860
1870
1854
George Boole publishes *The Laws of Thought*, the basis of Boolean Algebra and logic.
1848
California Gold Rush begins.

ASCII provides enough combinations to accommodate the number of characters in most western languages, but not enough for many non–western languages. Some of these languages (such as Chinese and Japanese) require thousands of characters. Some computers use other methods (like **Unicode**) that require two bytes (16 bits) to represent each character instead of one byte, thus increasing the amount of characters to as many as 65,536.

Computers are called virtual machines because they can be many different machines depending on their instructions. They can be calculators, paint systems, data managers, rolodexes, address books—almost anything. This is what distinguished Charles Babbage's Analytical Engine from every machine built before it. Unlike the Difference Engine, his previous machine, the Analytical Engine was designed to perform many different tasks. Where he (and others) had built different machines before to do one, specific task, this was the first single machine that could do many different functions. In effect, this machine was actually many machines in one.

Logic

It was George Boole in 1854 that distilled the concepts of logical thought and formulated them into rules based on *true* and *false*. In 1937, Claude Shannon devised a way for machines to follow these rules using logical algebra and binary numbers (0s and 1s). The most basic of these logic rules are **AND**, **OR** and **NOT**. By preparing a set of electronic switches to perform these processes, you have already built a crude computer.

There are three types of basic switch combinations or groupings used in computers. These switch combinations are called **logic gates** ▸56, 97. The three basic logic gates are: **AND**, **OR**, and **NOT**. The AND and OR gates need only two inputs and one output in their simplest forms, and the NOT gate has only one input and one output.

An AND gate will compare two signals and if they are both identical, then the gate will transmit a *true* signal. If the two incoming signals are different then the AND gate will transmit a *false* signal. An

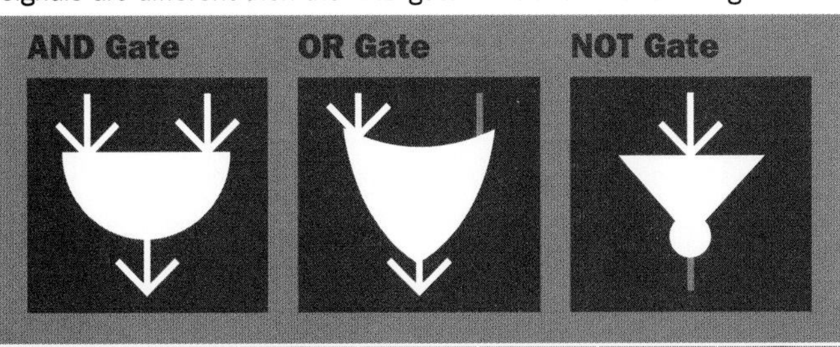
AND Gate
OR Gate
NOT Gate

1880
1890
1890
Census uses punched cards developed by Herman Hollerith in the 1880s.
1878
Telephone patented.
1883
First motor cars.

Logic

A pulse of electricity travels at the speed of light (186,000 miles per second). This means that in a ***nanosecond*** *(a billionth of a second) a pulse could travel almost 11" or across these two pages.*

In logic, ***true*** *is represented by a* ***1*** *and* ***false*** *is represented by a* ***0***.

AND Gate		OR Gate		NOT Gate	
Signals In	Signal Out	Signals In	Signal Out	Signal In	Signal Out
0 0	→ 0	0 0	→ 0	0	→ 1
0 1	→ 0	0 1	→ 1	1	→ 0
1 0	→ 0	1 0	→ 1		
1 1	→ 1	1 1	→ 1		

OR gate will transmit a *true* signal if either of the two incoming signals is *true* or if both signals are *true*. An OR gate will only transmit a *false* signal if both of the incoming signals are *false*. The NOT gate is the simplest; it just complements whatever the incoming signal is. If the incoming signal is a *true* it will transmit a *false*, if the incoming signal is *false* then it will transmit a *true*. A *true* signal is sometimes referred to as a **high** signal or an **on** signal and a *false* signal is, similarly, referred to as a **low** signal or an **off** signal. These relationships are easily defined in tables known as **truth tables**.

Manipulating the flow of current in a circuit allows the computer to simulate these logical statements. Computers use a device called a **transistor** ▶97–99 to control the current flow. A transistor is an electrical switch. By combining sets of these transistors together a **logic gate** can be built. This allows the transistors to simulate a logical statement.

Semiconductors

All metals conduct electricity (allow current to flow through), but some conduct it better than others. This means that it is easier and faster for electrons to flow through some metals than others. This is called **conductivity** and an element that conducts electricity is called a

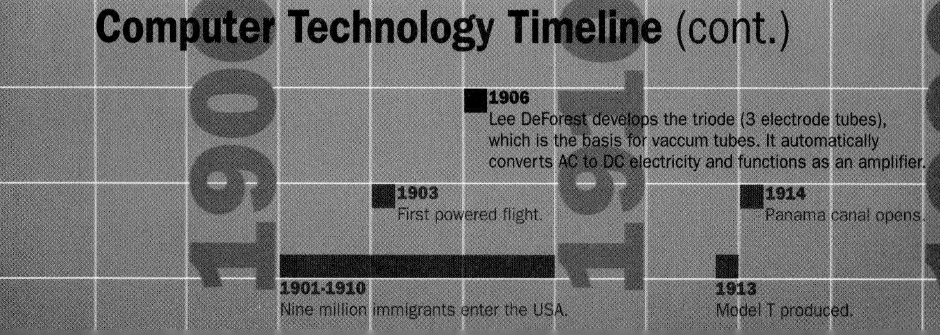
Computer Technology Timeline (cont.)
1900
1910
1906
Lee DeForest develops the triode (3 electrode tubes), which is the basis for vaccum tubes. It automatically converts AC to DC electricity and functions as an amplifier.
1903
First powered flight.
1914
Panama canal opens.
1901-1910
Nine million immigrants enter the USA.
1913
Model T produced.

Semiconductors

conductor. A **semiconductor** ▸97–99 is a material that allows current to flow only in certain circumstances. Current can be controlled in these metals more easily because the current flow is limited.

Inside the computer, data flows around in the form of electricity. Electricity or **electrical current** is electrons flowing through materials. Electric current typically flows through conductors and semiconductors, but under high voltage conditions, current can flow through anything. Lightning is a good example of current flowing through the atmosphere (normally, an insulator). The wires that go to your phone are an example of conductors. They are typically made of some sort of metal that is designed to conduct electricity at all times. A semiconductor is a type of material that falls between being a conductor (metal wire) and an insulator (plastics). A special group of semiconductors are based on Silicon. **Silicon** ▸99, 103 is special because when mixed with some elements it becomes a conductor and when mixed with others it becomes an insulator. Because of this special ability, Silicon is ideal for making computer chips.

Mixing Silicon with other elements is called **doping**. Doping Silicon with Boron (an element that has extra electrons) creates an electron–rich version of Silicon that conducts electricity better than pure Silicon. The extra electrons give it a negative charge. Doping Silicon with Phosphorus, an element short of free electrons, creates an electron–poor version. These two types of Silicon are called **n–type** ▸98 (Boron, conductor) and **p–type** ▸98 (Phosphorus, insulator). When these two types of semiconductors are brought together, a "space charge region" is created between them. This region is the basis for making electrical switches from semiconducting materials.

Metals are good conductors because they have free electrons that can flow easily. Bad conductors (called insulators), like rubber, plastic and glass, have few free electrons and won't release the ones they have easily if at all. Semiconductors conduct electricity poorly when pure but when certain impurities are added, they conduct electricity better. A semiconductor's positive or negative charge depends on the type of impurity added.

Analog Electronics and Sampling

Computers are **digital** ▸104 machines because they manipulate data as discrete units. Computers are also **binary** ▸45, 57, 90 machines because they only use two discrete units (1s and 0s). Machines that

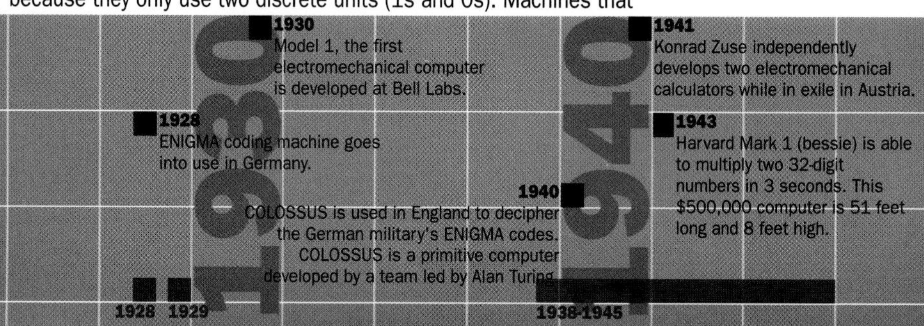

1930
1930
Model 1, the first electromechanical computer is developed at Bell Labs.
1928
ENIGMA coding machine goes into use in Germany.
1940
COLOSSUS is used in England to decipher the German military's ENIGMA codes. COLOSSUS is a primitive computer developed by a team led by Alan Turing.
1928
elevision transmission.
1929
Stock market crash.
1940
1941
Konrad Zuse independently develops two electromechanical calculators while in exile in Austria.
1943
Harvard Mark 1 (bessie) is able to multiply two 32-digit numbers in 3 seconds. This $500,000 computer is 51 feet long and 8 feet high.
1938-1945
World War II

Analog Electronics and Sampling

Silicon (the main element used in the production of electronic circuits) is extremely abundant. Sand contains Silicon. In fact, 28% of the earth's surface is covered with materials containing Silicon. In its natural state, Silicon is not very useful, but when refined with specific levels of impurities (called doping), Silicon conducts electricity in a highly controllable way.

Analog computers do exist but they have specialized functions since they are not as flexible with data as digital computers.

In the illustration to the right, the signal translates to the following binary sequence: 10111101000101011001011110

manipulate data in non–discrete units are called **analog** ▸64. These machines typically perform calculations (if at all) by measuring while digital machines calculate by counting. Analog machines can typically respond faster and with a greater capacity than comparable digital machines but with less flexibility.

Examples of analog devices include speakers and microphones, radios, telephones, televisions, cameras, and video discs. All of these devices process data as a continuous range of some physical phenomenon. Measuring and reproducing sound or light along a spectrum of wavelengths is an analog approach. Analog devices are very capable, but they cannot manipulate data like digital devices can. This limits the type of processes they can perform.

Analog devices (like televisions) receive and measure data in electrical, *analog* signals. In order for a computer to use these signals (or any other analog signals) it must convert them to *digital* signals. This is called **Sampling**. Scanners sample visual (analog) data and convert it to digital data. A microphone connected to a computer does the same with sound. Both of these devices have a special processor called an **Analog to Digital Converter** (ADC). ADCs measure the analog data at specific time intervals and record the intensity at each interval. This gives it a continuous flow of digital data in place of the analog data. This is how compact discs are made. The ADC samples the music at time intervals and records the values it hears. Once the music is converted to digital data, a computer could be used to manipulate it. For example, software can remove most noise without damaging the music.

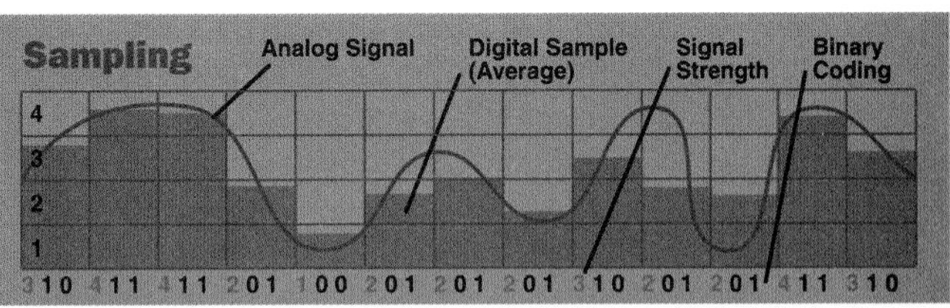
Sampling
Analog Signal
Digital Sample (Average)
Signal Strength
Binary Coding
4
3
2
1
310 411 411 201 100 201 201 201 310 201 201 411 310

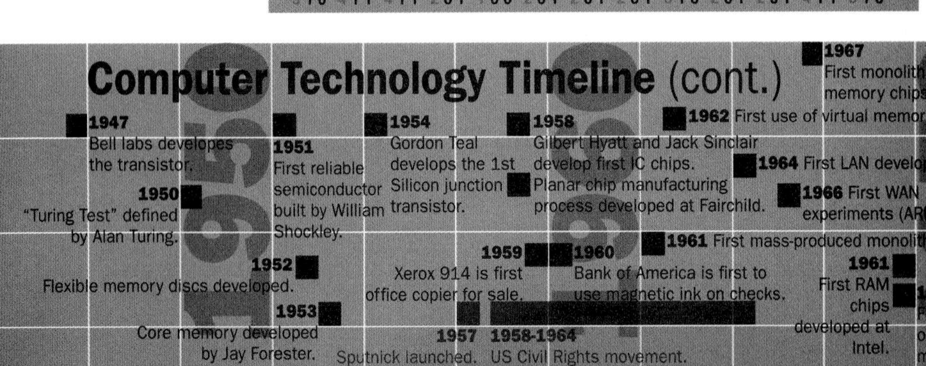
Computer Technology Timeline (cont.)
1947 Bell labs developes the transistor.
1950 "Turing Test" defined by Alan Turing.
1951 First reliable semiconductor built by William Shockley.
1952 Flexible memory discs developed.
1953 Core memory developed by Jay Forester.
1954 Gordon Teal develops the 1st Silicon junction transistor.
1957 Sputnick launched.
1958 Gilbert Hyatt and Jack Sinclair develop first IC chips.
Planar chip manufacturing process developed at Fairchild.
1958-1964 US Civil Rights movement.
1959 Xerox 914 is first office copier for sale.
1960 Bank of America is first to use magnetic ink on checks.
1961 First mass-produced monolith
1961 First RAM chips developed at Intel.
1962 First use of virtual memory.
1964 First LAN develo
1966 First WAN experiments (AR
1967 First monolith memory chips.

The disadvantage of translating analog signals into digital ones is that digital signals take up much more room to store. Digital music on compact discs would not have been feasible without the laser disc technology that allows large amounts of data to be stored in such a small space.

When the computer plays the music to speakers or displays images on a monitor, it sends the digital data through another processor called a **Digital to Analog Converter** (DAC). The DAC chip converts the data from digital to analog so that a speaker or television can use it. The merging of analog and digital technologies allows us to sample a variety of signals from the outside world, input them, manipulate them and output them again.

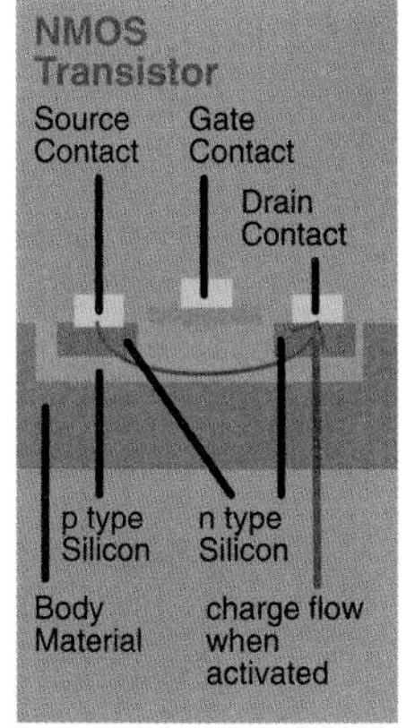

Not all transistors operate digitally (on and off). Those used in amplifiers and non–digital electronics can operate in gradual intensities, but these cannot be used for logic design.

Transistors

Processing, manipulating, "crunching," thinking—whatever you want to call it—is what computers do best. They can manipulate extremely large quantities of data at lightning speeds. At the lowest level, this data exists as pulses of electricity flowing through circuits of the computer's **chips**. These pulses are represented with the symbols **1** and **0** and correspond to a circuit being **on** or **off**.

At a higher or more abstract level, these calculations make it possible to perform very sophisticated operations, such as: compose music, manipulate images and predict weather forecasts. Everything, however, is ultimately accounted for in 1s and 0s.

The **transistors** used in computers are digital switches that have only two settings: on or off. Transistors turn electrical current on and off in logic circuits. These transistors are specially designed to go on and off very quickly and are the building blocks of **logic gates** ▶56, 93–94.

How easy it is for the transistors to turn on and off depends on many factors. The shape, size, configuration and **doping** ▶95 concentrations (amount of impurities) all affect how they perform.

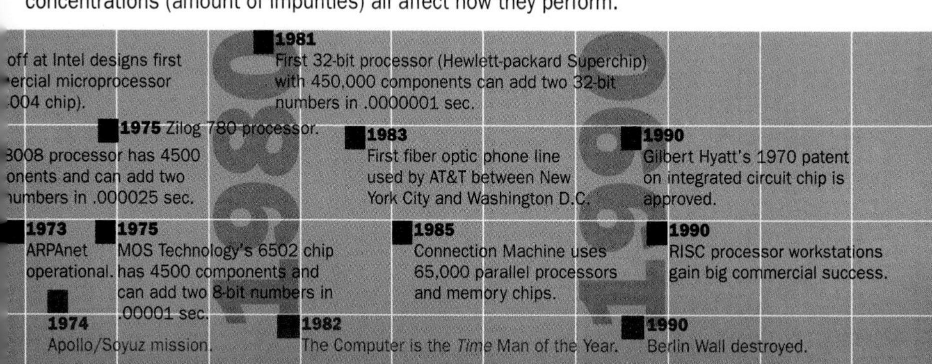

off at Intel designs first
ercial microprocessor
004 chip).
1975 Zilog 780 processor.
3008 processor has 4500
onents and can add two
umbers in .000025 sec.
1973
ARPAnet operational.
1974
Apollo/Soyuz mission.
1975
MOS Technology's 6502 chip has 4500 components and can add two 8-bit numbers in .00001 sec.
1980
1981
First 32-bit processor (Hewlett-packard Superchip) with 450,000 components can add two 32-bit numbers in .0000001 sec.
1982
The Computer is the *Time* Man of the Year.
1983
First fiber optic phone line used by AT&T between New York City and Washington D.C.
1985
Connection Machine uses 65,000 parallel processors and memory chips.
1990
1990
Gilbert Hyatt's 1970 patent on integrated circuit chip is approved.
1990
RISC processor workstations gain big commercial success.
1990
Berlin Wall destroyed.

Transistors

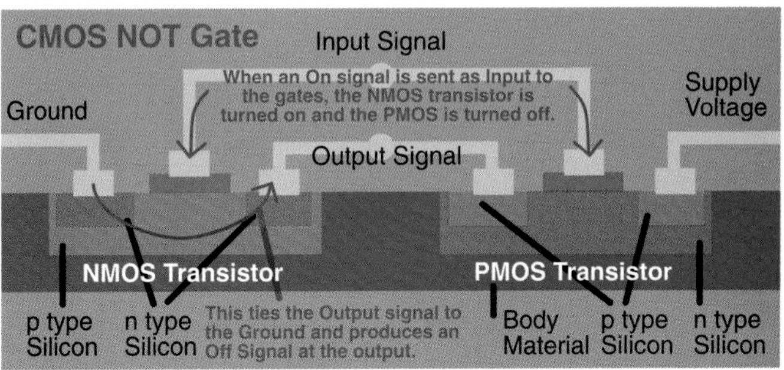
CMOS NOT Gate
Input Signal
When an On signal is sent as Input to the gates, the NMOS transistor is turned on and the PMOS is turned off.
Ground
Supply Voltage
Output Signal
NMOS Transistor
PMOS Transistor
p type Silicon
n type Silicon
This ties the Output signal to the Ground and produces an Off Signal at the output.
Body Material
p type Silicon
n type Silicon

*One of the most unsung pioneers of the computer was an Englishman named Charles Babbage. He was one hundred years ahead of his time in envisioning and building the first computer. His **Analytical Engine** was never finished because he could never find the support he needed. Completely mechanical, it used gears and levers where today's computers use electronics. To assist himself, he invented the concepts of the programmable machine, mass produced parts, diamond-tipped tools, and modern statistical theory.*

A transistor is made of **semiconductors** in a layered assembly on a chip. This assembly allows electricity to pass through only under certain conditions. This switching function of a transistor and the ability to control the current is the key to electronic logic.

A simple transistor is made with two types of semiconductors: p–type and n–type. A **p–type** semiconductor is made from Silicon doped with Boron. This gives the metal a positive charge. An **n–type** semiconductor is made with Silicon doped with Phosophorus or Arsenic and this gives it a negative charge. N–type semiconductors have extra electrons that carry the negative charge to any positive charge it can find. This means that electricity will flow from an n–type to a p–type easily. If the p–type material does not have enough positive charge, the electricity will not flow to it or through it.

Simple transistors are built by separating two pieces of **n–type** material with **p–type** material in a layered assembly. If the p–type does not have enough electrical charge, current will not travel from the first piece of n–type to the second. If it does, the current flows through the transistor easily. This simple flow/no flow or **on/off** logic is based on the actual current flow. Three wires are needed in a transistor: one to carry the electrical current to the transistor, one to carry it from the transistor, and one to control whether it passes between the first two. This is the formula for producing an **AND gate** (two signals in, one signal out). Other types of gates represent other rules of logic. For example, a **NOT gate** requires only one signal in to send a signal out.

The most popular type of gate in computer logic is the **NAND gate**. The NAND gate is a combination of an **AND gate** and a **NOT gate**. Most logic can be reduced into combinations of NAND gates. Also, NAND gates are readily constructed out of **CMOS** (Complemen-

CPU	Introduced	Bus Bit Size (address/data)	MIPS	Transistors (millions)
Intel 8088	1979	16/8	0.33	0.029
Intel 80286	1982	16/16	0.4	0.100
Intel 80386	1985	24/16	5	0.275
Intel 80386SX	1987	32/16	2.5	0.275
Intel 80486SX	1991	32/32	20	1.2
Motorola 68000	1980	16/16	0.5	0.068
Motorola 68020	1985	24/16	3	0.200
Motorola 68030	1987	32/32	5	0.300
Motorola 68040	1990	32/32	15	1.2
Mips R4000	1990	36/64	50	1.3
IBM RISC/6000	1990	32/64	55	NA
SunSuperSPARC	1992	36/64	75	3.1

tary Metal Oxide Semiconductor) semiconductor technology which is a preferred semiconductor technology because of its low power usage, gate densities, and fabrication capability.

The biggest problems with transistors is that they generate a lot of heat. Even though they are microscopic, because they are packed together with millions of other transistors, the combined heat generated can burn them out. The fan inside your computer is there to move air past the electronics and keep them cool. Heat is one of the biggest problems in putting more and more transistors closer together.

One way of making transistors perform faster is to use materials that allow electrons to flow through easier. Cooling special metals to super–low temperatures can achieve this. Semiconductors cooled to these temperatures (approximately –200° F) are called **superconductors**. Superconductors lose most of their electrical resistance when super–cooled and use very little power. Because they allow electrons to flow faster, the amount of electrons flowing increases. This builds up heat in the transistors and requires more cooling.

Super–cooling can be accomplished by a few different methods. Gases, like Freon, can be circulated around the electronic components, absorbing heat, and then cooled down again with water through a heat exchanger. This is similar to how a refrigerator or freezer works. Some computers actually have their electronics emersed in liquids, like liquid Freon, to reach super–cool temperatures and force bubbles through the liquid to move it around. The Cray–2 is known as "bubbles" because the bubbles of its liquid–immersion system can be seen behind glass cases.

*Instead of doping Silicon for semiconductors, developers are beginning to use Gallium Arsenide (**GaAs**) because it allows much higher speeds than p–type or n–type Silicon. GaAs also needs less cooling because it generates less heat. It is very brittle though, which makes it difficult to manufacture. A GaAs transistor can turn on and off in 230 billionths of a second (100 times faster than a Silicon transistor). Another material, Aluminum Gallium Arsenide (**AlGaAs**) is even faster. An AlGaAs switch can turn on and off in 2 trillionths of a second (ten times faster than GaAs). This is because electrons move through GaAs and AlGaAs faster than through Silicon.*

Superconductors are only in their infant stages of development. New ones can operate at –80°F but are still difficult and very expensive to manufacture.

CPUs

CPUs

When people use the term ***chip****, they are usually referring to the CPU.*

The six major parts of a CPU are: the ***ALU****,* ***registers****, a* ***clock****, a* ***program counter****, an* ***address decoder*** *and an* ***instruction decoder****.*

CPU enlarged and at actual size:

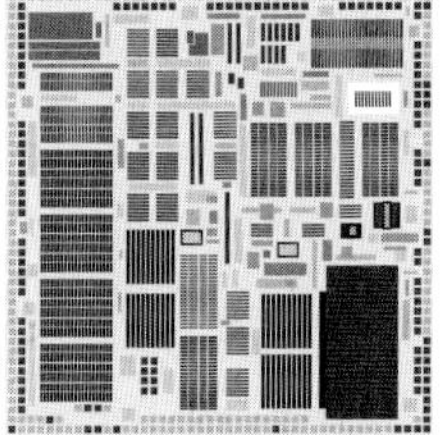

A common data voltage is five volts. Therefore, a five volt signal will represent a one and a zero voltage will represent a zero. When the voltage signal is between the two extreme voltages, say 2.5 volts, the signal is said to be UNKNOWN or unclear.

Actually, the clock usually runs at twice the speed of the CPU and system. These components count every other beat of the clock when they perform their function.

A **CPU** (Central Processing Unit) is the heart of a computer. The CPU is the chip that does the actual processing and calculations. It is a complex collection of many components.

Every CPU has six major components: the ALU, registers, a clock, a program counter, an address decoder and an instruction decoder. The **ALU** (Arithmetic Logic Unit) is the calculator that adds and subtracts two numbers. Most processors are only able to add and subtract. Multiplication, division and any other mathematic operations must be broken down into components of adding and subtracting. Some advanced CPUs can now multiply and divide directly, but these are still rare.

Registers are memory **cores** that keep data temporarily while the ALU is processing it. These cores are small but fast. Data is shuttled into the registers when the ALU needs it and out again when the ALU is finished with it. Data in the registers is **swapped** ▸45 to **RAM** (Random Access Memory) when it is no longer needed. Because other forms of memory are slower, the registers act as a type of buffer between the quick ALU and the comparatively slower RAM. This means that the ALU can be processing something while data is being swapped. Therefore, the ALU doesn't need to wait as often for the slower components to catch up.

The processor also contains a system **clock** that synchronizes the CPU and the entire system like a **metronome**. The clock has a quartz crystal that vibrates at a constant frequency. How fast the CPU operates is determined by the **clock speed** ▸103, 109–110 of the crystal. Clock speeds are measured in MegaHertz (MHz) frequencies such as 16MHz or 24MHz. This does not mean that all components operate at this speed. Most components are slower but can

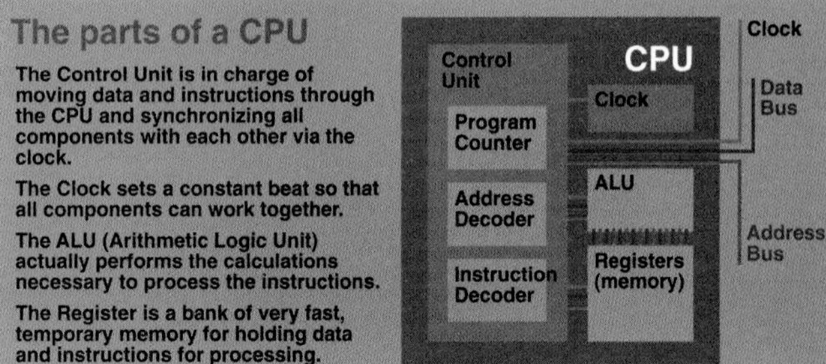
The parts of a CPU
The Control Unit is in charge of moving data and instructions through the CPU and synchronizing all components with each other via the clock.
The Clock sets a constant beat so that all components can work together.
The ALU (Arithmetic Logic Unit) actually performs the calculations necessary to process the instructions.
The Register is a bank of very fast, temporary memory for holding data and instructions for processing.
CPU
Control Unit
Program Counter
Address Decoder
Instruction Decoder
Clock
ALU
Registers (memory)
Clock
Data Bus
Address Bus

keep in step by synchronizing to the clock speed. Total system speed is called **throughput** and reflects the reality of data moving around the system under normal conditions. It is possible to have a higher throughput in a well–designed system with a slower clock speed than a poorly designed system with a faster clock speed.

The remaining three components are temporary logs and decoders that use specific aspects of the data or instructions. The **Program Counter** keeps the address of the instruction being used. The **Address Decoder** logs the address of the data being processed in the ALU and the **Instruction Decoder** actually interprets the instructions being performed. Typically, the instruction decoder will receive an instruction from the Program Counter to have two pieces of data processed by the ALU. The Program Counter acts as a bookmark in the program to keep the CPU's place while the instruction is carried out. Likewise, the Address Decoder keeps a bookmark in the location where the data came from.

As technology advances and better manufacturing methods are developed, CPUs are getting faster, more sophisticated and more tightly packed with components. Up to 1 million transistors are now routinely squeezed onto a chip the size of a fingernail.

If a computer's processor is said to be an 8–bit processor, it means that it can process eight bits (1 byte) at a time. Simplistically, it would be about twice as fast as a 4–bit processor, but there are many other factors that effect speed. It would be accurate to say that it was twice as **powerful** as a 4–bit machine, though.

Most CPUs are **CISCs** (Complex Instruction Set Chip). This means that they include instructions for many different types of operations in the **firmware** of the chip. This can slow down the operations of the chip because the library of instructions is so big. New chips with smaller instruction libraries are now being developed because the chips can run much faster. These **RISCs** (Reduced

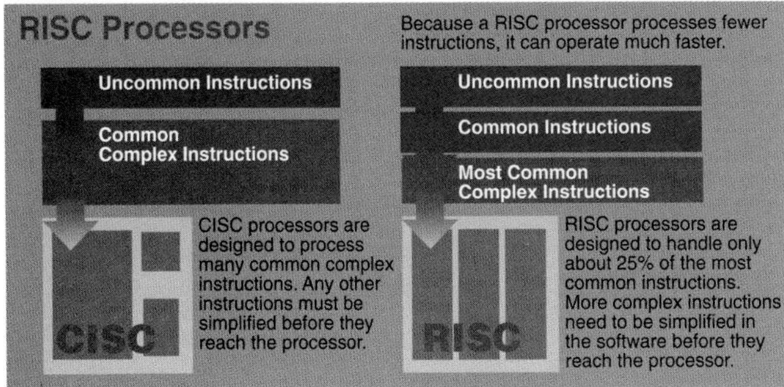

101

There are four ways to increase a computer's speed.

1. The first is to use high speed components and processors. This allows increased system speed (**clock speed** ▶100) *without slowing any components.*

2. The second is to use memory more efficiently. **Cacheing** ▶107 *and* ***Pipelining*** *are examples of this.*

3. The third is to decrease the distances signals must travel.

4. The fourth is to alter the computer's architecture for more efficient operation. This can be difficult to implement because it may require a whole, new approach to how computers operate. **Parallel processing** ▶112 *is one way to do this.*

RISC *technology was developed by a team led by John Locke at IBM, in the mid 70's. RISC instructions have identical lengths which make them easier and faster to process.*

Coprocessors

Even though a CPU's rated speed (measured in megahertz) might be high, this doesn't mean that the computer will run this fast. Many processes in the computer limit the speed CPUs run at. The system clock speed is usually set lower than the CPU's capabilities because other components may not be able to keep up with the CPU. These slower components cause the processor to wait until they have caught up. A measure of over–all system performance is important for accurate comparisons between different computer systems. **Throughput** ▶100 *is a loosely defined term for overall performance of operations. Usually, it takes into account memory speeds, I/O operations, writing to disc access times and other limiting factors.*

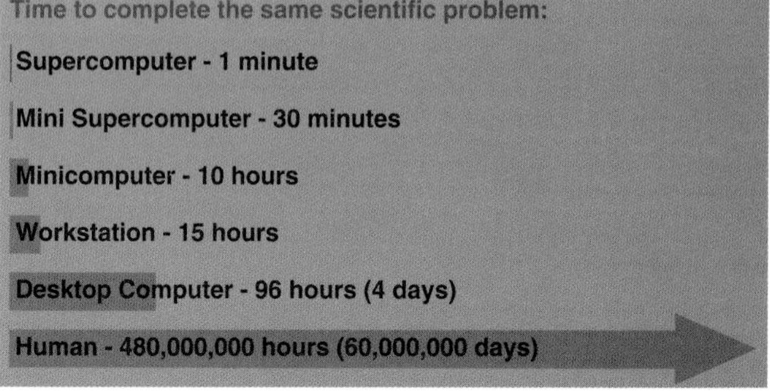

Instruction Set Chips) include the most common instructions needed (only about a quarter of those found on a CISC). This means, however, that more complex instructions must be simplified before than can be run by the CPU. This is done in the program itself. Programs must be **compiled** ▶53-54 specifically for a particular RISC chip so that they can run on that chip.

Coprocessors

Many computers use more than one processor to manipulate data. These other processors are called **Coprocessors** ▶46 because they handle special tasks and allow the main processor to operate more efficiently. Common coprocessors include DMA chips and FPU processors. A **DMA** (Direct Memory Access) ▶106, 111 chip can bypass the main CPU and provide direct communications between system **RAM** and other components within the computer. This means that the main CPU does not need to bother with moving large blocks of data around inside the computer. When data or instructions are needed, the DMA chip handles much of the moving .

I/O processors ▶47–48 handle data exchanges between the computer and **peripherals** ▶71. Any data entering and leaving the computer from a disc, diskette, network or other data source must, normally, interrupt the CPU's operations. An I/O processor can take over these functions and free the CPU to continue processing data and instructions.

FPUs (Floating Point Units) are chips designed especially to handle floating–point calculations. Floating–point calculations are based on exponents and require more complex processing. Most CPUs

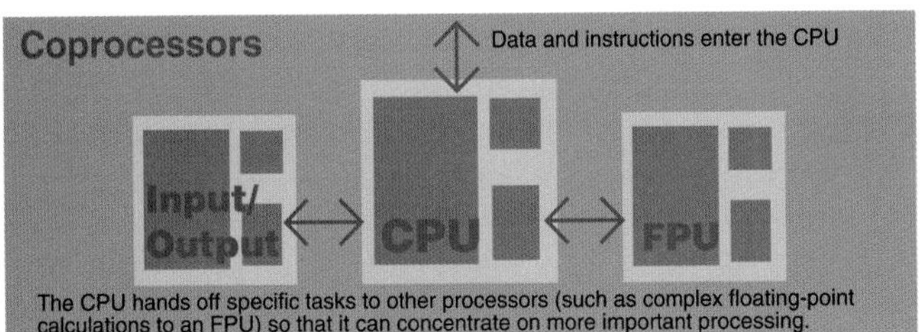

The CPU hands off specific tasks to other processors (such as complex floating-point calculations to an FPU) so that it can concentrate on more important processing.

have integer–based **ALU** ▶100 (Arithmetic Logic Units) instead of floating–point–based ones. This is fine for most operations, but **graphics**, **CAD**, and **music** applications (as well as many others) are heavily dependent on floating–point calculations. An FPU can process these types of numbers more easily and more quickly. Computers that have FPUs give these calculation tasks to the FPU, allowing the CPU to work on other things. The result is faster operations and more efficient work. Most newer CPUs have an FPU built into them.

Optical Circuits

The latest technology in computer circuit design involves **optical circuits**. Lasers and beams of light replace electricity flowing through the interconnects. This is very experimental technology. Optical switches block or let light pass through the circuits at the speed of light. Because light transmission has a much higher bandwidth than electricity, more data can be carried at once. This means that data can be transmitted at nearly one thousand times the rates of traditional electronic circuit designs. The drawbacks are that optical circuits generate much more heat and require more energy to operate. This technology is still in it's beginning stages and there are many limitations to be overcome before it will be found in commercial products.

Computer Performance	Megaflops	MIPS
Macintosh Quadra 900	2.8	15
IBM PC	1.5	15
NeXTstation	2.8	15
Sun SPARCStation2	21	30
Cray 1	80	160
CDC Cyber 2000	420	162
Cray X-MP/2	235	250
Cray 2	1,700	975
Cray Y-MP/2 C90	16,000	8,000

Megaflop = Millions of floating point operations per second.
MIPS = Millions of Instructions Per Second.

A CPU is rated in two ways. The first is its ***clock speed*** *measured in MHz (megahertz, millions of cycles per second). The faster the clock speed, the faster the CPU can process data. The second is its* ***word length*** *(number of bits it can process at once).*

Chips are built by layering levels of metals and semiconductors on top of a base material. The base material is typically a 6" diameter, .004" thick wafer of Silicon cut from a 2' long ingot. This ingot is 99.99999999% pure. The layers are added (or etched) one at a time over the surface of the wafer using masks to control exactly where the metals are applied. Chips use anywhere from 5–13 masks depending on the complexity of the design. Once finished, each wafer is cut into many identical chips. Each chip is then encased in a plastic box that allows it to connect to the system board or other devices more easily.

Storage

The price of computer memory is directly proportional to its speed and capacity. The faster and larger memory chips are more expensive than slower and smaller ones.

RAM is the most expensive common form of computer memory.

Memory which is said to be ***volatile*** *loses the data stored in it when the memory device loses power.*

Memory speed is measured in ***nanoseconds*** *or* ***ns****. A nanosecond is 1/1,000,000,000 of a second.*

There are several ways of storing data in a computer, but all share the same characteristics of storing it in a digital form (1s and 0s). Furthermore, this data is encoded with references to its location so that it may be easily found by the computer. Having a piece of important data is not useful if the computer cannot find it. The locations that refer to specific pieces of digital data in a computer are called addresses ▶45.

Data stored in memory need not be only numbers. While all data must be in binary form, it can represent any kind of information (sound, music, text, numbers, pictures, etc...) or instructions for operations.

RAM

There are primarily three types of memory used by computers: RAM, ROM and Storage Memory. **RAM** (Random Access Memory) ▶44 is the fast memory in which a computer stores data and instructions that it is currently using. It must be fast enough to keep up with the processor and spacious enough to store much of the data the CPU needs for its immediate operations. RAM is like a computer's thinking power. If the computer or CPU is a juggler, then RAM is its hands. The more hands, the more and faster the juggler can juggle. Therefore, the more RAM a computer has, the more it can handle at one time and the faster it can handle it. Sometimes, if there is not enough RAM available, a computer may not even be able to "think" about, or process, instructions because it cannot load everything it needs into RAM at once. This is like the juggler trying to juggle a ball too big for her to even hold.

Computer Memory Compared

Memory Type	Access-Time	Volatile	Erasable	Cost
DRAM	80 ns	Yes	Yes	Higher
SRAM/VRAM	20 ns	Yes	Yes	Highest
ROM	12 ns	No	No	Medium
EPROM	150 ns	No	w/UV	Medium
EEPROM	150 ns	No	Yes	High
Hard Drive	25,000 ns	No	Yes	Lowest

RAM

RAM is fast, but it is **volatile**. This means that when the power is turned off, the memory is wiped clean.

There are a few types of RAM that are used in specific circumstances: SRAM, DRAM, VRAM and Flash memory. **DRAM** stands for **Dynamic** Random Access Memory and the very process of reading its contents erases the data in it. In order to keep data in DRAM it is necessary to constantly be writing and rewriting it. This is fairly tedious but actually economical because these chips are relatively inexpensive compared to other forms of RAM. **SRAM** (**Static** Random Access Memory) does not need to be constantly rewritten in order to keep the data secure but is much more expensive than DRAM.

DRAM memory used in personal computers and workstations is put on a small board called a SIMM (Single In–line Memory Module). These boards can be installed into a computer simply by snapping them into available sockets to expand a computer's system memory. SIMMs come in 256K, 1MB and 4MB capacities.

VRAM ▶82 is a type of very fast RAM used for holding Video data displayed on a **monitor** ▶80–82. The VRAM stands for **Video** RAM. VRAM is used mainly on graphics, video and accelerator cards.

VRAM is typically a type of SRAM specifically suited to video applications.

Flash memory is a cross between RAM and forms of ROM. Specifically, it is constructed similarly to **EEPROM** ▶106 but is fast like RAM. The advantage of Flash memory is that it requires less energy to keep active because it doesn't erase so readily. Unfortunately, it is very expensive.

ROM

ROM (Read–Only Memory) is memory in which instructions are permanently encoded. This memory is in the form of a memory chip and is commonly used to start the computer. When the power is turned on the instructions in ROM are loaded into the computer's RAM first. These instructions are the computer's most basic ones. They usually contain only enough instructions to turn on, set–up and load the rest of the instructions from the disc. These instructions cannot be changed and do not erase when the power is turned off.

Computer and printer upgrades are sometimes made by simply replacing the ROM chips with newer ones that have more or improved functions.

ROM

There are a few types of ROM: standard ROM, PROM, EPROM and EEPROM. **PROM** stands for **Programmable** ROM and is a type of ROM that can be programmed after the chip is produced. Most ROM chips are produced with the instructions already encoded in them, but a PROM chip comes blank and the instructions can be programmed later. The instructions are "burned" into the chip electrically by sending them in coded form into the chip as pulses of electricity. Once these instructions are established in the chip they cannot be changed.

EPROM is **Erasable Programmable** ROM and, like PROM, is loaded with instructions after the chip is manufactured. Unlike PROM, however, the instructions can be changed by exposing the chip to ultraviolet light. This light erases the memory so that it can be reprogrammed.

EEPROM is **Electrically Erasable Programmable** ROM and instead of using ultraviolet light, it erases the instructions by using a stronger electrical current than normal. This can be easier to implement in many computers, although these chips are more complicated, and thus, slower and more expensive. Neither of these processes of erasing and reprogramming ROM are fast enough to be used instead of RAM.

Storage Memory

The third type of memory is Storage Memory. **Storage Memory** is used to store large quantities of data—much more than can fit in a computer's **RAM** or **ROM** at once. Storage Memory is also stable. This means that it does not erase when the power is turned off. **Hard drives**, **diskettes**, **CD–ROMs**, and other storage systems are all examples of storage memory.

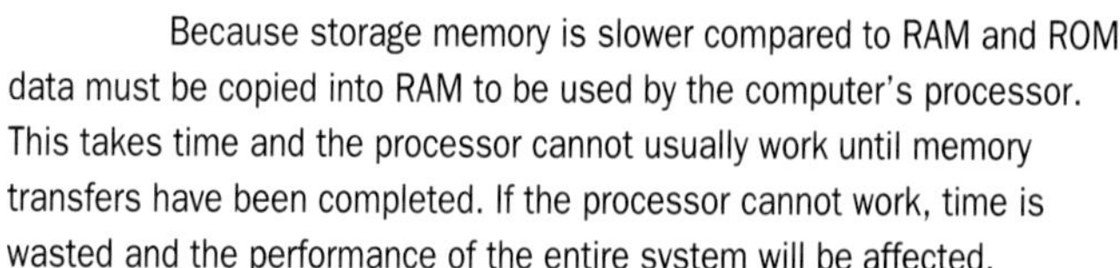

Because storage memory is slower compared to RAM and ROM, data must be copied into RAM to be used by the computer's processor. This takes time and the processor cannot usually work until memory transfers have been completed. If the processor cannot work, time is wasted and the performance of the entire system will be affected.

To decrease waiting on the part of the processor, some computers use special chips just for moving data around. A **DMA** (Direct Memory Access) chip is used to shuttle data from storage memory into RAM quickly. Since the processor can be working on other things instead, the entire system functions more efficiently. **I/O** (Input/Ouput) ▶102 chips do the same thing. These chips manage the moving of data between devices so that the CPU doesn't have to.

Some computers can use storage memory as a slower form of RAM. This is called **virtual memory** ▶47–48. If the computer's **operating system** ▶44–45 has virtual memory capabilities, it can use storage memory (such as a hard disc) to simulate RAM and trick the computer into thinking it has more RAM available than it does. This is especially useful when using huge files or doing complex calculations like those needed for **image manipulation** ▶11 or **computer-aided design** ▶19. Virtual memory is slower than traditional RAM because the access times of the hard disc or other storage devices are longer than those of chip-based RAM. However, it can sometimes be the only option for working on really big files.

With virtual memory, data in RAM is written to disc when there is no space in RAM left and new data is needed. When the data written to disc is needed again, it is swapped with data in RAM.

Cache Memory

Another way to allow processors to operate more efficiently is to use **cache memory**. This is high-speed memory that is much faster than the processor itself. The processor will keep the most recently used data and instructions in the **cache**. This allows the processor to grab them immediately instead of having to request them from storage memory or RAM which are both slower. Again, the entire system performance can be increased.

Cache memory has access times around 1 trillionth (1/1,000,000,000,000) of a second.

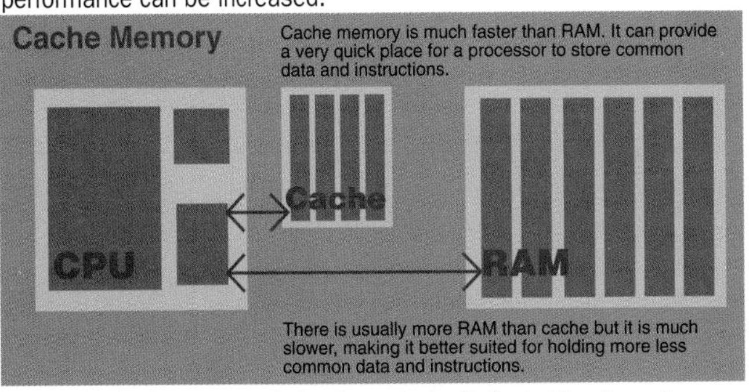

Cache Memory
Cache memory is much faster than RAM. It can provide a very quick place for a processor to store common data and instructions.
Cache
CPU
RAM
There is usually more RAM than cache but it is much slower, making it better suited for holding more less common data and instructions.

Cache memory is implemented with fast chips (usually, **SRAM** ▶105). Sometimes cache memory can be added to a computer on a small board similar to a **SIMM** (Single In-Line Memory Module). This board snaps into a special slot that can be accessed by the processor directly. This slot is sometimes called a **processor-direct slot**. Cache is expensive, however, and usually comes in small quantities.

Communications

John von Neuman was key advisor to the military and president during the 1940's. He championed computers and electronic technology and helped define the components of serial computers (like we use today). He was in a position to put great people and great technology together to produce even greater developments. This is why computers are sometimes called "von Neuman machines." Most computers follow the organization he helped formulate. **Parallel processing** ▸112 *computers are sometimes known as "Non–von" machines because they have a different fundamental organization.*

The transmission of data within a computer is a complex process that relies on the latest advancement of hardware and software engineering. The heart of the computer is the processor ▸100–102. Moving data to and from the processor is the key to manipulating data. The processor cannot perform any instructions if it can't get the data it needs. Also, it does no good to process data if it cannot be sent to the proper place at the proper time.

When you are talking with someone sitting next to you, you simply talk and the air around you carries your sounds to his ears. If the person you are talking to is many miles away you may need to use a telephone to communicate with him or her. The telephone system serves as a pathway between you and your partner. This telephone pathway ensures that no matter how far away you may be, the data is clear.

There are many electrical pathways within computers that allow components to communicate with each other. These internal pathways are microscopic wires instead of cables, etched between the devices that make up the computer. Basically, a computer is a data mover and manipulator and is involved in moving extremely large amounts of data around internally. To move this data around, the computer uses pathways known as **buses** ▸111. These are the "telephone lines" between different devices within the computer.

System Board

The computer's electronic components are organized on a board (called a **system board** or **motherboard**) that contains communication paths between them. This board is laid–out to provide the shortest possible paths between the components to allow them to communicate more quickly.

The major components on the motherboard are the **CPU** ▸100–102, any **coprocessors** ▸102–103, **ROM** ▸105–106 memory chips, slots for **RAM** ▸104–105 memory chips, and **ports** (connectors) to major components, such as the power supply, **diskette drives**, **hard drives**, or **peripherals**. The wiring systems that connect all of these components together are called the **buses** ▸111–112. All data, instructions and any other signals travel on the bus. The clock signal

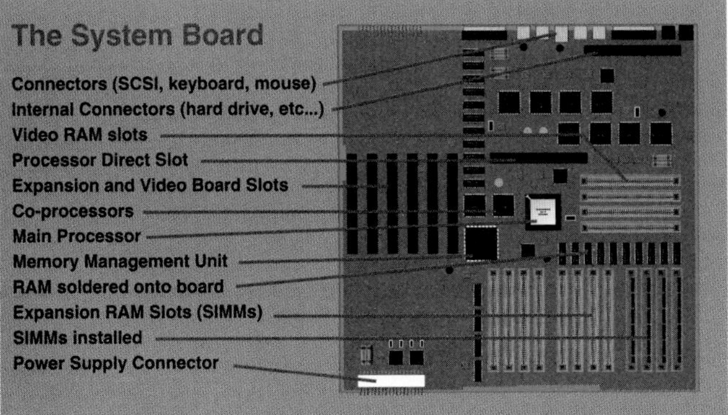

runs on a separate bus that synchronizes the components and separate ones for data and memory addresses. Data and memory addresses also run on separate buses.

As you can see on both the chip and board, there is an intricate lattice of buses between devices. These buses are the communication pathways that allow data to be transmitted within the computer.

Data flows around a computer as pulses of electricity on the bus. These pulses are measured as voltage changes. High and low voltage flows through the buses within the computer at close to the speed of light.

A voltage is a measure of electrical energy. For example, a new car battery will be fully charged and a dead car battery may have no voltage. We would then say that the new car battery has a value of one and the dead car battery has the value of ***zero***. *We are assigning the high voltage a data value of one and the low voltage a data value of zero.*

Clocking

With so many signals flowing within a computer, it becomes important to know when a signal has reached its destination. To aid in signal clarity and coordination, the computer uses a technique known as Clocking. **Clocking** is the use of an additional communication line to synchronize all of the others. The **Clock** is always understood to be the measuring stick for time intervals much like a metronome is in music. This allows the data inside the computer to be bundled, packaged, and stamped for a certain delivery time and place. For example, there may be four data lines going into a semiconductor device and one clock line. This makes a total of five lines entering the device. The device

Many types of connectors join equipment to the motherboard (and thus, the computer). One of the more common types is a ***SCSI*** *(Small Computer Systems Interface). Pronounced "scuzzy", this is a standard connector for personal computers that connects external equipment or peripherals, such as hard drives, printers and networks to the computer.*

Clocking

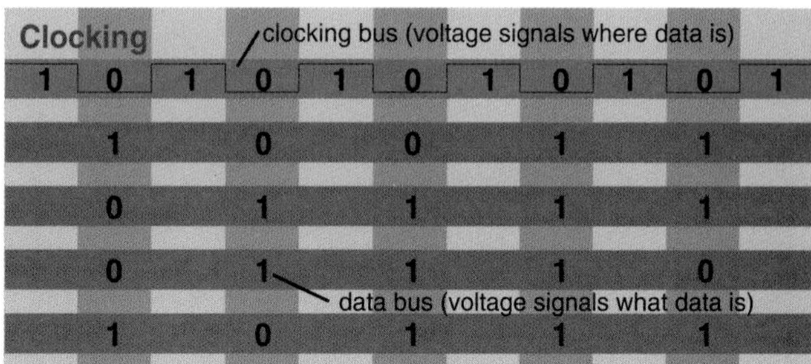

The clock is controlled by a crystal timing element that runs at twice the speed of the system or processor.

Usually, the longest interconnect (wire) on a bus determines the quickest clock cycle possible for that chip. If the clock cycle is faster than the time it takes any signal to transmit on the bus, the processor will get confused.

reads the data on the four incoming lines only when the clock line changes from zero to one. The same model is used for sending data. The sending device only sends data when the clock signal goes from zero to one. The result will be that all the data will be bundled together and the receiving device knows when all the data is in and is readable because it also has access to the clock line too. The trick of computer designers is to design a complex computer where they can turn the clock rate of a computer up so that all the data within the computer is transmitted flawlessly and quickly. One bit out of place and computers quickly become confused.

A commonly used term is **Wait State.** This is the amount of **clock cycles** (time) that a device must wait until the data it needs is available. Most high performance computer architectures often employ "zero wait state" architecture. This means that there is little or no time wasted by devices in the computer when transmitting data.

Something that computers are especially adept at is moving large amounts of data. There are certain characteristics about a computer that allows it to deal with large amounts of data. The first is that computers never tire. If someone asked you to read one page of a book, you could do it because this task is well within your range of capability. But if someone asked you to read a million books and find all the occurrences of the word *car*, this would be far from your personal capability. The computer, however, would not care, it would just start scanning. The second characteristic is that computers are very fast. If someone gave you a week to read a book, this would be relatively simple. On the other hand, if they asked you to read the whole book in the next three seconds, you would be incapable. The computer would not hesitate and would read the book and report back to the user when it was done. Computers are very good at handling large amounts of data quickly. Within the computer there are certain transmission structures that facilitate the computer's ability to process vast quantities of data.

The Bus

A **bus** resides on the **system board** ▶108 (or motherboard) within all computers. It can be thought of as a common highway that all the computer components live on. The bus supplies power, points of reference, clock signals, and data pathways for the data to flow. A bus consists of parallel lines of data pathways called interconnects.

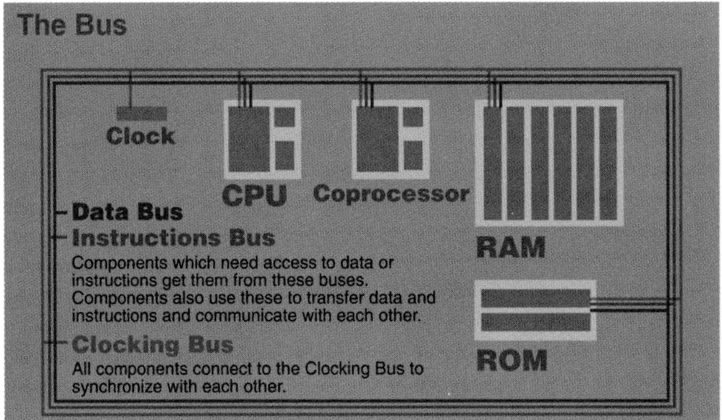

The Bus
Clock
CPU
Coprocessor
RAM
ROM
Data Bus
Instructions Bus
Components which need access to data or instructions get them from these buses. Components also use these to transfer data and instructions and communicate with each other.
Clocking Bus
All components connect to the Clocking Bus to synchronize with each other.

These are designed so that devices can **chunk** data into packets so that more can be manipulated at once. For example, an 8–bit bus can transfer twice as much data as a 4–bit bus. Bus structures range from 4–bits wide to 64–bits wide. The wider the bus, the more data that can flow at once.

Typically, a bus has three channels (pathways) for electrical signals. The first is the **data channel**. This is used for moving data between the different components. The second is the **address channel** which is used for transmitting the memory address locations for the data. The third is the **control** or **clock channel** which is used to keep consistent timing between all of the components.

In some computers there are multiple buses, which speed the flow of data even more. There are also **DMA Channels** (Direct Memory Access Channels) which are dedicated pathways for moving specific data around a computer and can greatly enhance the speed at which data flows through a computer.

Parallel Processing

If the channels are too close together, the signals can bleed into each other and garble the instructions. This is known as **crosstalk**. Crosstalk is only one of the many ways the signals on the interconnect can get disrupted.

CalTech's Hypercube is a parallel processing computer with 64 separate CPUs.

Parallel Processing

Parallel processing is when computers use more than one CPU to manipulate data and instructions. By letting more than one CPU work on a problem at once, the problem can get solved much faster—but not without creating some new challenges. It's hard enough to get a computer with one CPU to function efficiently. Two or more CPUs must coordinate the work they do. Each CPU must also have access to every component. This means that the bus must have a separate set of channels for each CPU, which complicates the design exponentially.

Another problem with parallel processing is breaking a problem into parts so that different CPUs can work on different parts at once. Coordinating the CPUs is like managing a team of people working on one complex project.

00011011	0
11011001	1
11010010	0
01101000	1

00011011
11011001
11010010
01101000
____
01111000

The top example is of ***parity checking****. The bottom one is an example of a* ***checksum*** *operation. The checksum takes less time to check than the parity check, but if there is a problem, it is not pin-pointed as closely. This means that all the data in the group will need to be recopied instead of only the incorrect bytes as in the case of the parity check.*

Note: Data rarely fails an integrity check.

Data Integrity

The accuracy (or integrity) of data in a computer is crucial. Because all information is decoded into complex combinations of 1s and 0s, missing even one bit can result in inaccessible data. Computers cannot be 90% accurate or even 99% accurate with data and still function. If a computer is not 100% accurate, the data it uses may be unidentifiable and unusable. A computer operates under the assumption that the data it uses is correct, but for critical processes, data integrity checks are employed to make sure that this assumption is true.

Computers use two methods to make sure they are copying data accurately. Both add 1s in data and compare the totals before and after copying. If the sum of the 1s is even, the ninth bit added is a 0. If the sum is odd, a 1 is tacked onto the byte. The computer only cares if the answer is even or odd, not how many 1s there actually are. A **parity check** is when the computer counts all of the 1s in each **byte** (eight bits) and adds a ninth bit. A **Checksum** is a method of adding an extra byte to a group of bytes as a reference to the number of 1s in the whole group.

The technology behind what you see and how you see it is changing rapidly. Computer screens (monitors ▶80–84) have already developed past the standards for broadcast television and are now driving the development of better television standards.

Typically, monitors have finer **resolution** ▶80, 88 than television sets. Although the standards for displaying data are different, both monitors and televisions use the same CRT (Cathode Ray Tube) technology.

The magnetic coils in a monitor create ***extremely low-frequency (ELF) magnetic fields*** *whose effects are under review by researchers. Some research suggests that these fields may not be healthy. Also, because the beams of electrons shoot straight out of the screen and computer users sit so much closer to their monitors than to televisions, there is some concern over the safety of CRT monitors. This probably concerns only users who spend long periods of time at their computer. While you shouldn't be alarmed at this information, you should begin to question for yourself the research concerning low-frequency emissions. See pages 41–42 and the* **bibliography ▶130** *for more information.*

CRTs

A **CRT** (Cathode Ray Tube) ▶80–84 is a large tube that forms the wide screen at one end and a small socket on the other. This tube is a vacuum tube. It has nothing inside it—not even air. On the surface of the screen is a coating of Phosphorus material that glows when heated (struck by electrons). In the socket is an electron gun (called a cathode ray gun) that shoots a beam of electrons toward the screen. The socket, itself, is surrounded by coils of magnetic wire. These coils are capable of guiding the beams of electrons toward specific spots on the screen. This is done magnetically; nothing touches the electron beam directly.

To create an image, the cathode ray shoots a beam toward the screen and the coils guide where it hits. The phosphors hit by the beam begin to glow. This is done very quickly.

There are two types of monitors that take different approaches to how they create images. A **vector monitor** ▶15 draws the outlines of objects by beaming the electrons at the screen along each of the object's lines. This creates a simple line drawing. A **raster monitor** ▶15 scans the entire screen, one row at a time, to fill the screen with an image. This is a slower process, but fast enough to work well. Televisions are raster monitors.

Color monitors operate the same way as monochrome monitors, except they have three electron guns instead of one. All colors capable of being shown on a color monitor can be made from the three colors of electrons in different intensities. Electron guns that

CRTs

control red, green and blue information each shoot a beam from the socket and are guided to the screen by the coils. Specific phosphors are used that can form these three colors.

Mixing colors with light is different than mixing them with paint or ink. In fact, colors made from light are mixed opposite than with paint. With paint and ink, the more color added, the darker the colors become. This is called a **subtractive color system** and colors tend to mix until they make black. With light, the more you add, the brighter the colors get. Full intensities of all three colors (red, green, and blue) result in white (not black). This is called an **additive color system**. Mixing different intensities of the light beams allows the monitor to make shades and a broad range of subtle colors.

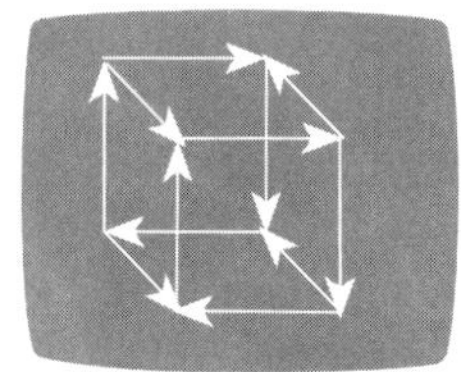

At top is an example of an image displayed on a vector monitor. At bottom is a raster image.

On the surface of the screen is a **mask** that creates a fine grid of cells called **pixels** ▶10, 80. Each pixel's location is known implicitly by the computer. The grid forms these cells so that the light doesn't blur and blend into adjacent areas of the screen. The mask makes the pixels distinct and the picture slightly sharper. Typically, a television set has about 64,000 pixels while a computer monitor may have as many as 9 million pixels (although 250,000 is average).

The main difference between a television screen and a computer monitor is the way they draw pictures. Images in a television are **interlaced.** The electron beam draws every other row on the screen (starting from the upper left corner) until it reaches the bottom of the screen. Then, it goes back to the top of the screen to draw every row it missed. A television does this 30 times a second—fast enough that we don't really notice this happening.

Most computers, however, draw every row of the screen from top to bottom without skipping. This difference has created challenges for developers who want to show television images on a computer or use television sets as a computer monitor.

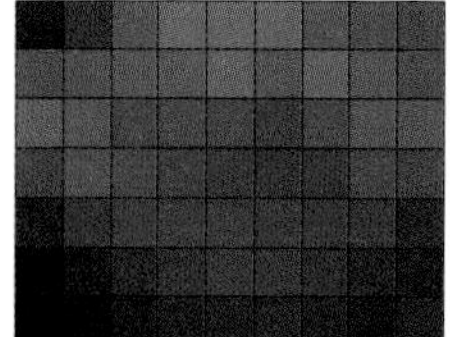

The top illustration shows a screen of pixels without a mask. The bottom one shows how a mask can make an image sharper.

Flat Screens

Although CRTs are the most common displays, other types of screens exist. Most are lighter and more compact and present none of the warnings of CRTs, but are costlier and more difficult to produce. The quality of these screens has not reached the levels of CRTs. Flat screens tend to be slower and coarser than CRTs.

Flat Screen Displays

Like **CRTs**, **Flat screen** displays have thousands of pixels. These pixels, however, are not merely a grid drawn on a screen but distinct, physical elements. Each pixel is like a tiny bulb that turns light on and off. There are three different technologies currently used in flat panel displays: AMLCD, Electroluminescent, and Plasma. All are currently more costly and complex than CRTs, but all produce thin, light displays—especially useful in portable computers.

Active Matrix LCD (Liquid Crystal Display) technology is used in digital watches. LCDs are produced by sandwiching an active, sensitive material between two pieces of glass with a separate transistor (switch) at each pixel. This material twists when the transistor provides voltage to it, causing the material to become opaque (dark). Thousands of pixels made from this sandwich of materials are combined to create a low–power display. Color AMLCDs are possible by sandwiching three layers of liquid crystals. Because there is no light emitting from these monitors, these displays do not use an **additive** color model like CRTs. AMLCDs build up colors by layering red, blue and yellow pixels in a **subtractive** color model. Often, a light behind these layers is used to brighten the display and make it more legible in dark places. This is called a fluorescent (pure white) **backlight** and is used with many monochrome and color displays.

Plasma displays have an active gas in place of an AMLCD's active liquid material. This gas glows when voltage is applied to it. Plasma displays are monochrome, consume small amounts of power and have slightly better contrast than LCDs. This makes them a little easier to read.

Electroluminescent displays use a phosphor film (like on the surface of a CRT) as its active material. So far, these have only been successful on small, monochrome screens. They offer slightly higher contrast but consume more power. Both Electroluminescent and Plasma displays emit light as the result of pixels glowing when charged.

On the horizon, AMLCD technology is promising to produce larger, full–color flat screens. AMLCDs are the most difficult and costly of the three technologies to scale up to larger sizes. However, they offer the best prospects for good color. Plasma displays are the easiest to scale up, but are not so great as color displays.

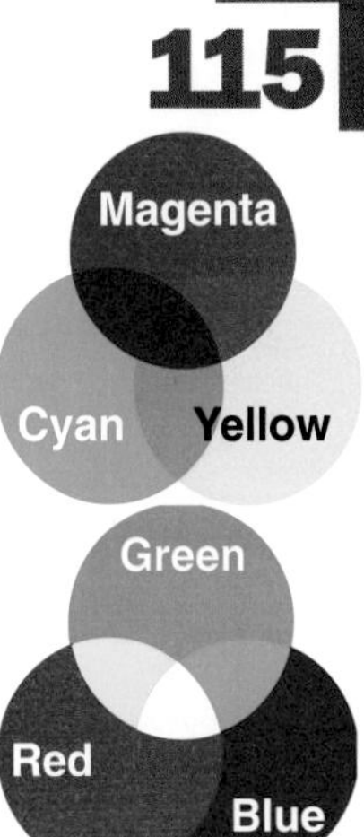

The top colors show how subtractive colors interact and the bottom colors show how additive colors interact.

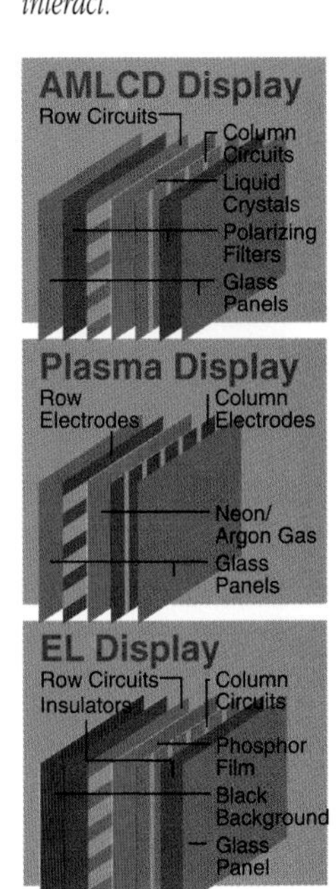

Evaluating Your Needs

When evaluating your needs, think about the following:

- *Will this computer need to be compatible with computers at your business?*
- *If so, what computers are used at work?*
- *What kind of work do you need to do with a computer?*
- *Will you need to travel with your computer?*
- *How many people will need to use this computer? Who are they? What are their needs?*
- *Is this computer expandable?*
- *Does software now exist for this computer that does what you need to do?*

To help you evaluate the capabilities computers can offer, see the **USES** ▶4 *section.*

Purchasing computer hardware and software is a lot like purchasing a car: both are substantial investments that require some thought and planning. These investments are not just of money and time, but can affect how well you do your work and how happy you are doing it.

Evaluating Your Needs

The first step is to evaluate what your **needs** are in a computer. If you plan on using a computer mainly for one specific use (**Computer–Aided Engineering** ▶19, biomedical imaging, or **word processing** ▶5–9, for instance) then you may want to evaluate the software available in that field and choose your hardware based on the software which feels the most comfortable. However, if you expect to use a computer to do many different things (writing letters, managing your finances, and creating music, for example) then you should evaluate hardware platforms that allow those capabilities first. Keep in mind that hardware (the actual, physical objects that you purchase) and software (the "programs" that offer specific uses) are both necessary. Great hardware and bad software will be terrible and disappointing to work with. Likewise, powerful software and inadequate hardware will make you want to throw the whole system out the window.

For the moment, disregard price. Evaluate a computer based on what it can do and what you need it to do. Buying a computer because you got a "good deal" on it and finding out that you can't use it—or don't like to—is a waste of money. If you were to buy an inexpensive car and found later you didn't like it, you could at least make do because it could still get you from point A to point B. But, if you purchase the wrong computer for the wrong reasons, it may not even be able to meet your basic needs.

Once you understand your needs (multi–use vs. specific–use, how often you are going to use it, what other computers or equipment it may need to connect with, how expandable it should be, what type of work you will be doing with it, how powerful your needs are, whether you *need* color—or just want it, whether it needs to be portable or not, etc...), your next step is to find the computer that fits those needs. Rank your needs by priority—what do you absolutely need and what can you live without. Now, start at the top of the list.

Remember, most computers are expandable, so that even if a model does not fit your needs exactly, there may be an add–on component that can help it to.

Computers are evolving quickly. The average speed of processors doubles every year. New features become available, present ones get faster, and better interfaces are continually developed. The only way to deal with this rapid development of technology is to buy the best computer you can afford that fits your needs, and use it fully. It will begin to become dated almost immediately, just like driving a new car off the dealer's lot, but don't let advertising or marketing convince you that your machine is worthless. When your computer is "out–of–date" and cumbersome, or cannot meet your evolving needs, you will know it. Until then, just because a new computer may come out that can out–pace yours does not mean that you must trade–up if your computer is still meeting your needs. For example, you do not, nor will you ever, need a supercomputer for word–processing.

Generally, it is safe to buy a computer that is two or three years old. Remember however, that a computer is not like a classic car that retains much of its value over time. Computers are only as valuable as they are useful.

Buy the best and fastest computer you can afford.

Buy a computer one level higher than you think meets your needs now. Once you begin to use a computer, you will discover things you want to do that did not occur to you before.

What to Buy

A good rule of thumb is to buy one level higher than you think meets your needs. This gives you some room to grow. You will find, once you start computing, that there are many more things that your computer can allow you to do than you originally thought. You can hedge your bet against the advancement of technology by buying a computer that is serious (not a toy or curiosity), expandable, has a great deal of good software available to use with it and has a history of upgrade paths and support for older models. Also, it may ultimately be important for your computer to connect to others, or at least share information with others. Evaluate how easily a particular computer can connect to others.

Presently, for personal computers, this narrows the choice between the Macintosh family from Apple Computer, Inc. and the IBM PCs, PS/2s and compatibles made by many different manufacturers. These two computer families are worlds unto themselves and have followers as devoted to their genre as they are opposed to the other family. These are the Hatfields and the McCoys of the computer world. In the world of workstations (substantially more powerful computers usually meant for business), there are numerous manufacturers

Sometimes, special software can be used on some computers to emulate a different computer in order to run software that would not normally run on it. An example of this is a program that might run on a Macintosh or NeXT computer that allows PC software to work. Within the emulator, the software and interface look just like they would on a PC. This can be like having two machines in one, but of course, it costs more.

What to Buy

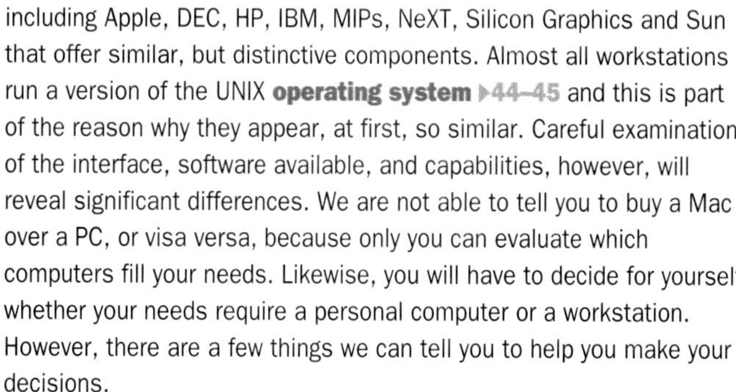

including Apple, DEC, HP, IBM, MIPs, NeXT, Silicon Graphics and Sun that offer similar, but distinctive components. Almost all workstations run a version of the UNIX **operating system** ▸44–45 and this is part of the reason why they appear, at first, so similar. Careful examination of the interface, software available, and capabilities, however, will reveal significant differences. We are not able to tell you to buy a Mac over a PC, or visa versa, because only you can evaluate which computers fill your needs. Likewise, you will have to decide for yourself whether your needs require a personal computer or a workstation. However, there are a few things we can tell you to help you make your decisions.

One of the things that differentiates computer families is *open* and *proprietary* architectures. There are benefits to each approach. IBM PS/2s and PC compatibles have an open architecture and their operating system (**DOS**) can be licensed to anyone from Microsoft Corp. This means that many manufacturers are able to produce "clones" that are just as effective and less expensive than the machines from IBM. Also, all of these clones work alike and can use the same software. Besides the often large price difference, these machines can vary substantially in quality and service. Usually, IBM's machines are more expensive but the possibility of getting a poorly made machine is much less. One drawback to the openness of the DOS operating system is that applications that run on DOS are vastly different to use—even if they perform the same functions. This leads to confusion and longer training time.

Get a list from the seller of the exact components in the machine. Many times, bargain equipment may include parts that don't perform up to the speeds of the processor and system. This makes your entire machine run slowly. Even though you buy a machine with a fast processor, if the rest of the parts aren't rated fast enough, you will not get the full benefits of its speed. This is especially important with IBM PCs and compatibles.

Apple took a different approach with the Macintosh. The system is proprietary and must be licensed by other manufacturers to produce similar machines (something Apple rarely does). This means that there are no "clones" for the Mac at cut-rate prices, but it also allows Apple to enforce standards and consistency. One of the biggest benefits to users is the consistency of operation between applications on a Mac—even between different types of applications. Users often find that by learning one application they have automatically learned 20%–30% of all other applications running on the Mac and sometimes 80%–90% of similar applications. This is a drastic reduction in training and operating time and it is well worth the extra price.

Recently, Microsoft (the creator of the DOS operating system) introduced Windows 3.1. This is a good **graphic–user**

interface ▶76–77 that runs on the DOS operating system and an attempt to bring some of the capabilities and advantages of the Macintosh to DOS computers. Many industry people agree that they have succeeded in transforming the interface of DOS machines into a much friendlier, easier–to–use, easier–to–learn and more capable interface. However, don't let anyone try to convince you that the features of Windows 3.1 are comparable to those of the Macintosh's System 7.1—or even System 6.0—software. The Mac has six years of development and refinement over Windows 3.1 and, at present, offers much richer, deeper, and more impressive features that still make it more friendly, more consistent and easier to learn. This is not to say that Windows 3.1 is bad. In fact, it is a fantastic programming feat that is transforming the PC compatible world. If you buy a DOS computer, consider Windows 3.1 a must and include it in any estimate when comparing prices of computers. Windows 3.1 may very well catch up to the richness of the Macintosh operating system but, for the moment, similarities are little more than skin deep.

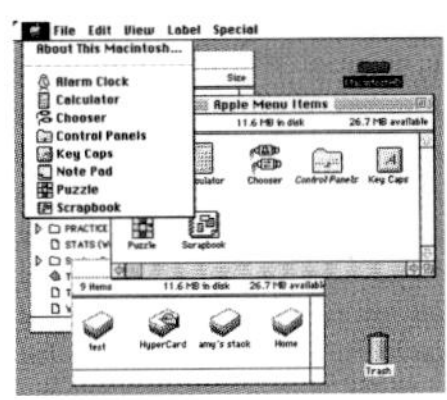

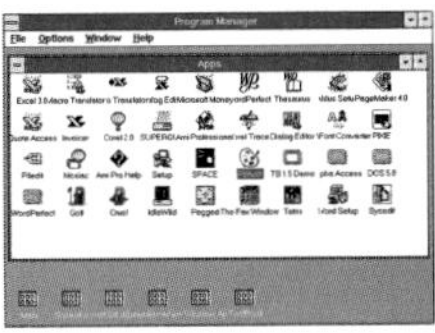

If you buy a DOS machine and are new to computers, consider Windows 3.1 mandatory. But make sure you get at least a 386 series processor to run it.

Remember, the most important feature in a computer is understandability. Do not skimp on this requirement. If you cannot figure out what is happening in your computer, all the snazziest of features will do you no good. This goes for software as well as for hardware. Ask a dealer if you can borrow a manual to read and see if you can understand it. It can be well worth the effort.

Plan on keeping your computer for at least 3–5 years. Realize that your computer's speed will eventually (and sometimes quickly) seem slow—no matter how fast it seems to be when you first buy it. As you learn how to use your computer more effectively, you will work faster but your computer will not. To avoid this, make sure your computer is expandable and can operate faster with added components in the future as you become more proficient.

Never buy a machine or software unless it does what you need now. Don't rely on promises of technology or features to come.

Buy two **drives** (a larger capacity unit such as a **hard drive** ▶62–63 or **optical drive** ▶66–67 and a drive for more portable media such as a $3^{1}/_{2}$" **diskette** ▶59–60 drive). You will quickly tire of working only with a diskette drive and may not even be able to work with many programs if you don't have a hard drive or similar large capacity drive. Consider 40 megabytes the minimum capacity for a hard drive (80MB if you are a serious or "power" user).

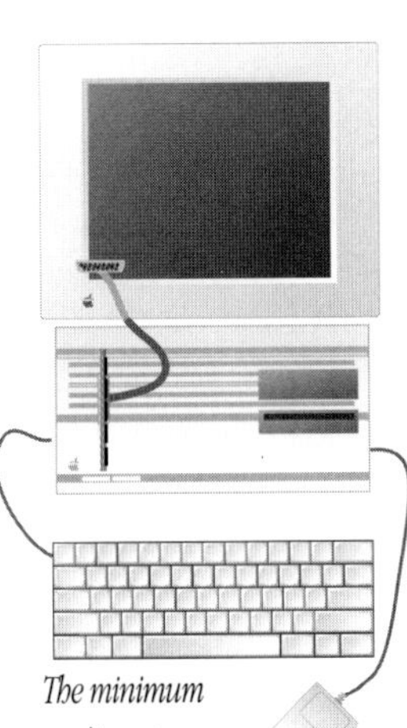

The minimum equipment you need is a CPU (computer), keyboard, monitor and video card, and possibly a pointing device (like a mouse).

What to Buy

Don't ignore your keyboard. You will spend the majority of your time interacting with your keyboard and the possibilities of straining your hands with extended use should be considered.

Only buy hardware and software that does what you need now. Don't rely on promises of future capabilities.

Consider 8-bit color the minimum if you are buying a color monitor.

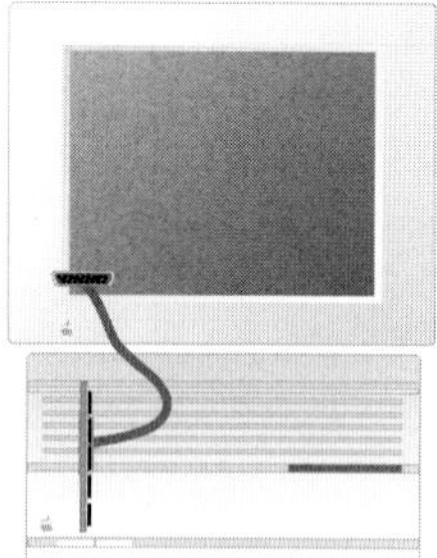

Don't buy a non-standard video card unless it's for a specific use (like CAD) that you need and know will work. Most monitors and software only support certain standards and may not work with all cards.

A workstation may need a much higher capacity hard disc (100MB–300MB) because the operating system requires so much more space than the typical personal computer.

If you are buying a portable computer, decide whether you need a transportable (a full computer that's easy to move to another spot to use), a laptop or notebook (a small computer that you can use on the go, such as on a plane or train) or a palmtop (a very small computer with limited functions, such as note–taking, address and appointment books and calendars).

Portable computers differ considerably in display quality, weight, power, battery life and features. Most can carry internal hard drives and almost all have diskette drives. Some even have internal modems and cellular modem/FAX capabilities. Make sure you understand how and when to recharge the battery and how to minimize your power consumption before your begin using one.

There is no difference between "personal" and "business" software—or hardware, for that matter. You will find that the needs you have in business are similar to those in your personal life (finances, correspondence, etc...). Some software labeled "personal" may be perfectly adequate for your business as well, whereas some software labeled "business" may have just the complement of features to organize your complex personal life. Business software does tend to have more features, but many times they are features you may never use—in business or at home. Evaluate software based on what it offers you and not how the label sells it.

Software is usually upgraded periodically with new features and capabilities. These upgrades also frequently fix problems in earlier versions. Don't think that you must use the latest, and usually more expensive, version but check to see what versions the **service bureaus** ▸10, 123 in your area currently support. Of course, if you need the capabilities in the latest version, definitely purchase it or upgrade. Registered owners of previous versions can usually purchase upgrades at a drastically reduced price. If an upgrade is announced within 90 days of your software purchase, write to the company and see if you can receive the upgrade for free (since it has been upgraded so recently).

Many computers come with software "bundled" with it. This means that it is included in the price. The system software or **operating system** ▸44–45 is mandatory and your computer is unusable without it. When you compare prices for different platforms, make sure you take into account system software, bundled applications included and other necessary equipment such as keyboards, monitors, pointing devices, etc.... One computer may look like a "deal" until you add up all the things it doesn't include.

Another necessary piece is a **video card** ▶80. In order to operate the monitor (or screen) that you buy for your computer, it may need a video card (sometimes called a graphics card). This is a board filled with **chips** ▶100 and electronics that allow your computer to communicate with the monitor. Video cards are specific to different monitors and not all monitors and video cards can be used in all computers. Some computers now have the electronics for operating a monitor built into the computer's electronics (such as the Macintosh IIci) and thus do not require a video card, but this is the exception rather than the rule. Some video cards allow you to use different types of monitors (grayscale, monochrome, color, and large sizes) with the same card so that as your needs change and you purchase a new monitor, you will not need to purchase another video card. This can be a strategic purchase.

If you are buying a color monitor, consider **8–bit color** ▶80–82 the minimum. This means that the monitor connected to it will be able to display 256 different colors at once. Anything less is not worth having color for. If you can afford it, 24 or 32–bit color will display over 16 million colors (more than your eye can differentiate) and will be a long–lasting standard.

When choosing a **monitor** ▶80–82, base your decision on the quality of the picture—much as you should when buying a television set. Is the picture sharp in all parts of the screen (including the sides and corners)? Is the picture sitting squarely in the screen or is it slightly tilted?

Other things you will need include a **keyboard** ▶80–81 and possibly a **mouse** or some other kind of **pointing device** ▶85–86. We are not yet to the era of affordable computers that do not require a keyboard. Make sure to include the price of the disk drive, keyboard, pointing device, monitor, video card and system software when comparing computer prices.

If you are buying a **modem** ▶73–74, purchase one with the highest **baud rate** ▶69 you can afford (2400 or 9600). This will save you time (not to mention patience) in transmitting data. Be careful,

72dpi 300dpi

1200dpi 2450dpi

Here are samples of the same type and images printed on four different kinds of printers. The first sample is from a 72dpi ***dot–matrix*** *printer. It is the most coarse and is not usually acceptable for business. The second is from a 300dpi laser printer. It is usually acceptable for business correspondance and proofing published pieces. The third sample is from a 1200dpi laser printer. It is possible to use this output for some publishing. The last sample is from a 2450dpi* **imagesetter** ▶86, 144. *This quality is mandatory for high–quality publishing and fine illustrations like those in this book.*

What to Buy

Don't let anyone convince you that the capabilities of Windows 3.0 are the same as the Macintosh.

There are some other great computers like the Commodore Amiga but they are not as standard, do not have as much software available for them and are not as easy to connect with other computers. However, some have specialties like multimedia, MIDI and video editing that may make them right for you.

Beware the IBM PS/1. It is expensive compared with similar systems from other manufacturers and not easily upgraded. It does come with software already installed and an easier interface than DOS, but it is not Windows 3.0 compatible.

There are many different standards for monitors and video boards in the PS/2 and IBM-compatibles. Only consider VGA or SuperVGA if you are buying a color monitor. Microchannel (MCA), EISA and AT are all standard **bus** ▶**111** *architectures but are incompatible.*

however. A few of the fastest modems may only be able to communicate at their highest speeds among themselves and not with modems from other manufacturers. A modem is only necessary if you need to send and receive information over phone lines. It is necessary if you plan to subscribe to and use an **on–line service** ▶**29**, electronic **Bulletin Board Services** ▶**29–30** or use **E-mail** ▶**28** without a network.

A **printer** ▶**12, 84–87** is a handy device, but it is also not always necessary. If you don't have a great need to print files from your computer often, you might be better off to take the money you would have spent on a printer and buy a better computer instead. Many copy stores have computers and laser printers on which you may print work. These are called **service bureaus** ▶**10, 123**. This may be a better use of your time and money. Explore the capabilities of the copy stores in your area. Which computers do they have? What software do they have? Which fonts? What are their prices?

Laser printed output is a must for professional correspondence, graphic design or desktop publishing. If you are going to do a lot of these, you will need frequent access to a laser printer. Dot–matrix printers are quickly becoming an endangered species as the prices for laser printers come down. Laser quality is so much better that you should only buy a dot–matrix printer if you absolutely cannot afford a laser printer or if the quality of the printed output is not important.

If you plan to be printing on multiple–layer forms, you will need an impact printer of some type. This may be a dot–matrix or other form of impact printer. Ask a salesman or check a buyer's guide for impact printers compatible with your computer.

When buying a printer, find out which ones are compatible with the computer you have or are buying. Not all printers work with all computers and not all printers have the same capabilities. What languages does the printer understand? If you are using **PostScript**™ ▶**12, 22–23** drawing software, a printer that doesn't understand PostScript™ will be useless. There are now PostScript clones on the market that are less expensive but generally slower. In fact, a software–based clone may be excruciatingly slow. Also, some clones may not be compatible with all equipment or be able to perform all capabilities. Have the salesperson explain and demonstrate exactly what the clone is and is not capable of. Also, have the salesperson explain how to change the ribbon or refill the toner. Changing the toner or ribbon on some printers is so complicated you may wish you hadn't bought it.

Color printers are available but are still expensive. Unless you have a lot of money, plan on using a **service bureau** ▶10 (a place that specializes in outputting computer files to color printers, slides and high–resolution output devices).

Ask the salesperson to explain what is required to set the system up and put everything together. Some systems are extremely simple to start–up with clearly labeled plugs and instructions that are easy to understand. Some also come with **hard discs** ▶62–63 formatted and **system software** ▶44–45 loaded. Other systems may require complicated attachments and software installation. Some systems come with tutorials (both software and book versions) to help you get started quickly.

When evaluating a dealer, ask them what to expect as a turn–around time when equipment is brought in for repair. Also, ask if they loan equipment out until it is repaired.

Only buy a dot–matrix printer if you cannot afford a laser printer or if output quality is not important.

Where to Buy

If you know exactly what you want, you may want to browse the advertisements in magazines for the best price. Otherwise, head straight for a dealer. There are many advantages to buying from a dealer, but keep your eyes open. Like any relationship, you need to be choosy. If the salesperson isn't making himself or herself clear, ask them to explain more carefully. If they are not interested in being clear or helpful, answering your questions, or treating you with respect, then leave. You can find a good dealer that you can begin to build a rapport with. This is strategic. A good dealer will help you make informed and appropriate decisions. They can offer you technical support, repair and service—as well as experienced advice. This is especially good if you are a novice because most manufacturers don't offer technical support or service—except through the dealer.

Many dealers also offer training courses and programs. If you find you just aren't getting the hang of the computer after you've bought it, this may be a wise investment.

Another avenue through which to buy a computer (and especially software and peripherals) is a mail order house. These usually offer the best prices, but they probably don't offer technical support or advice. They advertise in the trade magazines which you

Where to buy computer hardware and software:

- *Computer Store (dealer)*
- *Mail Order*
- *Want Ads (used)*
- *On–line ads*
- *Electronics Store*

Dealer prices should be between 10% and 15% over mail order prices. If higher, they better have fantastic service. A dealer's higher prices are worth it if they help you install the equipment or software and show you how to use it.

You can usually find great dealers close to a university or major college.

Where to Get Information

When ordering equipment or software by mail, get a list of exactly what components will be included (especially if it is a computer), keep all of your receipts and ask about the return policy. Most mail order firms have next-day delivery service and some even have same-day (although this is very expensive). Ask about your shipping options, and if you need anything to make the equipment or software work properly (like special attachments, cables, connectors or more software). If you do not receive what you ordered or it is damaged, refuse to accept it and call the mail order firm immediately. If you order by credit card, you have some additional protection if things don't work out because you can have your credit company help resolve any difficulties.

can purchase at any newsstand. Small ads in magazines and local newspapers are more risky. They may not have a refund policy or may not be accountable for faulty or wrong merchandise. Unless you have some experience, beware the ones that offer incredible prices for things—especially for RAM chips (**SIMMs** ▸105). These may not work properly or may be the wrong type for your computer and there may be no way to get your money back. If you do order something by mail, check the shipment when it arrives. If it is damaged, refuse to accept it and call the mail order house immediately. Also, remember that *lifetime warranty* only means *lifetime of the company that sells it.*

The support and information a good dealer can provide can be worth the higher price a dealer charges over a wholesaler or mail order house.

If you are buying on a budget (like most people), look in the want ads for used equipment. Evaluate it as if you were buying a used car—try it out, ask lots of questions, and look for any outward signs of damage or misuse. Many people sell their computers when new models arrive to get the latest and greatest and you can find some terrific bargains this way (if the used machine meets your needs). Also, there may be upgrade components that will allow you to upgrade an older machine to a newer, comparable model for a lot less.

If this is your first computer purchase, the want ads may not be a good place for you to buy. There are plenty of good deals in the want ads, but unless you already know something about computers, it is too easy to end up with something that doesn't fit your needs or a machine that is in bad condition. If you already have a computer and are thinking about selling it and buying a newer one, advertise in the want ads, on college bulletin boards, in college papers, and on electronic bulletin boards.

Department stores buy computers in volume and sometimes offer great deals if you know what you want and they carry it. The problem here is that there are rarely knowledgeable people on hand to help you make your decision and they usually offer terrible service (if any at all).

One of the best sources for information is the advice of an experienced friend, but be careful because his or her needs may not be the same as yours. Reviews in magazines are the next best source for information. See if any of the popular magazines has a review of the equipment or software you are interested in. Most magazines publish an index to the year's stories in December or January issues. Also, most libraries have indexes of many magazine stories on microfiche.

Where to Get Information

User groups can be a great resource for you whether you are a novice or expert. Most areas have groups of computer users that meet periodically to discuss equipment and software, offer support and advice, and sometimes offer discounts on software. Most user groups have libraries of shared software (called **shareware** ▸37–38) that are available to members. Try looking in local computer magazines for listings of user groups or ask a dealer. A user group is a great opportunity to make connections with knowledgeable people who have similar interests. If you make a commitment to participate you will build some valuable respect from the members but if you expect to just show up and get free help and free software you won't get very far.

There is an enormous amount of literature on computers. The best for evaluating systems are the trade magazines and buyer's guides. If you feel a little unsure of yourself, you might pick up a few magazines and read the articles to learn more about what products are available. Some good ones are listed in the **bibliography** ▸130.

Trade shows are another good source of information. These are usually held in major urban areas once a year. There are booths of companies offering software, hardware and services all in one place. Of course, the most difficult problem is trying to see everything and battle the crowds. They can be tiring but exciting and informative.

Good sources for information about computers:

- *Friends*
- *Co-workers*
- *User Groups*
- *Computer Magazines*
- *Dealers*

If you decide to buy a used computer, a good source is the Boston Computer Exchange. This is a group that helps match buyers and sellers. Ads with the group cost $10.00 and they take ten percent of the sale as a commission. They can tell you what the going rate is for your system and can be reached at:

PO Box 177
Boston, MA 02103
617 542-4412

Other Considerations

Warranties are important, but a manufacturer with a good reputation is better than one with a long warranty. Most hardware manufacturers have similar warranties anyway. A one year warranty should be the minimum you consider. Satisfaction warranties can be useful for software (in case you find out the software you've bought is of little use to you) but any other kind is pointless—software doesn't wear out as hardware does.

Other Considerations

We cannot stress enough the need for enough **RAM** ▶104 *memory in your computer. Not only can it allow you to open large files and run sophisticated software, but to some extent it can make your computer perform faster. Usually software publishers give minimum RAM requirements but these may be excruciatingly slow. Count on needing about twice the amount their minimums state. Fortunately, RAM is getting less expensive but it is still more expensive than storage memory such as a diskette or hard disc.*

Because the information on a disk is stored magnetically, you should protect your data by keeping your disks away from sources of magnetic fields. These include magnets, stereos, motors, television, and power supplies. Do not lay your disk down on your monitor or computer. And of course, keep liquid, dust and direct sunlight from your disks as well.

Beware of **beta software** ▶36. This is software that is still in the process of being developed and while it probably won't ruin your system, you may lose some information. Only experienced users should fool around with beta–software and never let someone convince you to buy it.

Many applications now come with **tutorials** and templates that help you learn how to use the software. These can be real aides for inexperienced users. Some companies offer free **demos** that run on your computer to show you what their software can do and how it works. This is usually only for sophisticated software. They will not let you actually work (or save your work) so you are not getting the software for free. However, they are great tools to help you evaluate if the software will meet your needs. Contact the manufacturer to see if they offer demos of the applications you are interested in.

There are also many ways to get training for different computers or specific applications. Most community colleges offer courses in the most popular applications and systems. Also, many user groups and community organizations offer training. You can find out about these in local computer magazines or from knowledgeable dealers in your area.

With software, you actually purchase a *right* to perpetually *use* the application, not the actual **source code**.

Many applications are **copy–protected.** This means that measures have been taken to prevent users from using unauthorized copies. Many of these measures can make the software bothersome to use—even if you legally own the right to use it. Software copying is illegal if you don't actually own the code (this goes for applications, utilities, and fonts, as well). Because software is so easy to copy, you are, basically, on an honor system. Definitely make a back–up copy (for your own use) and store it in a safe place, but giving it to a friend is not acceptable. Legally, every computer must have a separate, purchased copy of every piece of software (unless the software is **freeware** ▶37–38). There are few exceptions. If you have many machines that use the same software, call the manufacturer and ask about **site–licensing**. This will allow you to get a volume discount.

Many manufacturers do not offer **technical support** if you have a problem. They rely on the dealer to help you (if you bought through a dealer). If you bought your computer through some other means, a dealer may or may not help you. User groups usually can help you with many problems (as well as offer advice). If you are calling a software manufacturer for technical support, check your **manuals** thoroughly before you call to make sure the answer isn't there somewhere. When you call, make sure you know exactly what kind of software and hardware you are using and what versions of software (especially system software) are installed on your machine.

Buying a computer is an important process, but a valuable and, hopefully, exciting one. No matter what computer you finally buy, subscribe to a good computer magazine and seek out others who use similar equipment and are doing similar things. The connections you make with others can be sometimes more important and more rewarding than those you make with your computer.

After You Buy

Chances are that you will never think about computer **repairs** ▸18 until your computer needs fixing. While computers are getting more reliable everyday, there are things you can do to prevent most problems. First, fill out and send in all of your product registration cards. This will mean you will start to get a lot of annoying junk mail, but you will also receive information on upgrades and repairs.

There are a few accessories you might consider for your computer. A **surge protector** isolates your computer from problems in your home or office power system such as voltage spikes. Computers are more sensitive to power irregularities than appliances. Power supply in urban areas tends to be more stable and regular, but if you live in a remote area, the little expense for a surge protector could save you a great deal of money and heartache if something should happen.

Most computers have some sort of vents or fan to cool the computer circuits. These vents should not be covered so that air can get through, but with air comes dust. It is a good idea to keep a **dust cover** over your computer when it is not in use.

If your computer does get dusty or dirty you can do most of the cleaning yourself. The **screen** will constantly attract dust because it has a negative charge when it is on. Use a slightly damp rag but don't use a window cleaner solution. Never spray anything directly on the screen or use anything abrasive.

The protection that surge protectors offer does not last forever. It wears out over time and, unfortunately, cannot be checked easily.

Save the cartons and packaging your equipment comes in. If you move, you'll want to pack it into the original packaging to keep it safe during transport.

After You Buy

If the company you shipped your equipment to for repairs goes bankrupt (and it has happened before), take a deep breath and remain cool. Many times this will make it difficult to get your equipment back—repaired or not. If you can manage to contain your anger and frustration when dealing with representatives from the company, you will get a lot further. Remember that they are just as angry and frustrated. Try to talk to the manager and be ***very*** *persistent. Try to be extra nice to those you speak with (chances are they are not to blame for the company's failing) and offer to make compromises. Offer to pay postage and only send copies of receipts. Be creative. Sending a batch of cookies is bound to put them on your side and keep you in their minds. Remember, getting your equipment back is important and may take a lot of work.*

The **keyboard** is a problem because of all the tiny openings facing up. If you don't drink or eat over your keyboard, you should be fine. If anything wet does fall into the keyboard turn your computer off immediately, unplug your keyboard, turn it upside down and let it drain. Take your keyboard into a dealer or service center and have them clean it. A glass of lemonade is probably not covered by your warranty.

You can clean your computer by wiping it down with a slightly damp rag. A light glass cleaner is probably fine for cleaning, but don't spray anything directly on the computer and only clean it when it's off.

Use a **screen saver**. This software will automatically blank out the screen on your monitor (or put on some pattern) after a specific interval of inactive time. If the same image remains on your computer for a long time the image could burn into your screen. This will result in a permanent ghost image.

Shelter the computer from direct sunlight as it will add to the heating problems of the circuits and eventually fade the plastic. Also, prevent any hard shocks to the computer such as dropping it or anything onto it. Remember that the **hard drive** ▶62–63 is spinning at 3600RPM and 2 microns from the drive head. Any sharp bump to the computer (or even the table) could cause it to crash.

After a few years, think about purchasing a self–cleaning device for your diskette drive. The device will look like a standard disk and will clean the drive heads when inserted into your computer.

Most computer warranties last one year. If you depend on your computer everyday you may consider getting an **extended warranty** to cover your computer beyond the typical coverage. Some warranties include loaner systems if yours must sit in the repair shop for days. Check them out carefully. It might be a good idea to get an extended warranty on a **monitor** because they are expensive to repair.

Repairs

If something does go wrong with your system, stay calm. Almost anything can be repaired. The first thing to do is to consult the troubleshooting section of your computer's **manual**. Sometimes the problem can be fixed simply by restarting the computer. There are also many **utility applications** ▶18 that can help your retreive lost data in the event of a disk crash or if you accidentally erased something.

If you have a software problem call your dealer—many

problems can be solved over the phone. If you have a hardware problem (broken part, shorted keyboard, etc...) call your dealer and make an appointment to bring your system in. It is a good idea to bring in everything so that your dealer can see it connected and working together (sometimes what appears to be a problem in one thing turns out to be a problem in something else). Some problems the dealer can fix on the spot and others will require you to leave it for a diagnosis. Tell your dealer if the data on the hard drive is backed–up or not and if the computer has had any other problems.

It is usually less expensive to replace parts than to try and fix them (if it is even possible).

The biggest risk with equipment failure isn't the destruction of the equipment but important data that may be impossible to replace. Backing–up data regularly is the best way to ensure that data is secure.

Software problems may be easier to fix. Sometimes, different pieces of software conflict with each other. The remedy may be to not use them together or to take one out entirely. Call the software publisher after your have thoroughly explored the software manual for an answer. A lot of software is shipped with small **bugs** (problems) that may occur from time to time. The publisher may have a fixed version already out or planned. If not, you may have to wait for the next major revision of the software. Stay in contact with the publisher and make sure they know about the bugs you have found.

Serious problems are fairly rare but minor ones are bound to occur. If you can manage to keep your calm and you sense of humor, you will probably find many people willing to help you.

Books

Alan Turing, The Enigma
Andrew Hodges © 1984
Touchstone, Simon & Shuster, Inc.
New York City, NY
ISBN 0–671–52809–2
Biography, Alan Turing, History
This is a great account of the life and works of one of the most important and tragic pioneers of computers. It builds a good understanding of how important and innovative Turing's developments were in his day.

The Art of Human–Computer Interface Design
Ed. Brenda Laurel © 1991
Apple Computer & Addison–Wesley, NY
ISBN 0–201–51797–3
User Interface Design
This is the best book on current thinking and technology regarding interface design. The articles cover the latest theories and are written with style and life.

Computer Comfort
Melissa Mayfield ©1990
1117 Woodland Ave, Menlo Park, CA
Ergonomics, Computer Injuries, VLF Radiation
This is a well–written and presented book and HyperCard stack explaining computer–related injuries and how to prevent them.

The Computer Glossary—7th Edition
Alan Freedman, ©1989
The Computer Language Company, Inc. & Prentice Hall
ISBN 0–941878–02–3, 0–13–1644831

Computer Models of the Mind
Margaret A. Boden, ©1988
Cambridge University Press, Cambridge, MA
IBSN 0–521–27033–2

Computer Lib/Dream Machines
Ted Nelson, Microsoft Press
ISBN 0–914845–49–7
General and Personal Computing
This self–published book has turned more people on to computers than perhaps any other. It is rich, weird, informative, wild and always fascinating. You may be bewildered at first but this book is very personal and actually reads fairly easily.

Computer Pioneers
Laura Green, ©1985
ISBN 0–531–04906–X
Biographies, History

The Computer Pioneers: The Making of the Modern Computer
David Richie ©1986
Simon and Shuster, New York CIty, NY
ISBN 0–671–52397–X
Biographies, History
This book is a great account of the history of those who made computers a reality. It is filled with interesting and obscure information on these personalities and how they accomplished what they have.

A Computer Perspective
Charles and Ray Eames ©1973
Harvard University Press, Cambridge, MA, **ISBN 674–15626–9**
Timelines, History, Technology
This remarkable book is a historical account of achievements in the computer world from the beginning to 1973. Organized as a timeline, it includes fantastic information and visual references to events.

Computer Power and Human Reason: From Judgement to Calculation
Joseph Meizenbaum (author of ELIZA), ©1976, W.H.Freeman, San Francisco, CA **ISBN 0–7167–0463–3**
Artificial Intelligence

The Cuckoo's Egg
Clifford Stoll, ©1990, Pocket Books, NY, **ISBN 0–671–72688–9**
Computer Crime, Security
This is an exiciting and true story about an astronomer tracking a German "cracker" invading some of the most sensitive research labs, corporate centers and military bases in the United States. It is an extraordinary and detailed account and very well told.

Cyberpunk
Katherine Hafner and John Markoff ©1991, Simon and Shuster
ISBN 0–671–68322–5
Computer Crime, Security
This is an intriguing book on three contemporary cases of computer crime. While it is very clear in the language used who the authors liked and didn't like, the accounts are extremely detailed. These cases of three different groups of "crackers" are probably only prophecies of more to come.

The Difference Engine
William Gibson and Bruce Sterling
©1990, **ISBN 0–553–07028–2**
Science Fiction, History, Society
This science fiction novel poses the question: "What would the world be like if Charles Babbage was successful in developing the first computer in the 1820s?" It does an interesting job of answering it and has some good insights about how computers fit into our own society today.

The Elements of Friendly Software Design—Second Edition
Paul Heckel © 1991
SYBEX, Alameda, CA
ISBN 0–89588–768–1
User Interface Design, Copyrights
This is probably the best introduction to user interface design for anyone new to the field. It covers most of the important issues with clarity and good examples. The section at the end on Mr. Heckel's own copyright battles are particularly interesting.

Godel, Echer, Bach: The Eternal Golden Braid, Douglas R. Hofstader, ©1989, Basic Books, New York City, NY, **ISBN 0–394–75682–7**
Artificial Intelligence, Mathematics
This fascinating but difficult book lays some of the groundwork for a thorough understanding of artificial intelligence and parallel processing. Its style and format are enjoyable but the discussions are complex and daunting for anyone new to these topics.

High Tech, Window to the Future
Gene Bylinksky, Charles O'Rear and Lawrence Bender ©1985
Intercontinental Publishing Corp. Ltd., Hong Kong, **ISBN 0–962276–001–5**
Biographies, History, Technology
This book is filled with beautiful photos and interesting information about the personalities and companies responsible for the computer industry in Silicon Valley.

Historical Dictionary of Data Processing: Biographies
James W. Cortada, ©1987,
Greenwood Press, New York
ISBN 0–313–25651–9
Biographies

The Home Computer Revolution
Ted Nelson ©1977
distributed by The Distributors,
South Bend, Indiana
General and Personal Computing

Macintosh Bible—3rd Edition
Sharon Z. Aker and Arthur Naiman
©1990, **ISBN 0–940235–12–9**
General Computer, Macintosh
This book is specific to Macintosh computers but there is really nothing else like it. It is extremely easy to read and learn from and even comes with free updates.

Neurocomputing: Foundations of Research
James Anderson and Edward Rosenfeld, ©1988, MIT Press, Cambridge, MA **ISBN 0–262–51048–0**
Artificial Intelligence, Neural Networks

The New Alchemists: Silicon Valley and the Microelectronics Revolution
Dick Hanson, ©1982, Little, Brown, Boston, MA
History, Technology, Biographies

Portraits in Silicon
Robert Slater, ©1987 MIT Press
ISBN 0–262–69131–0
Biographies, History

Secret Guide to Computers, 14th Ed.
Russ Walter © 1990
TEL 617 666 2666
ISBN 0–939151–14–6
General Computing, Components and Computer Platforms
This incredible and overpowering guide is written and self–published by an amazing man. He covers historical and contemporary information on all aspects of personal computers—and more. He also makes himself available for technical assistance by phone at all hours and every day.

Tools for Thought
Howard Reingold ©1985
Simon and Shuster, New York City, NY
ISBN 0–671–49292–6
Society and Technology
Howard Reingold writes in a rich and informative way. The issues he raises and the topics he discusses are well–covered and interesting.

Note: If you are looking for the book entitled ***The Little Mac Book*** *(a terrific beginner book for Macintosh users), be careful to get the right one. There are two different books by the same title with the same price, but written by two different authors and published by two very different publishers. The original one (and the one most people mean when recommending it) is written by* ***Robin Williams*** *and published by Peachpit Press.*

Pamphlets

Improving VDT Work—The Report Store
$15.00
TEL (913) 842.7348
Ergonomics, ELF Radiation
This is a report on how to minimize your exposure to emissions from video display terminals and cathode ray tubes.

The VDT Book: A Computer Guide to Health
$6.00, New York Commitee for Occupational Health and Safety, 275 7th Avenue, New York City, NY 10001
Ergonomics, ELF Radiation
Another guide to the topic of lowering exposure to electromagnetic radiation from monitors.

Understanding Computers Series
Time–Life Books, Alexandria, VA
General Computing, Components, Technology
This series of computer books is a first–rate and exhaustive source of explanations of the most important aspects of computers. Because of the size of this series, the information is much more in–depth than we could hope to provide. This is a good place to start if you are interested in learning more about almost anything you read in this book. Your local library should already have this series.

Magazines

Byte
Monthly
McGraw Hill Information Services
This is a great monthly magazine that discusses issues about the world of computers: new products, special topics, technology, cultural issues, etc.... It is not oriented toward users of any particular family of computers.

Computerworld
Weekly
IDG Communications
This magazine can easily overpower someone with its amount of information. It covers all types of computers from personal to mainframes and tracks developments in many differect fields. It is not specific enough for most readers, but if you want to follow the computer industry, this is a good start.

Computer Currents
Every Two Weeks
IDG Communications
This free magazine can be found in computer stores and newspaper racks in major metropolitan areas. It has timely information and many ads for bargain equipment. It is a great source to find user groups, swap meets and BBSs in your area.

Infoworld
Monthly
IDG Communications
This magazine covers news on almost every aspect of the computer industry: articles of general interest as well as technological advances, business and communications, but concentrates on the workstation market.

MacUser
Monthly
Ziff Davis Publishing
Another monthly Macintosh magazine, MacUser tends to be more *how–to* oriented (both for novices and experts) and carries more product comparisons but less in–depth information than MacWorld. Both MacUser and MacWorld actually complement each other as Macintosh sources.

MacWEEK
Weekly
Ziff Davis Publishing
This is a weekly magazine for the Macintosh community and focuses on business and industry information. MacWeek specializes in late–breaking news and rumors of up–coming products. It is a good source for current information but it isn't geared toward new users.

MacWorld
Monthly
IDG Communications
This is a great magazine for anyone with a Macintosh computer (or interested in one.) MacWorld has product comparisons and articles on a broad range of computer issues. The editorials tend to whine, but the information is invaluable.

Microtimes
Every Two Weeks
BAM Publications Inc.
This free magazine is similar to *Computer Currents* in topics, but covers less popular computers as well (Amiga and others).

NewMedia Age
Monthly
Hypermedia Communications
TEL 415 573 5131
This is an informative slice of articles concentrating on multimedia computing and products. It includes insightful reviews and editorials.

NeXTWorld
Quarterly
IDG Communications
This is **the** source of information on everything happening in the NeXT community.

PC/Computing
Monthly
Ziff Davis Publishing
Another good monthly PC magazine similar to *PC World*.

PC Letter
TEL 415–592–9192
This magazine covers major shifts in the PC industry, news, new products, business method, financial trends, and both industry and computer perspectives of current events.

PC Magazine
Monthly
Ziff Davis Publishing
Another good monthly PC magazine similar to *PC World*.

PCWeek
Weekly
Ziff Davis Publishing
Like MacWeek, this weekly magazine covers current business and industry information related to IBM PCs and clones. Again, this is not really for new users or those not interested in the computer industry.

PC World
Monthly
IDG Communications
This monthly magazine is the main source of information for IBM PCs and clones. It is very similar to MacWorld in the information and topics it covers (but for PCs instead of Macintoshes).

Publish
Monthly
PCW Communications
501 Second Street
This is a good magazine concentrating only on the developments of computers and technology in the desktop publishing industry. It covers both IBM PC and Macintosh computers, equipment and software.

Newsletters

BCS Update
Monthly
Boston Computer Society, Inc.
TEL 617–367–8080
A general personal computer magazine that features articles on microcomputers and its workings, software, product development, and interviews.

BMUG Newsletter
Semi–Annually
Berkeley Macintosh Users Group
Although there are many user groups for different computers across the country, BMUG is a standard with which to measure all others. Their newsletter is now more of a catalog and directly filled with advice, recommendations, insight, reviews and tips. It is directed only at Macintosh computers, but there should be similar offerings from user groups that focus on PCs, Amigas, NeXTs, or other equipment. These are usually the best information your money can buy on any budget.

Business Week Newsletter for Information Executives
Semi–Monthly
McGraw–Hill, Inc.
This is a well written, but very expensive ($495/year) newsletter that highlights major trends and important information. Only industry professionals or corporate libraries should worry about a subscription, though.

Electronic Frontier Foundation News
TEL (617) 864.0665
Internet: effnews–request@eff.org
This is a newsletter that concentrates on the coming electronic village and the impacts it is having on our society. EFF tracks law suits related to computers and technology, violations of constitutional rights and other social problems resulting in a rapidly changing technocracy.

Seybold Outlook on Professional Computing
Monthly
Seybold Group
FAX 408–746–2448
Like the Business Week Newsletter, this report is equally well–written, slightly less expensive and covers the same, basic topics. Seybold also offers two other reports highlighting the electronic publishing and digitial media industries.

Almost all of the magazines listed here, as well as many of the books, should be available at your local library.

A card or board that can be placed into a computer to improve the performance of the CPU.

Active Matrix (Liquid Crystal Display) A special type of LCD display used in **flatscreen** displays that incorporates a **transistor** at each **pixel** for fine, fast control.

The specific location of a byte of data kept in a computer's memory.

Algorithm
A specific approach to a problem or a step–by–step procedure in software to accomplish a task.

Analog
Any physical property indexed, controlled, or represented by another physical property capable of representing it accurately. Usually refers to a system that codes data by measuring voltages, rather than discrete signals (digitally).
Analog Computer
A computer that manipulates and represents data by some physical means other than digital (such as variable voltage or turning gears).

A software program that performs a specific task, such as word–processing, database management, etc....

The study of how to make computers do things that, traditionally, people are better at. Aspects of certain software that allow a computer to "think", "learn" and make decisions or mimic lower forms of human intelligence.

(American Standard Code for Information Interchange) A system used to represent letters, numbers, symbols, and punctuation as **bytes** of **binary** signals (1s and 0s).

A unit of measure of data transmission approximately equal to bits per second.

(electronic Bulletin Board Service)

A period near the end of the software development cycle used to work out problems before the software is released for general distribution.

A system with only two possible states, such as on or off, 1 or 0, high and low.

A CPU th t is similar to another CPU at its most basic level. This means that software running one would have no trouble running on the other.

The smallest unit of data in a computer (or any digital machine) symbolized as either a 1 or a 0 and represents a pulse of electricity (voltage) in the circuits.

A display in which each pixel on a screen is represented in RAM with a special bit or group of bits in data.

A system of mathematics that represents logical expressions, such as NOT, OR, AND, etc... in the circuits of a computer. Developed by the mathematician George Boole in 1854.

A problem or incompatibility in hardware or software. Originated from the Mark I computer program at Harvard. Moths would be attracted to the vacuum tubes and cause them to burn out, stopping the computer.

Wiring or cables that carry signals around inside a computer, or between computers and other devices.

A measure of data equal to eight **bits**.

A portion of memory or disk space set aside for quick access to the most recently used data by the processor.

Computer–Aided Design is a category of applications used to design and develop products and buildings on a computer.

(Computer–Aided Engineering)

CalTech ▶112
CAM ▶19
Computer–Aided Manufacturing is a category of applications used to control machine tools and manufacturing equipment with computers in order to produce products designed with computers.
Camera–ready art ▶24
Artwork that is ready to make photographic negatives for printing plates.
Card ▶21, 23
Carpal–Tunnel Syndrome ▶41
A repeptitive–strain disorder that affects the wrist and hand and can cause permanent damage if not treated.
Cartridges ▶63, 66, 144
A high–volume form of removable storage.
CAT ▶19
(Computer–Aided Testing.)
Cathode Ray Tube ▶41–42, 80, 113–115
See CRT
Cellular Modem ▶74
A device that allows a computer to connect with other computers over cellular telephone systems.
CD–I
(Compact Disc–Interactive) A format for storing different types of information (graphics, video, sound, text...) in a compatible form on a compact disc.
CD–ROM ▶25, 65–66, 106
(Compact Disc–Read Only Memory) A format for storing information digitally on a compact disc.
Chip ▶43, 47, 50, 97, 103, 106, 121
An integrated circuit, usually manufactured on a very small piece of silicon that contains **transistors**, **logic gates**, and other electronics.
Circuit ▶91, 97
A route for electricity to flow through.
Circuit Board ▶43
A board that holds chips and other electronic components connected by circuits that carry signals between them.
CISC ▶101
(Complex Instruction Set Chip)
Clock ▶100, 109–110
An electronic component that emits consistent signals, like a metronome, that paces a computer's operations.
Clock channel ▶111
Clock cycle ▶110
Clocking ▶109–110
Clock speed ▶100–101, 103
Clones ▶118
CLUT ▶81, 82
(Color Look–Up Table)
CMOS ▶99
(Complementary Metal Oxide Semiconductor) A low–power **semiconductor** device that contains both p–type and n–type **transistors**.
CMYK color model ▶81, 82
(Cyan, Magenta, Yellow, blacK)
COBOL (Computer Language) ▶52, 55
COLOSSUS ▶55
Command ▶57-58
An instruction to the computer from either the user or software.
Command Line Interface ▶75–76
Commodore Amiga ▶122
Communications Application ▶17, 27
Compiler ▶53, 55, 57, 102
A piece of software that translates instructions written in a high–level language into a lower–level language or machine language so that the processor can understand them.
Compression Utilities ▶23, 28
Applications that squeeze data into smaller files by coding them into special formats that take less space.
Computer
A programmable (changeable) device that accepts input, manipulates data and outputs data in some form.
Conductor (Electrical) ▶94–95
Control channel ▶111
Coprocessor ▶46, 102, 108
An extra processor designed to process specific tasks for the central processor.
Copy–protection ▶36, 126
Copyright laws ▶35–36, 40
Core
An ancient term for a ring of metal (traditionally ferrite) that hangs at the juncture of two wires and was the basis of computer memory for many years.
CPU ▶45, 50, 100–102, 104, 108, 112
(Central Processing Unit) The basic "chip" that processes the instructions in a computer. A CPU consists of a logic unit, a control unit, a clock, and memory. Also called a **processor**.
Crash ▶18, 63
Crosstalk ▶112
CRT ▶41–42, 80, 113–115
(Cathode Ray Tube) A popular type of display that shoots electrons through a tube to a phosphorescent screen to display information (like a television set).
Cursor ▶83–84
A symbol on a computer screen that acts as a pointer for some action taking place.
DARPA ▶35
DAT drives ▶66
Data ▶52
Data channel ▶111
A wiring system used to transmit data between different components in a computer.
Data compression ▶23, 28
See **Compression Utilities**
Data integrity ▶112
Database ▶17, 21–25, 29, 48, 77
An organized set of data with structured routines for storing and retrieving.
Database Publishing ▶24
Dealers (Computer) ▶123–124
Deallocation ▶45
The process in which the **operating system** clears **RAM** memory to make room for new data.
Demonstrations (of software) ▶126
Desktop Publishing ▶10, 13, 20, 86
Difference Engine ▶93
Digital ▶14, 94, 104
A system of discrete symbols used to represent and manipulate data.
Digital Computer
A computer that represents and manipulates data in discrete increments.

Digital to Analog Conversion (DAC) ▸97

Digitize
To convert or represent data (such as a picture, sound, text, etc...) in digital form.

Directory ▸59, 62, 65

Disc ▸47, 62, 76
A plate of magnetic material used to store data in digital form.

Disc Drive ▸62
The physical mechanism that accepts, reads and writes data to a disc or diskette.

Disc Recovery Utility ▸62

Disk ▸21, 59, 66, 70, 106, 108, 119
Short for diskette, an easily transportable disc.

Display ▸47, 75, 80
Another term for *monitor* or computer screen.

Dither ▸81, 86
A way of assigning colors to **pixels** in order to display an image with fewer colors than it requires.

DMA (Direct Memory Access) ▸102, 106, 111

Document
Anything you create with an application that resides in the computer. Normally refers to a file created with a word processing or page–layout application.

Doping ▸95, 97, 99
The process of adding impurities to a substance to change its characteristics.

DOS ▸118–119, 122
(Disk Operating System) This operating system was developed in 1981 by Microsoft Corp. and is the standard operating system for IBM–compatible personal computers (also called MS–DOS for Microsoft–DOS).

Dot–Matrix printer ▸84–85, 121–122

Double–Page Display ▸80

Douglas Engelbart ▸35, 78

Double–Sided Diskette ▸59

DPI (Dots per Inch) ▸84, 88
This is a measure or resolution or detail used for screens (*monitors*) and printers.

DRAM ▸105
(Dynamic Random Access Memory) A form of RAM that requires continuous electricity to keep its contents stored and intact.

Drawing Application ▸11

Dust Cover ▸127

Dvorak Keyboard ▸78

Dye Sublimation Printer ▸86

Dynabook ▸35

Education Applications ▸17

Edutainment ▸15
Combining important information with exciting ways of presenting it.

EEPROM ▸105–106
(Electrically Erasable Programmable Read–Only Memory) The data stored within these **ROM** chips can be erased and replaced with new data by applying an electric current.

Electroluminescent Display ▸115

Electromechanical
Anything composed of both electronics and mechanical (physical, moving) parts.

Electron ▸99, 113–114
A particle of matter that affects electricity and electrical current.

Electronic Frontier Foundation ▸40
An organization dedicated to protecting the electronic and first–amendment rights of the public.

Electronics
Components that use electrical voltage to represent data and manipulate signals.

ELF) Extremely Low–Frequency Magnetic Fields ▸41, 113

E–mail
(Electronic Mail) The process of sending and receiving messages via computers.

Encapsulated PostScript (EPS) ▸23, 142

Engelbart, Douglas ▸35, 78

ENIAC ▸50
(Electronic Numerical Integrator And Computer) Built in 1946 at the University of Pennsylvania, this was one of the first electronic computers.

Entertainment Applications ▸13

EPROM ▸37, 106
(Erasable Programmable Read–Only Memory) The data stored within these **ROM** chips can be erased with ultra–violet light.

Erasable Optical Disk ▸66–67
A portable, erasable disk that uses both magnetic and optical technology to read and write data.

Ergonomics ▸39
The study of fitting equipment to people so that it is easier to use and does not cause harm to users.

Ethernet ▸73
A network of high–speed transmission cables and software.

Expert System ▸33–34
An area of **Artificial Intelligence** that allows a computer to make decisions based on a set of organized rules created from a **knowledge base** about a particular subject.

Eyestrain ▸40

FAX Modem ▸74

Fiber Optics
Thin glass fibers that carry digital signals in fast pulses of light much like wires carry electricity.

File ▸76
Distinct data created with an application and stored in computer memory.

File Format ▸5, 19, 22–23, 85, 88

File Server ▸71, 73

Film Recorder ▸10, 12

Firmware ▸50, 101
Internal software in chips that control the operations of that chip.

Flat File Database ▸21

Flat Screen ▸114–115

Flat–Bed Plotter ▸87

Floating–Point Calculations ▸58

Floppy Disk ▸59
A transportable, light–weight diskette with a flexible disc encased in either a flexible or rigid plastic case. See *diskette* or *disc*.

Flash Memory ▸105
Electronic memory similar to RAM that does not erase when the power is turned off.

Floptical
A portable, erasable magnetic disc using optics to track data stored magnetically.

Flowchart ▶58
A diagram of a piece of software's problem–solving process.
Fonts ▶11–12, 85–86, 143
Formatting (Diskettes) ▶60
FORTRAN (computer language) ▶55, 59
Forums (electronic) ▶30
FPU (Floating–Point Processor) ▶102
Fractals
Mathematically–generated shapes that can resemble the characteristics of random, real–world elements.
Fragmentation (disc) ▶18
Freeware ▶30, 37–38, 126
Function Keys ▶19, 81
GaAs ▶99
Games (computer) ▶13
Gateway ▶72
Gigabyte (GB)
A unit of memory measure equal to 1024 megabytes (1,073,741, 824 bytes).
Goldberg, Adele ▶35
Grammar Checker ▶8
Graphics Accelerator ▶82, 121
Graphics Pad ▶83
Grayscale ▶23, 80–82, 87–88
Levels of gray and not just black or white.
Groupware ▶27, 68–69
Software that allows several people working on the same things to better interact and communicate.
GUI ▶35, 76, 79, 82–83, 119
(Graphic–User Interface) A type of interface between the user and computer that represents processes and objects as visual symbols in a two–dimensional environment.
Hacker
Someone who is devoted to writing software or experimenting with the workings of a computer. Often used *inaccurately* to mean someone who uses computers mischievously.
Hand–Writing Recognition ▶9
Hard Disc ▶18, 29, 60–63, 66, 73
A magnetic disc for storing data.
Hard Drive ▶60–63, 106, 108, 119, 128
A device that stores and reads data on a magnetic disc.
Hard Error ▶60–61
A physical irregularity in a disc or diskette that prevents data from being magnetically stored in that spot.
Hardware ▶36, 116, 120
The physical parts of a computer.
Hex (Hexadecimal) ▶55, 90
A coding system with sixteen discrete symbols (0–9, A–F) used to write software.
HDTV
(High Definition TV) A new format for broadcast television that allows increased resolution and better sound.
HIFF ▶23
High–Level Language (computer) ▶52, 56
High–Density Diskette ▶60
Holiday, Stephen ▶78
Host Identification ▶34
HyperCard™ ▶25
Hypercube ▶112
HyperTalk™ ▶53
Hypertext/Hypermedia
▶23, 24–26, 29–30, 35, 78
Software that allows users to explore and create their own path through written, visual and audio information. Capabilities include being able to jump from topic to topic at any time and follow cross–references easily.
IBM PS/1, PS/2 ▶122
Icon ▶76
A graphic or pictographic symbol used to represent an abstract or concrete object or process in the computer.
Image Manipulation ▶11, 107, 142
Imagesetter ▶10, 12, 86, 121, 144
Industrial Applications ▶20
Inference engine
The part of an **expert system** that contains the logic with which a computer makes decisions using information from the knowledge base.
Infotainment ▶13, 17
Initialization (diskettes, discs) ▶60
Ink–Jet Printer ▶85
Combining important information with exciting ways of presenting it.
Input ▶57
Data entered into a computer, or the process of entering such data.
Input/Output (I/O) port ▶47–48, 102, 107
A component on a circuit board that allows input or output devices to be attached and through which data flows.
Instruction ▶51, 53-54, 106, 108–109
An order to the CPU to perform a task (usually consists of a basic operation). Sets of instructions form the basis for programs and other software.
Instruction Decoder ▶100–101
Integer Calculations ▶57-58
Integrated Circuit (IC) ▶56
Electronic circuits manufactured on a single, very small piece of material, usually silicon, from a variety of layers of metals.
Integrated Packages ▶17
Interactive ▶14–15, 18
Software that responds quickly to certain choices and commands a user makes.
Interface ▶26, 119
Interlaced Video ▶16, 64, 88, 114
Internet ▶38, 73
Interpersonal Computing ▶68
A new term for computer hardware and software that allows different users with separate computers to communicate and share resources.
Interpreter ▶54
A piece of software that reads instructions written in a high–level language and decodes it for the processor to execute at that time.
I/O (Input/Ouput) ▶47–48, 102–103, 107
The devices and processes that support the input and ouput of data in a computer.
IPC (Inter–Process Communications) ▶17, 48
These operating system features allow applcations to communicate send messages back and forth and share data.

ISDN ▸74
(Integrated Services Digital Network) A standard protocol (format) for digital telecommunications transmissions. ISDN is an international standard for transmitting digital information (text, sound, voice, data, video, etc...)
Isopoint ▸84
Joystick ▸75
Kay, Alan ▸35
Kernel
The core elements and instructions of an operating system (especially UNIX).
Keyboard ▸41, 47, 75, 78, 120–121, 128
A device that allows the user to input alpha–numeric information into a computer via a set of keys (like a typewriter).
Key Combination ▸19, 79
Kilobyte (KB)
A standard measure of data used with memory. Equal to 1,024 bytes (2 to the tenth power).
LAN ▸70
(Local Area Network) A group of computers connected so that they may share resources like peripheral devices, and possibly, access to other computers.
Languages, Computer ▸51–55
A well–developed system of statements and commands used to compose software for use by a computer.
Large–scale integration (LSI)
A manufacturing process that shrinks the size of **transistors** and other electronic components so that many can fit in a very small space on a chip.
Laser ▸65–66, 87
(Light Amplification by Stimulating Emission Radiation) A device that focuses light into a concentrated beam.
Laser Printer ▸10, 85, 121–122, 142–143
A printer that uses a laser to electrostatically charge small points of a toner–based printing engine that usually results in high resolution printing on paper.
Layout Application ▸6, 10, 143
LED Display (Light Emiting Diode) ▸42
Letter Quality ▸84
Light Pen ▸75, 83–84
A pen–shaped stylus connected to a computer that allows the user to input data or point to a location on the screen using light as the visual cue.
Links ▸25
Connections made between two or more separate pieces of information or processes (nodes), especially in a **hypertext** system.
Liquid Crystal Display (LCD) ▸42, 115
A digital display composed of numerous diodes that turn opaque when stimulated with electricity. Encased in plastic or glass, these diodes can be turned on (opaque) and used to display text, graphics or pictures. Common in digital watches.
Logic gate ▸56, 93–94, 97
An electronic component that is capable of directing the flow of electricity in a circuit based on signals from the computer that correspond to logical relationships, such as AND, NOT, and OR.
Look–Up Table ▸81–82
Also see *CLUT*
Machine language ▸55
A low–level coding system of statements and commands to the **CPU** that instructs it on how and when to manipulate data.
Macintosh ▸84, 122, 142–143
Macro Utilities ▸19, 79
Mail Merge ▸8, 24
A process of printing a database of addresses into a letter template automatically so that each letter does not need to be types individually.
Mainframe computer ▸47, 68–69
Traditionally, a very large and powerful computer that processes data for many users at once. No particular power or speed can be used to distinguish a mainframe from other computers since the average power and speeds are always rising (today's minicomputers are as fast as yesterday's mainframes and tomorrow's minicomputers will be as fast as today's mainframes). Typically, mainframes are connected to large memory devices and many **peripherals**.
Manuals ▸126–128
Mask (Monitor) ▸103
Mask (Silicon) ▸114
Megabyte (MB) ▸61, 92
A measure of computer memory equal to 1,048,576 bytes.
Megaflop
(One Million Floating–point Operations Per Second) A measure of a **CPU**'s performance.
Megahertz ▸100, 103
Memory Management ▸45–46, 104
Menu ▸76
A list of possible commands accessible in a graphic–user interface.
Microchip
A small Integrated Circuit (IC) chip.
Microcomputer
A smaller, sometimes portable computer used by one person. Also called a personal computer.
Microprocessor
A chip that contains all of the components of a **Central Processing Unit** (CPU).
MIDI ▸14
(Musical Instrument Digital Interface) A standard for formatting musical data that is understood by almost every digital musical instrument and computer music software.
MIFF ▸23
Minicomputer
A larger and more powerful computer than a microcomputer. Can be called a workstation and may serve several usesr at a time.
MIPS
(Millions of Instructions Per Second) A measure of a **CPU**'s processing speed.
Modem ▸27, 30, 69, 73–74, 121
A device that allows a computer to transmit data over phone lines to and from other computers.
Modifier Keys ▸79
Monitor
▸80–82, 105, 113–114, 120–121, 127
A display device on a computer, usually a **CRT (Cathode Ray Tube)**.

Monochrome ▶80–82, 115, 121
Motherboard ▶37, 65, 108–109, 111
Mouse ▶35, 47, 75–79, 83–84, 121
A small screen–pointing device that a user moves on a horizontal surface to control a **cursor** on the screen.
MS–DOS >118–119, 122
see ***DOS***
Multimedia ▶13, 17, 23, 29, 64
Combining sound, video or many other media into one presentation.
Multi–Tasking ▶46
Music, Computer ▶14
N-Type (Semiconductor) ▶95, 98
NAND gate ▶98
Nanosecond ▶94
An extremely small unit of measure for time used to measure a computer's operations corresponding to a billionth of a second (.000000001 second).
Natural Language Processing/ Recognition ▶35, 89
The abilities of a computer to recognize, understand and respond in natural "human" language.
Net Modem ▶73
Network ▶28–29, 37, 70–73
Neural Network ▶34–35
A system that interprets a collection of discrete inputs to produce a response. Usually provided with the ability to adjust its interpretations of the inputs based on past performance.
Nibble ▶92
A rarely used measure of data corresponding to four **bits** or half of a **byte**.
Node ▶72
A separate piece of information within a **hypertext** system or a separate device on a local or wide–area network.
NOT Gate ▶98
NTSC ▶16, 88
(National Television Standards Committee) This is the standard form in which television pictures are transmitted in for the USA, Mexico, Canada, and Japan. It displays 525 scan lines at 30 frames per second.
Object Code ▶54-55
Object–oriented ▶56
A type of programming language that is highly structured so that programs are written as collections of discrete objects. Each object is responsible for manipulating its own data.
OCR ▶19, 76
(Optical Character Recognition) Software that is capable of translating pictures or scans of handwriting into edited with a computer.
Octal ▶90
A system of counting in Base 8 (using only the numbers between 0 and 7).
On–line ▶25, 29–30, 122
On/Off ▶91, 98
Operation Sun Devil ▶43
Operating system
▶44–45, 49–51, 62, 75, 82, 107, 118–121
The software in a computer that contains the instructions necessary for running the computer's system operations, including memory management, **system calls**, and instructions to the processor.
Optical Circuits ▶103
Optical Discs ▶65–67
Optical Drive ▶119
Output ▶57
Data transmitted to the user or to memory that has been processed by the CPU.
P–Type (Semiconductor) ▶95, 98
Packets ▶69, 73
Page Description Language ▶12, 85
Paged Memory Management ▶46
PageMaker™ ▶12, 143
Paint Applications ▶10
PAL ▶88
(Phase Alternation by Line) This is the television transmission standard in Western Europe, China, India, Austrailia, New Zealand, Argentina and parts of Africa. It displays 625 scan lines at 25 frames per second.
Paperless Office ▶30
Parallel processing ▶46, 101, 112
Using more than one CPU to process parts of a problem concurrently rather than one CPU to process the entire problem itself.
Peripheral ▶69, 71, 102, 108–109
A piece of hardware connected to a computer (usually by a cable, such as a disk drive, a printer, or a scanner) that gives the computer certain external capabilities.
Parity Check ▶112
Partitions (hard drive) ▶62
Pascal (language) ▶55
Passwords ▶40
Pen–Based Interface ▶76
Pipelining ▶101
A method of processing different instructions simultaneously and not waiting for pther parts to be completed before proceeding.
Pixel ▶11, 80, 114–115
(Picture Element) The smallest controllable spot on a display screen.
Personal Computer ▶117–118
Any computer designed to be used by one person at a time and designed to be fairly easy to use and understand.
Plasma Display ▶115
Platform ▶5, 22, 25
Plotter ▶87
Pointing Device ▶75–76, 83, 120–121
Portrait Display ▶80
Ports ▶108
Physical connections on the **circuit board** that allow other devices and components to connect to the computer.
PostScript™ (language)
▶12, 22–23, 35, 85, 122, 143
Posture ▶39
Presentation Applications ▶13
Printer ▶12, 73–74, 84–87, 121–122
Processor ▶44, 47, 54, 58, 82, 100–102, 104, 107–108, 117
See also *CPU*.
Program ▶4, 57
A set of instructions written in a computer language that tells the computer how and when to manipulate data.
Program Counter ▶100–101
Programming ▶52-53, 56, 57-58
PROM (Programmable Read–only Memory) ▶106
A type of ROM memory chip which has changeable instructions.

Time-sharing ▶47
Token Ring ▶70, 72
A type of **Local Area Network** that connects computers and other devices one after another in a ring of cables. A **token** is passed between the computers on the ring and only the computer with the token can send a message at one time.
Toolbox ▶50
Touch Screen ▶84
A monitor that is able to act as an input device by recognizing a user's touch.
Trackball ▶83–84
Tracks (disc) ▶59–64
Trade Shows ▶125
Transistor ▶94, 97–99
An electronic switch that controls the routing of signals in a circuit.
Trojan Horse ▶37, 39
True Color ▶81–82
Truth Tables ▶94
Turing, Alan ▶32–33, 55
Turing Test ▶33
A criteria of **artificial intelligence** stated by Alan Turing that a computer can be considered intelligent if it can fool a person into thinking that it is another person.
Tutorials ▶126
Type ▶50
Typeface ▶12
Typography ▶12, 50
Unicode ▶91
A type of character coding system that uses two **bytes** (instead of one, like **ASCII**) to describe each character. This provides 65,536 possible characters and is necessary for describing many non–Roman language characters to a computer (such as in Japanese and Chinese).
UNIX (operating system) ▶50, 118
Upgrades ▶105, 127
User Group ▶125
A group of people interested in a specific type or brand of computer or software who share tips, information, advice and activities.
User Friendly
A term used to define anything that has been designed with the user's needs and capabilities in mind.
User Interface ▶75
The area in which the user and computer interact.
Utilities ▶18, 24, 128
Vacuum tube
An electromechanical type of switch, typically about 1 million times larger and less energy efficient than a **transistor**.
Vaporware
A term for software (and sometimes hardware) that is discussed or advertised but is not yet available.
Variable ▶56–57
Vector-Tracing (monitor) ▶15, 113–114
A method used by some monitors to draw object outlines on the screen.
Very-High Density Diskette ▶60
Video Capture Board ▶88
Video Processors ▶82
Video Card ▶62, 80, 82, 88, 121
Video Disc ▶64
Video Editing ▶16
Virtual Interface ▶77
A computer interface that simulates a three–dimensional space in which the user can interact.
Virtual Memory ▶47, 50, 107
A means of using memory space on a disc to simulate a seemingly inexhaustible amount of **Random Access Memory** available to a processor.
Virtual Reality
An artificially constructed space in **software** in which to interact with others or a computer.
Virus (computer) ▶37–39
VLSI
(Very Large–Scale Integration) A manufacturing and design process that allows great quantities of electronic components to be put on a single chip. Approximately 1,200,000 transistors can be put on a ¼" square chip at the time of this writing.
Voice Mail ▶28
Any messaging system that allows the user to leave a recorded message to another person.
Voice Recognition ▶89
Volumes (disc) ▶62
Von Neuman, John ▶108
VRAM (Video Random Access Memory) ▶82, 105
Wafer
A slice of purified silicon on which many chips are manufactured.
WAN (Wide Area Network) ▶28, 73
A network of connected computers that covers a great geographical area.
Wait-state ▶110
Warranty ▶125, 127–128
Window ▶76
A work or display area in a **graphic–user interface** that responds to distinct and complete actions.
Windows 3.1 ▶119, 122
A graphic–user interface for the DOS operating system produced by Microsoft.
Wire-frame Model ▶19
Word Processor ▶5–9, 17
Workstation ▶118
A computer designed to meet all of one person's needs (typically more powerful than a personal computer). Commonly used for financial, scientific, or industrial applications.
Worm (computer) ▶38–39
WORM drive ▶65
(Write Once, Read Many) A disc that allows information to be written only once by the user, but can be retrieved many times.
WYSIWYG ▶6
(What You See Is What You Get) Refers to computer interfaces that display things the way they will eventually look if printed out (pronounced Wizzywig).
Xanadu ▶24
Xerox PARC ▶35, 73
Zones ▶72

Colophon

The steps we went through to create this book entirely with computers are outlined below.

Research, Writing and Editing

Nathan Shedroff, J.Sterling Hutto, Ken Fromm

This book was written and edited on Apple Macintosh II and IIci computers. Black and white **proofs ▶85** were output on an Apple Personal LaserWriter IINT **laser printer ▶85, 121-122.** Files were circulated both on paper and **cartridges ▶63** during the writing and editing process.

The **word processing software ▶5-9** used was Claris MacWrite II. Correct Grammar from Lifetree Software was used to aid editing.

Illustrations

Nathan Shedroff

The illustrations in this book were designed and produced on the Apple Macintosh IIci. Colors were specified and trapped for four-color process printing and saved as **Encapsulated PostScript™ ▶12, 122-123** files. Proofs were output on the Apple Personal LaserWriter IINT. Aldus FreeHand 3.0 was used to create these illustrations.

Photographs

Rachel Olson, Photographer
Sanjay Sakhuja, Digital PrePress International (scanning)

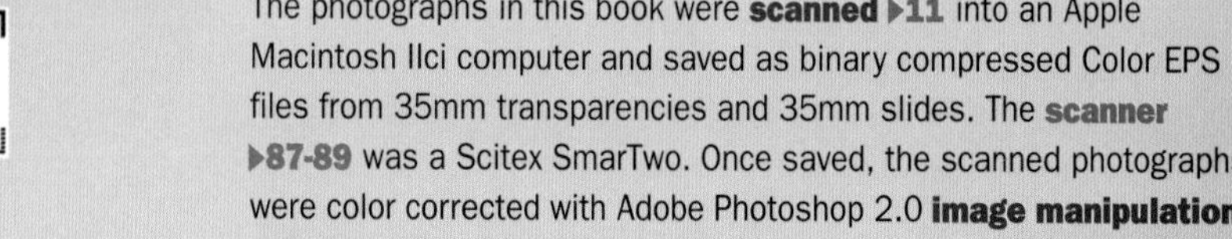

The photographs in this book were **scanned ▶11** into an Apple Macintosh IIci computer and saved as binary compressed Color EPS files from 35mm transparencies and 35mm slides. The **scanner ▶87-89** was a Scitex SmarTwo. Once saved, the scanned photographs were color corrected with Adobe Photoshop 2.0 **image manipulation software ▶11**.

Graphic Design and Production

Nathan Shedroff

The artwork, text and photographs were imported into Aldus PageMaker 4.01 **page layout application ▸10** for design, layout and production on an Apple Macintosh IIci.

The text was imported and flowed into columns. The **index ▸132** was created semi-automatically within this application and expanded to function as a glossary as well. The chapters were created as separate files and linked together to form a complete book.

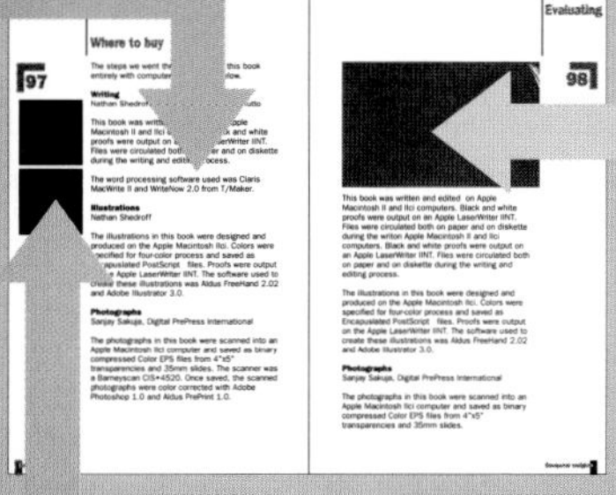

97

Where to buy

The steps we went th[illegible] this book entirely with computer[illegible]low.

Writing
Nathan Shedrof[illegible]

This book was writt[illegible]pple Macintosh II and IIci [illegible]k and white proofs were output on [illegible]erWriter IINT. Files were circulated both [illegible]r and on diskette during the writing and editi[illegible]ocess.

The word processing software used was Claris MacWrite II and WriteNow 2.0 from T/Maker.

Illustrations
Nathan Shedroff

The illustrations in this book were designed and produced on the Apple Macintosh IIci. Colors were [illegible]ecified for four-color process and saved as [illegible]apsulated PostScript files. Proofs were output [illegible] Apple LaserWriter IINT. The software used to [illegible] these illustrations was Aldus FreeHand 2.02 and Adobe Illustrator 3.0.

Photographs
Sanjay Sakuja, Digital PrePress International

The photographs in this book were scanned into an Apple Macintosh IIci computer and saved as binary compressed Color EPS files from 4"x5" transparencies and 35mm slides. The scanner was a Barneyscan CIS+4520. Once saved, the scanned photographs were color corrected with Adobe Photoshop 1.0 and Aldus PrePrint 1.0.

Evaluating

98

This book was written and edited on Apple Macintosh II and IIci computers. Black and white proofs were output on an Apple LaserWriter IINT. Files were circulated both on paper and on diskette during the writon Apple Macintosh II and IIci computers. Black and white proofs were output on an Apple LaserWriter IINT. Files were circulated both on paper and on diskette during the writing and editing process.

The illustrations in this book were designed and produced on the Apple Macintosh IIci. Colors were specified for four-color process and saved as Encapsulated PostScript files. Proofs were output on the Apple LaserWriter IINT. The software used to create these illustrations was Aldus FreeHand 2.02 and Adobe Illustrator 3.0.

Photographs
Sanjay Sakuja, Digital PrePress International

The photographs in this book were scanned into an Apple Macintosh IIci computer and saved as binary compressed Color EPS files from 4"x5" transparencies and 35mm slides.

The graphics and photographs were imported, resized, cropped and placed in the page layout.

Fonts

ITC Franklin Gothic and ITC Garamond families were used in the design of this book. All **fonts ▸11-12** are Adobe PostScript™ fonts.

Black and white page proofs were printed on Apple Personal LaserWriter IINT and LaserWriter IINTX printers. Color proofs were output on a QMS ColorScript 100 **color laser printer ▸85-86, 122.**

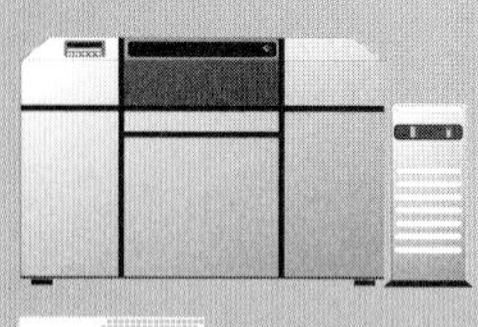

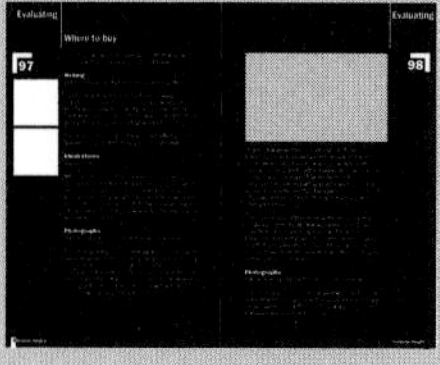

Separation

Kelly McKiernan, Z PrePress

Once the chapters were completed, the files were transported to the service bureau on Syquest **cartridges ▶63**. The files were separated and output as film negatives on an Agfa SelectSet 5000 **imagesetter ▶10, 12, 86, 121** with Aldus PrePrint 1.5 .

The negatives were proofed by making Fuji Color Art color proofs and checked for proper separation density and quality (Thanks to Brett Waters and Doug Ballinger at Metagraphics).

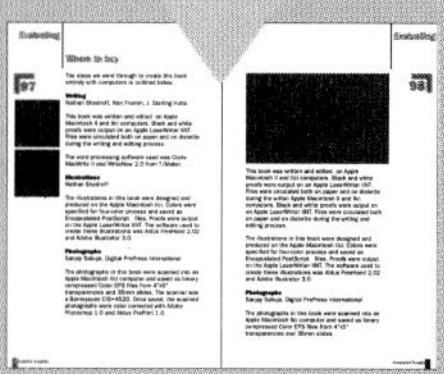

Printing and Binding

R.R. Donnelley and Sons, Joel McCabe (Representative)

The separated film was sent to the printer and run as a 4-color print job on a web press. The printed pages, arranged in signatures, were transported to the bindery where they were bound.

Special Thanks

We would like to thank Norma Laskin, Alan and Phyllis Shedroff, Michael Everitt, Jane Rosch, Francesca Freedman, Steven Bernsen, Craig Alexander, Peter Levy, Maria Guidice, Scott Smith, Joe Masarich, Rajan Dev, Joe Hutsko, Nell Paulk, and Aaron Solomon for their help and support.

Thanks also to Rudolph Langer, Dianne King, Margaret Rowlands, Joanne Cuthbertson, Sharon Crawford, and David Krassner of Sybex.